Tuesday's Gone

Voting, Elections, and the Political Process

Series Editors: Shauna Reilly and Stacy Ulbig

Receptive to studies in the American and comparative settings, the *Voting, Elections, and the Political Process* series examines the broadly defined electoral process. The series seeks scholarly monographs and edited volumes that investigate the ways in which voters, candidates, elected officials, parties, interest groups, the media, and others interact in the context of electoral politics. Works with a focus on individual attitudes and behavior, institutional and contextual influences, and the legal aspects of the electoral process are welcome. This series accepts interdisciplinary work using a variety of methodological approaches.

Recent Titles

Tuesday's Gone: America's Early Voting Revolution by Elliott Fullmer

The 2020 Presidential Election in the South edited by Scott E. Buchanan and
    DuBose Kapeluck

The Trifecta in Voting Barrier Causation: Economics, Politics, and Race by Shauna Reilly

An Unprecedented President and the Prospect for American Democracy by Arthur Paulson

The Resilient Voter: Stressful Polling Places and Voting Behavior by Shauna Reilly and
    Stacy Ulbig

*Unconventional, Partisan, and Polarizing Rhetoric: How the 2016 Election Shaped the
    Way Candidates Strategize, Engage, and Communicate* edited by Jeanine E. Kraybill

The 2016 Presidential Election: The Causes and Consequences of a Political Earthquake
    edited by Amnon Cavari, Richard J. Powell, and Kenneth R. Mayer

Tuesday's Gone

America's Early Voting Revolution

Elliott Fullmer

LEXINGTON BOOKS

Lanham • Boulder • New York • London

Published by Lexington Books
An imprint of The Rowman & Littlefield Publishing Group, Inc.
4501 Forbes Boulevard, Suite 200, Lanham, Maryland 20706
www.rowman.com

86-90 Paul Street, London EC2A 4NE

British Library Cataloguing in Publication Information Available

Library of Congress Cataloging-in-Publication Data Available

ISBN: 978-1-7936-5206-5 (cloth)
ISBN: 978-1-7936-5208-9 (pbk.)
ISBN: 978-1-7936-5207-2 (electronic)

To my wife and best friend, Jenna

Contents

List of Figures and Tables   ix

Acknowledgments   xi

Introduction   1

1   The Early Voting Story   11

2   Early Voting and County Turnout   35

3   Early Voting and Individual Turnout   75

4   Early Voting and Down-Ballot Roll-Off   87

5   Early Voting and Racial Inequity   101

6   Early Voting and Presidential Nominations   113

Conclusion   133

Bibliography   145

Index   163

About the Author   169

List of Figures and Tables

FIGURES

Figure 0.1	Early Voting in the United States, 2021	4
Figure 2.1	Early Voting Site Density and Turnout, 2012	50
Figure 2.2	Early Voting Site Density and Turnout, 2016	51
Figure 2.3	Early Voting Site Density and Turnout, 2014	61
Figure 2.4	Early Voting Site Density and Turnout, 2018	61
Figure 3.1	Early Voting Site Density and Probability of Voting, 2014 (Full Model)	80
Figure 3.2	Marginal Effects on Turnout (in Percentage Points), 2014	80
Figure 3.3	Early Voting Site Density and Probability of Voting, 2016 (Full Model)	84
Figure 3.4	Marginal Effects on Turnout (in Percentage Points), 2016	84
Figure 6.1	Marginal Effects on Support for Hillary Clinton across Four States, 2008	127
Figure 6.2	Marginal Effects on Support for Hillary Clinton across Three States, 2016	129

TABLES

Table 2.1	Early Voting and County Turnout, 2012 and 2016	52
Table 2.2	Early Voting and County Turnout in Large vs. Smaller Counties, 2012 and 2016	54
Table 2.3	Early Voting and County Turnout (with Interactions), 2012 and 2016	57
Table 2.4	Early Voting and County Turnout, 2014 and 2018	62

Table 2.5   Early Voting and County Turnout in Large vs. Smaller
            Counties, 2014 and 2018   66
Table 2.6   Early Voting and County Turnout (with Interactions),
            2014 and 2018   69
Table 3.1   Early Voting and Individual Turnout, 2014   78
Table 3.2   Margins Analysis of Early Voting Site Density and
            Turnout, 2014   79
Table 3.3   Early Voting and Individual Turnout, 2016   82
Table 3.4   Margins Analysis of Early Voting Site Density and
            Turnout, 2016   83
Table 4.1   Early Voting and Ballot Roll-Off in Ohio Supreme
            Court Races, 2010   94
Table 4.2   Early Voting and Ballot Roll-Off in Ohio Partisan
            Races, 2010   95
Table 4.3   Early Voting and Ballot Roll-Off in Ohio Races, 2018   98
Table 5.1   Demographics and Early Voting Site Density, 2012
            and 2016   105
Table 5.2   Demographics and Early Voting Site Density, 2014
            and 2018   108
Table 5.3   Demographics and Early Voting Site Density (with
            State-Fixed Effects), 2012–2018   110
Table 6.1   Early Voters in National Election Pool Exit Polls
            (Democratic Party Primaries), 2008 and 2016   123
Table 6.2   Predicting Support for Hillary Clinton in Democratic
            Party Primaries, 2008   126
Table 6.3   Predicting Support for Hillary Clinton in Democratic
            Party Primaries, 2016   129

Acknowledgments

I have been researching early voting and its effects since 2010. Through many long days of exploring state archives, chatting with county clerks, and collecting quantitative data, I have crossed paths with scores of helpful people. This book has undoubtedly been strengthened by these interactions.

In particular, I am deeply grateful to have studied at Georgetown University, where numerous colleagues offered helpful mentorship—particularly at the early stages of this project. My dissertation committee chair, Clyde Wilcox, deserves special thanks. Valuable discussions with many others—including Michael Bailey, Furman Daniel, Dan Hopkins, Micah Jensen, Jon Ladd, Jim Lengle, Yu-Ming Liou, Andrea Mayer, Jon Mummolo, Paul Musgrave, Hans Noel, Seth Petersen, Zacchary Ritter, Mark Rom, Jack Santucci, Michele Swers, and U Jin Wong—also greatly enhanced the book.

Since 2013, I have had the pleasure of working at Randolph-Macon College. My colleagues in the political science department—Tom Badey, Lauren Bell, Richard Meagher, and Brian Turner—have been both helpful and supportive. Grants distributed by the College's Committee on Faculty Development—through both the Walter Williams Craigie Endowment and the Rashkind Family Foundation Endowment—have allowed me to commit countless hours to this project.

My research has been strengthened by the critical advice provided by voting behavior scholars. Barry Burden, Paul Gronke, Michael Hanmer, Michael McDonald, Shauna Reilly, and Daniel Smith have been both gracious and thoughtful in their comments and critiques. I have also received sound guidance from Lonna Atkeson, Brian Brox, Moshe Haspel, Peter Miller, Scott McClurg, Robert Stein, and many others.

Various organizations provided prompt and helpful assistance when I contacted them about their data, perspectives, or tools. These include MapChart, the National Conference of State Legislatures, the Roper Center for Public Opinion Research, the U.S. Census Bureau, the U.S. Election Assistance Commission, and Verified Voting. In addition, dozens of county clerks provided their unique perspectives free of any compensation or reward.

Jenna Fullmer is far more than a supportive and loving spouse. A successful political consultant and small business owner, her insights and professional resources have been invaluable assets for this book (as well as in my broader career as a political scientist).

Finally, our precious daughter, Lily, is a constant source of joy, inspiration, and clarity. On those days when I could not find the data, the code, or the words, she was a welcome reminder that life is still good.

Introduction

On November 3, 2020, the world watched in anticipation as former vice president Joe Biden challenged incumbent Donald Trump for the presidency. In a campaign held amid a deadly pandemic, a struggling economy, and rising partisan polarization, enthusiasm was unusually high. Voters stood in lines at fire halls, school gymnasiums, and civic centers to cast their respective ballots, often receiving customary "I Voted" stickers as they departed. It was Election Day, the day when the presidency and hundreds of other federal, state, and local officeholders around the nation would be democratically chosen. For presidential campaigns, it had been this way since 1845, when Congress certified the first Tuesday after the first Monday of November as the national day of selection for presidential electors.

In reality, however, November 3 was more a culmination of a long decision process than a decisive day. With the United States ravaged by the COVID-19 outbreak, nearly two-thirds of voters—over 100 million Americans—had opted to cast their ballots through the mail or at early voting sites before Election Day. Eager to vote and concerned about reported backlogs at the U.S. Postal Service, millions submitted absentee ballots as early as September. As a result, their votes would not be informed by late events or developments in the campaign, including the presidential candidate debates, President Trump's COVID-19 diagnosis, or the nomination and confirmation of Supreme Court Justice Amy Coney Barrett.

Understandably, media accounts covered the rush of Americans casting early ballots. Long lines at some early voting sites were highlighted, while journalists sought meaning in the partisan composition of the early electorate. But while the surge of pre-Election Day voting was indeed unprecedented, the truth is that early voting had been a major factor in U.S. elections long before 2020. Over one-third of votes were cast early in both 2012 and 2016.

This included all votes in two states—Oregon and Washington—and large majorities in many more. For decades, but especially since 2008, political campaigns had actively sought to mobilize supporters to vote early, understanding that a vote *cast* is always better than a vote *expected to be cast*. By 2020, county clerks in most U.S. states were well accustomed to processing vote-by-mail (VBM) requests and managing early voting sites at libraries, schools, and even shopping malls. While early voting received a sudden burst of attention in 2020, its gradual expansion had been transforming U.S. elections for a generation.

Early voting undoubtedly made the 2020 election safer for citizens, though the broader normative consequences of its emergence remain a matter of debate. For some, it serves as a necessary reform to ease the administrative burden on elections officials. With voters distributed across several weeks, lines are generally lessened and logistical problems can be identified before Election Day. Many also believe that early voting promises to increase voter participation by providing citizens with ample opportunities to cast ballots. Given that voter turnout in the United States lags other industrialized democracies, this is an important consideration. Comparing the most recent national elections held in each of the 35 member nations of the Organization for Economic Cooperation and Development, U.S. turnout—which was unusually high in 2020—still ranks just 24th (DeSilver 2021).

But not everyone is convinced that early voting's benefits outweigh its costs. Critics argue that early voting decreases the civic nature of Election Day, and therefore the quality of American democracy itself. Some claim that the diminished importance of Election Day may *depress* overall turnout. Others lament that when some voters participate before a campaign has completed, they inevitably do so with less information (or at least access to information) than their peers. With some states commencing early voting more than six weeks before Election Day, it is possible that some voters will regret their choice(s) by a campaign's close. In this sense, the decline of simultaneous voting means that election outcomes may not accurately match the collective preferences of a determinate majority (or plurality) at any particular point in time. Rather, with citizens casting ballots over lengthy periods, elections become more "a series of decisions made by different majorities" (Thompson 2004). By contrast, some argue, citizens who vote at the same time do so "on equal terms" with equal access to information about candidates; in doing so, their collective decisions are best assured to have legitimacy. Beyond concerns about information asymmetries, critics worry that early voting increases the cost of campaigns, creates down-ballot roll-off, and widens racial disparities in polling access.

In the chapters that follow, I apply new approaches to assess the development and implications of early voting through a series of empirical inquiries.

Addressing both intended and unintended consequences, I conclude that while early voting certainly creates new challenges and complications, these pale in comparison to its capacity to increase both convenience and participation in U.S. elections.

EARLY VOTING TODAY

The terms surrounding convenience voting are often applied in different ways by academics, the media, and even states and localities. In this book, *early voting* serves as an umbrella term for pre-Election Day voting options available to all registered citizens, regardless of the mechanisms through which votes are cast. *No-excuse absentee voting* suggests that any registered voter is permitted to request and submit a ballot through the mail without citing a reason for doing so. *Early in-person voting* is distinct, as any registered voter may cast their ballot at a physical location before Election Day. These locations can include external sites established by municipal officials, as well as local elections offices themselves. A program allowing voters to visit an elections office, request an absentee ballot, and complete and submit it on site falls under the definition of early in-person voting. In this book and elsewhere, early in-person voting sites are often simply called *early voting sites* (or locations) for short. Finally, *universal VBM* means that every registered voter throughout a jurisdiction is automatically mailed a ballot in the weeks before each election.

As Figure 0.1 indicates, 42 states and the District of Columbia allow all registered citizens to vote before Election Day.[1] This number has grown steadily since 1978, when California became the first state to offer early voting in the form of no-excuse absentee ballots (Bomboy 2016). Today, 30 states offer *both* early in-person sites and no-excuse absentee voting to registered citizens. An additional seven states offer early in-person sites, but require a valid excuse (e.g., disability, work travel) in order for a voter to receive an absentee ballot. Five states—Colorado, Hawaii, Oregon, Utah, and Washington—now employ universal VBM programs. Eight states offer no form of pre-Election Day voting for most citizens, though those with valid excuses may still request and submit absentee ballots (National Conference of State Legislatures [NCSL] 2020a). In 2020, all non-early voting states except Mississippi temporarily offered no-excuse absentee voting or early voting sites to all voters due to the COVID-19 pandemic, but these policies expired after that year's election (Harrison 2020).

Increased early voting access has predictably led to a huge growth in the number of Americans participating before Election Day. According to the 1992 Current Population Survey (CPS), only 7% of voters cast early ballots

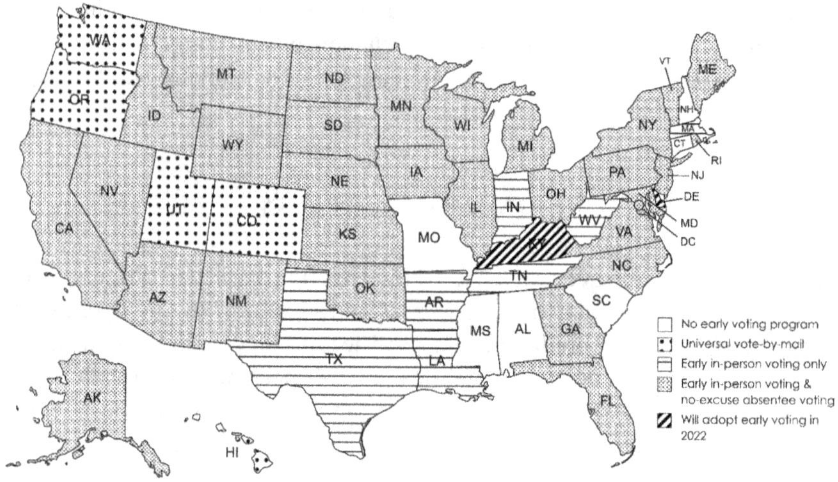

Figure 0.1 Early Voting in the United States, 2021. Notes: Kentucky will adopt only early in-person voting in 2022, while Delaware will adopt both early in-person and no-excuse absentee voting. *Source*: Created by Elliott Fullmer using the MapChart website and data from the National Conference of State Legislatures (2021).

that year (U.S. Census 1992). Most did so out of necessity, as a majority of states still lacked physical early voting sites or no-excuse absentee programs. In the 1990s, however, early voting entered a "new phase" (Gronke and McDonald 2008). New laws began to appear throughout the United States, predominately in the western part of the country. From 1992 to 2004, the percentage of early votes among all ballots cast increased by an average of 4.25 percentage points per presidential election, reaching 20% by 2004 (Gronke and McDonald 2008). In 2008, the figure soared to over 30% of the electorate, including a strong majority of voters in several states (Heimlich 2012). In 2016, at least 47 million ballots were cast early, representing nearly 35% of the electorate (McDonald 2016). In 2020, records were shattered as over 100 million Americans (about 64% of all voters) cast early ballots (McDonald 2020). Whether this number represents a COVID-driven anomaly or a new normal remains to be seen.

GENERAL OBJECTIVES OF THE BOOK

Voting has long commanded the attention of political scientists. Riker (1982) summarized the view of countless others, calling voting "at the heart of both the method and the ideal of democracy." Hanmer (2009) offers a more mechanical assessment, commenting that "Voting, at a minimum . . . allows citizens the opportunity to hire and fire their representatives." Given its existential importance to democracy, changes to voting rights and laws carry particularly high stakes. Women's suffrage, the end of Jim Crow, and the Australian ballot not only changed administrative practices; they also served as transformative developments for American society more generally.

In recent years, early voting has undoubtedly altered U.S. elections. One reporter even called it "the most radical change to American voting culture since the abolition of poll taxes" (Issenberg 2012). Early voting means new options for voters, a new set of procedures and responsibilities for election clerks, and new opportunities (and challenges) for political candidates and operatives. The central purpose of this book is to examine the implications of these substantial changes. Decades after its introduction, has early voting enhanced the quality of American democracy, or has it failed to achieve its goals and instead brought troubling unintended consequences? Such an inquiry not only has academic value, but practical implications as well. While early voting is now an entrenched part of U.S. elections, it remains an evolving institution. Even before the COVID-19 outbreak, state and local officials frequently considered and implemented changes to their programs. A better understanding of early voting's efficacy in U.S. elections serves to inform future discussions regarding its adoption, modification, and implementation.

While researchers have studied early voting since the 1990s, the focus has generally been limited to aggregate analyses on voter participation. Naturally, researchers—myself included—have sought to determine whether a reform aimed at increasing turnout has actually accomplished its goal. The turnout literature can benefit from new approaches that recognize the important role of state and local (mostly county) implementation of early voting programs. Furthermore, while the turnout question is important, too little focus has been paid to potential complications of early voting. Assessing the full effect of a reform requires that attention be paid to both its intended and unintended consequences. With these considerations in mind, I have organized the book around several key objectives.

First, I explore the rapid development and diffusion of early voting across the states since the 1980s. State legislative archives and news accounts provide valuable insights into why states chose to adopt such reforms. I also examine the politicization of electoral reform (including early voting) that has emerged since the 2000s, as well as the legal dynamics that have affected recent efforts to cut early voting in several states.

Second, early voting advocates hope (and believe) that it can increase voter participation. I develop new approaches and models to assess if (and importantly, under what conditions) early voting appears to achieve this effect. While others have explored this question, the existing literature fails to account for important differences in early voting implementation across states and counties. Applying new data from the Election Assistance Commission (EAC), the CPS, and other sources in recent presidential and national mid-term years, I offer a more refined approach.

Of course, early voting does not operate in a vacuum. Its development has coincided with the emergence of other state and local policies that both promote and deter voting. Twenty-one states allow citizens to register on the same day in which they vote, while 20 now automatically register most eligible adults. While these changes have eased the voting process, many states have also taken actions that make voting more difficult. Some have begun requiring photo identification (something over 10% of adults lack) in order to vote, purged voter rolls, and reduced polling places and equipment. The complex environment in which early voting has emerged and developed makes isolating its effects a difficult endeavor. The models developed in this book are designed with these challenges in mind.

Third, as I previously noted, it is well-documented that public policy changes produce unintended consequences. It is quite possible that a law can achieve its central objective(s), while also creating new issues and problems in the process. Examples abound in the study of American politics. The binding presidential primaries and caucuses mandated by the McGovern-Fraser Commission in 1971 produced numerous unintended consequences. These included new advantages for particular candidates and their supporting factions within the respective political parties (Joslyn 1976; Lengle and Shafer 1976; Maisel and Lieberman 1977; Marshall 1979; Hammond 1980; Geer 1986, 1989; Ansolabehere and King 1990), increased party factionalism (Kamarck 1987), and disadvantages for the Democratic Party (Cavala 1974; Kamarck 1987; Wattenberg 1991). The Bipartisan Campaign Reform Act (BCRA) of 2002 banned "soft-money" contributions, resulting in the rise of 527 groups, or tax-exempt organizations able to raise and spend unlimited sums for political advocacy purposes (Valdemoro 2005). Finally, research has suggested that the No Child Left Behind (NCLB) Act of 2001, designed to lessen the "achievement gap" in student performance in elementary schools, led to a narrowed curriculum, an overemphasis on test-taking skills, and the removal of important areas of focus in the classroom (Granowsky 2008). Assessing the full implications of any policy requires that attention be paid to both its intended and unintended effects. I explore several potential pitfalls of early voting laws that have been largely overlooked by researchers. These include increased racial disparities regarding voting access and greater levels of roll-off in down-ballot races.

Fourth, I explore the degree to which early voting has altered political campaigns and their outcomes. With a large percentage of citizens casting ballots early, campaigns now operate in a modified strategic environment. Some may find it useful to mobilize voters during the early voting period before their support diminishes. Relatedly, voters may cast a vote for a preferred candidate during their state's early voting window, then come to regret their decision as additional information about the candidates is revealed. In an era of heightened partisan polarization, the number of voters susceptible to regret is arguably more limited in general elections. But in intraparty contests (party primaries), the potential is greater because support for candidates is more volatile. Applying both qualitative and quantitative methodologies, I explore whether early voting appeared to aid or hurt certain candidates in two recent presidential nomination contests.

CHAPTER OUTLINE

I address the above research objectives through six empirical chapters. My studies rely on multiple methods of inquiry, including considerable quantitative analyses, archival research, case studies, and personal interviews. Chapter 1 offers a brief history of voting rights in the United States, including the process through which early voting evolved from a limited opportunity for the military, elderly, and expatriate communities to a widespread right for a vast majority of Americans. I explore state legislative archives from Texas and other Western states, as early in-person voting first blossomed in these areas in the late 1980s and early 1990s. Through analyzing these records and local media accounts, I identify low voter turnout and election administration problems as the primary catalysts for early voting's initial adoption. Regarding the latter, the infamous 2000 presidential election led many additional states to streamline their administration efforts. Early voting served as one mechanism to make the process easier, as it would reduce lines and allow problems to be identified before a flood of voters arrived on Election Day.

Early voting has also expanded because it has been generally popular with both voters and administrators. States have demonstrated a learning effect, as legislators have cited programs in other states as cause for adopting early voting in their own state. Nevertheless, programs have not always been supported by lawmakers. While the adoption of early voting was overwhelmingly bipartisan in most states, it has increasingly been the subject of partisan fights in recent years. In particular, Republicans have recently (since the 2008 election) sought to limit early voting efforts in numerous states. Furthermore, in several New England states, early voting adoption has been slow due (mostly) to logistical concerns.

In chapters 2 and 3, I explore how well early voting laws have achieved one of their primary objectives: *expanding the American electorate*. Reformers have long argued that reducing the costs of voting should lead to higher participation rates. Early voting effectively lowers costs by offering citizens the opportunity to cast ballots when it is most convenient for them. Despite this logic, empirical research on early voting's turnout effects has been mixed. In fact, most newer analyses have reported that the independent effect of early voting on participation is nonexistent, negligible, or even negative (Fitzgerald 2005; Highton 2005; Gronke et al. 2007; Primo et al. 2007; Scheele et al. 2008; Larocca and Klemanski 2011; Burden et al. 2014).

In chapter 2, I introduce a new approach for measuring the effect of early voting on turnout. I argue that the simple availability of early voting does not necessarily constitute a notable reduction in the costs of voting. Some early voting programs offer far greater conveniences than others. Counties within early voting states differ greatly in how they implement early in-person voting. While some offer a multitude of locations to voters, many provide just one. In my view, early in-person voting only makes voting more convenient if locations are ample throughout one's locality. I therefore break from past research and create a measure of early in-person voting availability at the county level. To account for intercounty differences, I rely on EAC data from over 2,000 U.S. counties on the number of early voting sites available in several recent national elections. I then measure the effect of early voting sites (per capita) on county turnout.

Of course, early voting programs differ in other ways. A small number of states mail ballots to all registered voters. Others provide early in-person sites, but have declined to provide no-excuse absentee voting options. Some states offer over six weeks of early voting, though others have only a few days of it. While these state differences have received a bit more scholarly attention than those regarding early in-person sites, they too demand greater scrutiny. I account for each of these factors in my turnout models.

Controlling for a wide range of other known influences on participation, I find that early voting sites had a significant and positive relationship with voter turnout in the 2012, 2014, 2016, and 2018 elections. Across many specifications, the relationship holds with remarkable consistency. Substantively, the findings suggest that adding an additional early voting site for every 1,000 voting-age residents increases turnout by two to three percentage points. In urban counties, the effect is larger, as an additional site per 10,000 residents often yields comparable (and sometimes larger) gains. I also report that universal VBM and no-excuse absentee laws, as well as longer early voting windows, appear to boost turnout.

In chapter 3, I expose these findings to new scrutiny. I utilize individual-level data from the 2014 and 2016 CPS to determine whether individual citizens residing in counties with more expansive early voting options become more likely to vote. While I addressed this question in chapter 2, county-level data should be interpreted cautiously due to ecological inference concerns. Examining the turnout question through individual data on over 30,000 citizens adds an important robustness check. Ultimately, my analyses confirm those reported in chapter 2 regarding early in-person sites, as individuals residing in counties with more site density were significantly more likely to vote in the 2014 and 2016 elections. While my positive findings regarding universal VBM laws and turnout are also confirmed, the effect of no-excuse absentee laws is a bit less consistent than in chapter 2. Finally, longer early voting periods are no longer linked to higher turnout in the CPS analysis.

In addition to studying the effectiveness of early voting in achieving its objectives, I focus on several unintended consequences it may be producing. Each has been referenced as a possible effect of early voting laws by researchers, though the literature has focused comparatively little attention on them. Chapter 4 explores the role of early voting in creating higher levels of down-ballot roll-off. Specifically, roll-off occurs when a voter submits a preference for the race at the top of the ballot (typically president or governor), but fails to do so for one or more lower offices. Many political operatives and journalists have voiced concerns that some early voters are participating before they have full information about the candidates. Indeed, candidates for down-ballot offices often do not even begin campaigning until the few weeks or month before Election Day. The logic follows that if many voters participate before campaigning for some offices has peaked or even begun, then they may be more inclined to skip these races when filling out a ballot. In particular, roll-off may occur more in nonpartisan races where a voting cue is missing. I explore this potential unintended consequence through a county-level analysis of Ohio in 2010, determining that early voting is associated with higher levels of roll-off in some circumstances, including state supreme court elections and a variety of partisan statewide offices. A brief follow-up analysis of the state's 2018 elections suggests that heightened roll-off has (for the most part) remained an issue in heavy early voting counties.

Chapter 5 tackles a challenge issued by Gronke and McDonald (2008) regarding racial inequities and early voting. The authors suggest that heavily non-Hispanic White counties offer more early voting opportunities than those with higher percentages of minority citizens. Again utilizing EAC and Census data, I find that heavily Black counties (though not heavily Hispanic counties) have indeed been underserved in terms of early in-person voting sites across multiple elections. Early voting is therefore creating a racial disparity in terms of access to the polls, something that could justify federal intervention under the Voting Rights Act.

Chapter 6 explores campaign effects and information asymmetries in the electorate caused by early voting. Those who vote before a campaign has concluded do so without any information about the candidates or political environment that may emerge between their vote and Election Day. I believe that this effect may be most notable during presidential nomination contests, as candidate support tends to be more fluid and information about candidates is often limited when early voting begins. In particular, I believe early voters should be more likely to support early front-runners and those with high levels of name recognition. Further, I suggest that campaigns may view early voting as an opportunity to accumulate votes in a favorable state while their candidates' popularity is high, blunting the negative effects of momentum from later contests.

Focusing on the 2008 and 2016 nomination contests, I find that Hillary Clinton's campaign (in both cases) designed a strategy to take advantage of her front-runner status during the early voting period in several states. Applying exit poll data, which includes a substantial numbers of early voters, I find that Clinton indeed benefited from early voting in both 2008 and 2016. These findings suggest that early voting has changed the competitive environment during nomination contests and created new strategic considerations for political campaigns.

Early voting is a complex, varied, and evolving institution. Identifying its cumulative effect on U.S. elections requires the collective effort of many scholars. I cannot submit that this book fully answers the important questions before us. Instead, it builds on existing work by offering new approaches, analyses, and insights in the hopes of adding a few pieces to a challenging puzzle.

NOTE

1. Delaware and Kentucky will each institute early voting in 2022, bringing the number of early voting states to 44. Delaware will allow *both* early in-person voting and no-excuse absentee voting, while Kentucky will only offer the former.

Chapter 1

The Early Voting Story

Like many features of U.S. elections, early voting is a decentralized practice. For the most part, it has emerged and developed at the state and local levels of government. Early voting is not the product of a federal constitutional amendment, an act of Congress, or a landmark Supreme Court decision. Rather, it has diffused—and is diffusing—throughout the United States by virtue of mostly quiet state and county legislative activity guided by various motivations.

Decentralization has always been a central feature of voting in the United States. The roots of local autonomy stem from colonial days, when "virtually every substantive aspect of voting was under local control and varied considerably from one place to the next" (Ewald 2009). While many New England colonies adopted paper ballots and permitted secret voting by the 1680s, voice voting was prevalent throughout the South until the ratification of the Constitution (Morgan 1988). Voter eligibility also lacked uniformity in the colonies. In South Carolina, a justice of the peace was responsible for certifying citizens as naturalized, a requirement for voting. Meanwhile, Pennsylvania had much more relaxed standards, as German immigrants were permitted to both vote and serve in government without naturalization. Religious requirements were present in many colonies, though Rhode Island was founded largely on the basis of religious freedom and had fewer restrictions. While most colonies held elections on a single day, New York and Virginia were known to hold three or five-day elections, particularly if bad weather developed (Ewald 2009). Many colonies lacked formal age, sex, or residency restrictions. These decisions were instead left to small towns and county governments, who authorized a wide variety of standards. Some towns allowed widows with property to vote, while others even allowed Native Americans and free Blacks to participate in elections (Crews 2007).

The Constitution did little to break the decentralized nature of elections. While the Guarantee Clause required each state to have a republican form of government, states had considerable flexibility when it came to interpreting and implementing popular rule. States were permitted to choose their presidential electors in any fashion they wished (a right they still enjoy). In the presidential election of 1789, only six of the 13 U.S. states allowed any sort of popular vote to choose their electors to the new Electoral College. In fact, it was not until 1832 that nearly all states allowed citizens to choose electors through a popular vote.[1] States had differing policies with regards to suffrage for non-property owners; while Pennsylvania allowed all White men to vote in 1776 (Ratcliffe 2013), North Carolina limited voting to property-owning White men until 1856 (Schmidt et al. 2009). Finally, the Constitution left the responsibility of funding and conducting elections to state and local governments. Hall and Tokaji (2007) have aptly referred to local election administration as "the country's oldest unfunded mandate."

Article I, Section 4 of the Constitution does give Congress the ability to alter the "Times, Places and Manner" of U.S. House and Senate elections, though Congress has generally opted to exercise this power sparingly. Voting reforms at the national level have often followed the initiative of one or more states. While the 19th Amendment guaranteed women the right to vote, 15 states had already done so by the time it took effect. Women in Wyoming had been voting since 1890 (Keyssar 2001). The 26th Amendment expanded suffrage to all 18–20-year-old citizens; in doing so, the United States required all states to follow the model set by Alaska, Hawaii, Georgia, and Kentucky, which had already permitted those under 21 to participate in elections (Neale 1983).

In more recent times, state and local governments have remained the primary catalysts of voting reforms. In addition to early voting laws, states have continued to adopt, modify, and enforce widely different policies regarding felon disenfranchisement, voter identification at the polls, and registration requirements. Furthermore, while the national Help America Vote Act (2002) sought to standardize voting machines, registration records, and poll-worker training across the United States, the law offered considerable latitude to states and localities in implementing new programs.

Some believe the decentralized nature of elections and voting in the United States is detrimental to the democratic process. Hochschild (2003) has said that the effect of varied local election laws and practices ranges from "amusing to appalling." Former Federal Elections Commission Chairman Michael Toner agreed, calling "the state of election administration in this country . . . an embarrassment" ("Interlude," 2006). Writing the day after the 2020 election, Lee Drutman and Charlotte Hill of New America, a respected Washington, DC think tank, wrote, "Voting in America is a mess. It is unfair, insecure, and too complicated. As a result, most Americans distrust our elections—and unfortunately, they have some good reasons for their skepticism" (Drutman and Hill 2020).

Others have defended the decentralized nature of elections, arguing that local autonomy provides citizens with a greater sense of civic engagement and stronger feelings of ownership over the electoral process. Supporters have also pointed out that state and local governments have often used their autonomy to act as effective laboratories for voting reforms, including aforementioned changes regarding women's suffrage and youth voting (Ewald 2009).

EARLY VOTING EMERGES

The early voting revolution did not begin in the states until the late twentieth century, and it initially evolved slowly. In 1978, California became the first state to allow no-excuse absentee voting. In essence, any registered voter could request a ballot through the mail several weeks before Election Day. No longer would one need to offer evidence of special circumstances. The percentage of Californians voting absentee increased over the next few election cycles, but it was still not a particularly high share. In 1984, about 7% of the state's voters requested and submitted an absentee ballot, and a large chunk of these individuals presumably did so out of necessity (California Secretary of State 2012). During the 1980s, other states followed with liberalized absentee rules, including Oregon and Washington (Gronke et al. 2008).

While never mistaken as a haven of progressivism, Texas has been called a "pioneer" state for early voting in the United States. The label is a fair one, as Texas was the first state to authorize early in-person voting for all citizens. In 1987, House Bill (HB) 612 was enacted in the Texas House, creating what officials described as "no-excuse voting by personal appearance." Similar to California and other states, voters would no longer need to provide a reason if they wished to vote before Election Day. The notable difference was that voters were provided physical locations where they could cast a vote in the weeks preceding Election Day. In most counties, the locations consisted of the permanent office(s) of the local elections official. HB 612 passed in the Texas Legislature without much controversy. It received a unanimous 8–0 vote in the House Committee on Elections and was ultimately adopted by a voice vote in both chambers (Texas House 1987). The bill's passage was scarcely mentioned in the state's major newspapers.

A report issued by the House Committee on Elections soon after the bill's passage suggested that increasing voter participation and convenience, as well as reducing voter fraud and intimidation, were the motives behind the legislation. The report expressed clear concerns for the state's chronically low turnout rate, which is cited as 44th in the nation. While members of the legislature argued that the early voting reforms should improve the convenience of voting and yield higher rates of participation, the committee report acknowledged that the turnout problem in Texas was largely one of voter registration, as 40% of the eligible population was not even registered. The committee advocated a "motor voter" approach, whereby registrants could be added to the rolls when applying for a driver's license, a provision that became federal law in 1993 (Texas House 1988).

Regarding voter fraud, the report noted that cases of abuse had been observed with the state's absentee voting program. In particular, there appeared to be some degree of "preying on elderly citizens," as many applications were "requested" by elderly citizens in nursing homes who were "unable to vote." While many elderly citizens had no choice but to vote via absentee ballots, some in the legislature saw these issues as a red flag. In order to lessen the volume of absentee voters, they sought a transition to early in-person voting, where convenience could be maintained but voting would occur in person. The new policy would also help election administrators, who had reported that increasing numbers of absentee ballots were difficult to verify in the time allotted (Texas House 1988). Texas therefore continued to require that voters have a valid excuse (e.g., disability, work travel) in order to receive an absentee ballot.

In reviewing the law's effectiveness following the 1988 elections, the committee judged that it was "well received by both the general public and the local election officials implementing and administering it" (Texas House 1988). In response to its popularity, Governor Ann Richards signed Senate Bill 1234 (SB) in May 1991, which set a minimum standard for the number of early voting locations provided by each county. In some counties, including the populous Harris County (Houston), up to 25 early voting sites were mandated. Similar to the 1987 law, the bill was not contentious along partisan lines. A motion to suspend debate passed 31–0 in the Texas Senate and the bill ultimately passed in both chambers by a voice vote (Texas Senate 1991).

The law and its expansion quickly gained a momentum of its own, as citizens became accustomed to it. There seemed to be little suspicion that one political party was benefitting from the program more than the other. Media accounts cited unnamed political operatives as being uncertain about partisan consequences, though both sides actively sought to benefit from the new rules. The NAACP, Houston Area Urban League, and other Democratic-leaning groups provided free transportation to students and elderly citizens to early voting sites (Bernstein and Zuniga 1992). Republicans sought to utilize their fundraising advantage in the state by spreading mobilization efforts, including a "massive phone bank operation," across the several weeks of early voting. Texas Democrats were typically unable to match this effort ("Texans Begin Early Voting," 1992).

Before the 1992 elections, concerns about turnout were apparent in the state's administration of the early vote program. Lawmakers ordered the opening of additional early voting sites in Harris County because it had demonstrated a pattern of lower turnout than other metropolitan areas (Greene and Bernstein 1992). County Republican Chairwoman Betsy Lake dismissed complaints from within her party that too many locations were in Democratic-leaning urban districts. She stated, "If they want to go vote, people are going to vote" (qtd. in Bernstein and Zuniga 1992). In fact, it was Anita Rodeheaver, the county's longtime Democratic clerk, who publicly opposed both early voting and the mandate for additional sites. She argued that low voter turnout was "a Harris County phenomenon that won't be increased by adding polling places. . . . People don't want to vote until Election Day. Period. In their own precincts" (qtd. in Greene and Bernstein 1992). Rodeheaver also lamented the cost of the expansion, which she anticipated to be about $250,000 to cover additional temporary workers, telephone lines, and other expenses at the new sites.

In general, however, early voting was popular in Texas, and other states began to take note of the state's innovative approach. Representative Bob Holmes, the Democratic chairman of the Governmental Affairs Committee in the Georgia General Assembly, argued that Georgia should replace absentee voting with physical early voting locations, as these would be less susceptible to voter fraud. Unlike absentee ballots sent to a home, early in-person voting occurs in the presence of election officials, he argued. Citing that early voting had been adopted successfully in Texas (Osinski 1993), Holmes held hearings during the 1994 legislative session, though Georgia would not adopt early voting until the 2000 election cycle.

Other states acted much more swiftly, particularly those in the West. In Nevada, a 1991 law allowing no-excuse absentee voting passed 21–0 and 39–2 in the state assembly and senate, respectively. Within two years, a broader early voting law—establishing physical locations throughout the state—was approved by 21–0 and 42–0 margins (Nevada Legislature 1993). That same year, the Republican-led Colorado Legislature approved an early voting law—featuring no-excuse absentee ballots and physical sites—on a bipartisan basis. Republican Donetta Davidson, chief elections officer in the Colorado Secretary of State's office, was integral in motivating the legislature to approve early voting as a way of "making voting more convenient" (Anderson 1994). During the 1992 campaign, however, Democrats appeared to capitalize on the new program. In a series of rallies, Reverend Jesse Jackson led hundreds of residents to the Denver Election Commission to vote early. He stated, "Today we have this splendid opportunity in Colorado. . . .

Having 20 days to go downtown to vote makes more sense than one day. . . .
What's going on here in Colorado now is one of the most advanced steps in
the country" (qtd. in Yang 1992).

Meanwhile, Kristin French, communications director for the Bush-
Quayle presidential campaign in Colorado, expressed disapproval that
early voting began before the first presidential debate had even been held,
noting, "The people haven't had a chance to look at everything yet, to hear
all there is to hear" (qtd. in Yang 1992). The pessimism about early voting
apparently did not extend to President Bush himself, who voted early in his
native Texas.

New Mexico approved early voting in 1993 with the support of legislators
from both parties. After several election cycles, Republican Party Chairman
John Dendahl argued that it "is a good way for people to cast their votes"
(qtd. in Holmes 2002). Denise Lamb, chair of the state Bureau of Elections,
said in 2002 that she suspected early voting had effectively increased turnout
or at least stabilized a decrease in voters. She stated, "Making absentee an
option has kind of stabilized what you might see as a kind of decline in participation that's taken place in other states" (qtd. in Holmes 2002).

In 1997, New Mexico's neighbor, Arizona, passed a law making early
voting access mandatory across the state's counties. It had been optional
since 1993. The new law was sponsored by Sue Grace, a Republican, and
passed 29–0 in the senate and 59–0 in the house, again indicating that it
was not a controversial measure (Arizona State Legislature 1997). Both
the New Mexico and Arizona measures allowed any voter to either receive
an absentee ballot or vote at a physical early voting site. Most states who
would adopt early voting in the years that followed would ultimately—if not
immediately—grant both options to voters, though some followed the Texas
model and chose to simply offer physical sites. Others claimed to only offer
no-excuse absentee voting, but because they allowed voters to visit an elections office and complete a ballot *on site*, they technically met the criteria for
an early in-person voting program.

With early voting growing by the year, the U.S. Supreme Court in 2000
effectively defended the constitutionality of the new laws. In June, justices
rejected an appeal of earlier federal court decisions (including one from
the Fifth U.S. Circuit Court of Appeals) upholding the Texas law. The suit
had been brought by the Voting Integrity Project, which argued that federal
law required congressional and presidential elections to take place only on
Election Day, the Tuesday after the first Monday in November. The appeals
court, however, argued that this was not necessarily true. Their February
2000 decision stated, "Because the election of federal officials in Texas is
not decided until Texas voters go to the polls on federal Election Day, we
conclude that the Texas early voting scheme is not inconsistent with federal

election laws." Without much fanfare, state autonomy with respect to early voting had been upheld ("High Court," 2000).

EARLY VOTING EXPANDS

While early voting was popular in the places that had adopted it, as of 2000 it remained limited to a minority of states. Twenty states offered early voting in the form of either (or both) no-excuse absentee ballots or early voting sites. The circumstances of the 2000 presidential election, however, quickly led other states to consider laws allowing voting before Election Day. It is well-documented that the election was a disaster in the state of Florida. As Republican George W. Bush and Democrat Al Gore fought a legal battle over recounts and spoiled ballots, the nation caught an unfortunate glimpse of a state with numerous election administration problems. By no means was Florida the only state deserving of criticism; it was just the one to receive the limelight. Florida's problems included the improper disenfranchisement of voters, confusing ballots, long lines, and vast administrative inconsistencies both across and within jurisdictions. Following the election, the state considered a number of election reforms in an effort to clarify the process for voters, make voting more convenient, and ease the stress of election administrators.

In 2002, the state legislature approved early voting by a wide margin, and it was signed into law by Republican Governor Jeb Bush. The law was quickly judged a success. Courteney Strickland, director of voting rights for the ACLU, stated, "It took a lot of pressure off polling places and allowed for better management. . . . Now we have to make sure early voting is something that stays" (qtd. in LaPolt 2002). Given its popularity, most considered the law a permanent fixture of campaigns. Hillsborough County Supervisor of Elections Pam Iorio commented, "It will be the way it's done in the future . . . because it's more convenient to the customer, and the customer is the voter" (qtd. in Tobin 2002).

Politically, the Republican Party appeared to claim an advantage. Under new laws that allowed anyone to request an absentee ballot, the party sent thousands of application forms to their registered voters. Operatives then followed these mailings with house visits and telephone calls, hoping to mobilize as many voters as possible before Election Day. Similar to Texas years prior, Democrats had no similar effort because they often lacked the necessary financial resources. In some counties, Democrats did not even seek lists of which voters had requested but not returned absentee ballots, information that county officials willingly make available. Republicans in Escambia County retrieved the lists and "harvested those votes," while "the Democrats didn't ask." In 2004, as his brother crisscrossed the state seeking a second term as president, Jeb Bush defended the early voting law, stating, "I think it's great. . . . It's another reform we added that has helped provide access to the polls and provide a convenience. And we're going to have a high voter turnout here, and I think that's wonderful" (qtd. in Graham 2012).

In 2004, lines remained long during the early voting period in some Florida counties, notably in Miami-Dade and Broward, where more than 110,000 people voted before Election Day across 20 local elections offices. However, clerks from around the state commented that voters seemed rather patient and content while enduring lines. One story referred to waiting voters as "more like fans clamoring for concert tickets than citizens exercising the right to vote" (qtd. in Tobin 2002). This perhaps suggests that when voters can select the day and time that works best for them, waiting is easier to endure because voting is not being crammed into a busy schedule.

West Virginia was another state that authorized early voting in light of the 2000 election. Cindy Smith, team leader of elections for the Secretary of State's office, said the primary reason was voter convenience. She noted that "the whole purpose of the law is to make voting more convenient. . . . People can now vote around their schedules rather than trying to fit it in on one day" (qtd. in "Elections Officials Hope," 2002). Legislators also felt that administration problems could be better addressed through early voting than the absentee process. To provide an incentive for voters to show up early, the state continued to require an excuse to vote absentee via the mail.

Following the 2004 election, other states explored early voting as a solution to ease congestion and long lines on Election Day. Tim Storey, a senior analyst with the National Conference of State Legislatures (NCSL), summarized the atmosphere: "The enduring image in many places of the 2004 election was just the long lines that voters were waiting in, and that is probably one of the top priorities that states are going to look at . . . ways to effectively manage the number of voters. . . . The population continues to grow, and so it's a matter of resources and commitment." Storey said that his office received calls from many states seeking information on early voting programs in other states, noting that "they are looking for ways to make it easier for voters to cast their ballots" (qtd. in Magers 2004).

Michigan, a perennial swing state in presidential elections, saw record lines in 2004. This inspired Secretary of State Terri Lynn Land to advocate a new early voting law. Her spokesman, Kelly Chesney, said, "She sees early voting in person and no-reason absentee as a possible remedy for those longer lines. . . . She would like to make it easier for all voters" (qtd. in Magers 2004). Under Michigan law, only those (1) 60 and older, (2) with a disability, (3) out of town on Election Day, or (4) with religious reasons could acquire an absentee ballot. While Democratic Governor Jennifer Granholm supported an early voting law, it ultimately stalled in the Republican-led legislature.

Oakland County Clerk William Caddell, who supported expanded early voting, said lawmakers were discouraged by the fact that voters could cast their ballots and then change their minds before Election Day, when it would be too late. Some believed that Republicans were resistant because Democrats could more easily mobilize their political base, including young voters, union workers, and racial minorities, if given additional time (Eggert 2004).

Some Republicans in the legislature supported early voting. Senator Beverly Hammerstrom, a Republican from Temperance, said, "Anything we can do to make it easier for people to vote, I think we should do." She believed that the existing absentee system was dysfunctional, as it incentivized lying by voters who wished to vote before Election Day. University of Michigan professor Michael Traugott commented on the partisan implications of a potential law, stating, "Our research shows there is no partisan advantage. . . . The most important predictors of whether a person votes or not is psychological—whether they think the election is important and whether their vote counts" (qtd. in Eggert 2004). Nevertheless, enough Republicans in the legislature blocked the initiative and early voting was not approved in Michigan until a successful ballot referendum in 2018.

Similar debates occurred in Missouri, as the state legislature approved a measure establishing procedures for early voting, but never actually authorized the policy. In the months leading into the 2004 election, St. Louis Mayor Francis Slay sought to implement early voting in the city to ease the burdens of Election Day. The city designated $75,000 to help pay for sites at designated locations. But Republican Secretary of State Matt Blunt refused to interpret the state's law as allowing early voting and blocked the effort (Mannies 2004). In 2011, the state legislature passed an unambiguous early voting law, though Democratic Governor Jay Nixon vetoed it because it included provisions forcing voters to present photo identification at the polls (Lieb 2011).

Ohio was another state that was heavily scrutinized after the 2004 election. National Association of Secretaries of State communications director Meredith Imwalle singled out Ohio, noting that the state "saw lines that were eight and nine hours long" (qtd. in Magers 2004). In Gambier, Ohio, a polling place had to stay open until 4 a.m. to accommodate everyone. Rita Yarman, deputy elections director in Knox County, which includes Gambier, says early voting would have prevented this inconvenience. Ohio Secretary of State Ken Blackwell, a Republican, acknowledged momentum for early voting, stating, "Because of the broad number of people who experienced this inconvenience, I don't think the full-court press for change is going to let up" (qtd. in Drinkard 2004). Indeed, in 2005, the Ohio House passed a law allowing early voting by a vote of 60–36, while the Senate approved the measure 21–11. Each chamber had a solid Republican majority at the time of passage and the bill was signed into law by Republican Governor Bob Taft, suggesting that partisan attitudes were different from those seen in Michigan and Missouri (Ohio General Assembly 2005).

In 2005, the Democratic-led Maryland Legislature also approved a law allowing early voting. State Republicans strongly opposed the measure, arguing that it lacked necessary safeguards to prevent abuse. Delegate Christopher Shank, the lower chamber's minority whip, said, "Given that Maryland does not require photo identification for voting, this is ripe for fraud" (qtd. in Rein 2008). Republican Governor Bob Ehrlich promptly rejected the bill, though the legislature was able to override his veto. It appeared as though Maryland would have early voting in time for the 2006 midterm elections. In June 2006, Maryland Senate President Mike Miller defended the new law, stating, "The important aspect of early voting is that working men and women can actually vote on Saturday. . . . They don't have to take off work on Tuesday to vote" (qtd. in "Maryland Early Voting," 2006). Democrats were unapologetic about their hopes of increasing turnout among groups traditionally supportive of them. Delegate Sandy Rosenberg, a Democrat from Baltimore, said the law was necessary because "younger people are less likely to stand in long lines on Election Day" (qtd. in Rein 2008). In the months after passage, the heavily Democratic legislature established 21 early voting sites, mostly in urban areas where their support was concentrated (Rein 2008).

But plans were stifled in August 2006 when the law was struck down by the Maryland Court of Appeals.[2] Judges, including some appointed by Democratic governors, ruled that it was illegal for Maryland elections officials to open polling stations during the week before Election Day because the state constitution strictly set the timing of elections. In addition, the new law also improperly permitted voters to cast ballots outside of their precincts. While early voting defenders cited 10 other early voting states with similar provisions in their constitutions, the Maryland judges were unwilling to consider conditions outside of the state (Mosk 2006). The legislature then moved to have a referendum to amend the state's constitution and allow early voting. The measure was placed on the 2008 ballot, where it passed with slightly over 70% of the vote (Farr 2010). When Bob Ehrlich, ousted from office in 2006, ran again in 2010, he cast his ballot early (Wagner 2010).

THE NEW ENGLAND EXCEPTION

The New England region mostly resisted the national move toward early voting in the 1990s and 2000s. Vermont and Maine had early voting sites and no-excuse absentee policies by 2001, but the region's other four states— Connecticut, Massachusetts, New Hampshire, and Rhode Island—continued to offer no options for most voters to cast their ballots before Election Day. In 2016, Massachusetts finally adopted early in-person voting sites, but it continued to restrict absentee ballots unless a valid excuse was provided. Rhode Island approved both no-excuse absentee and early in-person voting in 2020. As of 2021, Connecticut and New Hampshire continue to resist all forms of early voting.

The region's unique election administration customs arguably make early voting more challenging to implement. While most states have county election management, New England conducts its elections at the town level, reflecting the long tradition of autonomous self-government in the region's cities and towns. Connecticut, for example, has 169 towns, each of which has its own municipal government responsible for conducting elections. If early voting were adopted in the state, sites would need to be established in each town in order for these entities to maintain control over the electoral process. According to one report, adding just three days of early voting would increase administrative costs by about 60%, placing a disproportionate burden on small towns (Weeks 2009).

Maine, who also conducts elections at the town level, allows early voting. Citizens may appear at a municipal clerk's office in the month before Election Day, receive an absentee ballot, and complete it on site. Maine has considered expanding its offerings to include more expansive vote centers in the weeks before Election Day, but it has hesitated because small towns may have difficulty staffing the necessary number of workers. In 2007, the state conducted a pilot program whereby nine towns offered expanded early voting. Each municipality had to choose a single location that was large enough to handle estimated turnout and accessible to people with disabilities. While feedback was largely positive, many town clerks expressed reservations about expanded early voting. A clerk from Bar Harbor stated, "Small municipalities . . . cannot be running an election 14 to 30 days prior to Election Day and maintain the daily operations of a clerk's office." The Freeport clerk offered that "the logistics of setting up and preparing for Tuesday (Election Day) are large and important. To have us all totally exhausted going into Tuesday because there is too much to accomplish on Monday, has become problematic" (qtd. in Maine Secretary of State 2007).

Massachusetts adopted an early voting law in 2014 (it went into effect in 2016) that largely mirrored the Maine program. The law provided for 12 days of early voting in presidential and national midterm election years. Voting would take place at the office of the town clerk. Upon the law's decisive passage, clerks from around the state immediately expressed concern. Nancy Blackmer, president of the Massachusetts Town Clerks' Association, remarked, "Everyone's budgets are being cut all the time. I hope it doesn't mean we're going to have to come up with more money to implement it" (qtd.

in Schoenberg 2014). Asked about the cost to municipalities, Governor Deval Patrick said, "Cities and towns, like all of us, have a responsibility for making voting easier. Frankly, that's something everybody is committed to" (qtd. in Massachusetts 2017). Ultimately, the state addressed the clerk's concerns, appropriating funds to cover additional expenses borne by towns. In 2016, State Auditor Suzanne Bump and Secretary of the Commonwealth William Galvin determined that towns would be reimbursed $1.06 million, while the figure jumped to $1.14 million in 2017. Given that Massachusetts had a state budget nearing $40 billion in 2018, early voting appeared to be a bargain. In 2016, the first year early voting was offered, nearly 30% of the state's voters cast ballots before Election Day.

The tradition of small towns conducting elections indeed makes early voting more difficult because economies of scale cannot be realized. Rather than a single county pooling resources to offer convenience voting in the weeks before Election Day, New England states—given their current system, which few wish to change—must conduct this effort in each individual town. As Massachusetts has demonstrated, however, this problem can be greatly mollified with relatively modest investments by state governments.

UNIVERSAL VOTE-BY-MAIL

The Pacific Northwest states of Oregon and Washington were the first to entirely eliminate physical voting and move exclusively to absentee ballots. In 1998, Oregon citizens approved universal vote-by-mail (VBM) in a statewide initiative. Ballots would be mailed to all registered voters weeks before Election Day. Several years after its adoption, the Secretary of State's office claimed that Oregon's approach "raises voter participation, decreases costs and increases the overall integrity of the election process" (qtd. in Gronke 2005). Several studies initially found that the change increased turnout (Southwell and Burchett 2000; Southwell 2009), though that finding could not be replicated in subsequent analyses (Gronke and Miller 2012).

Washington, after years of observing Oregon's policy, became the second state to offer universal VBM. The state gradually implemented the policy on a county-by-county basis during the 2000s, and in 2011 finally mandated that all counties move to this system. In 2013, Colorado approved universal VBM, but decided to complement mailed ballots with some early and Election Day polling sites. Unlike the early voting programs approved in Western states in the early 1990s, the vote was markedly partisan. In fact, no Republicans in either the Colorado House or Senate supported the measure before it was signed by Democratic Governor John Hickenlooper. In chapter 2, I report that Colorado's "kitchen sink" approach increased turnout in both 2014 and 2018.

Colorado's neighbor, Utah, also began implementing universal VBM at the county level in 2012. Unlike in Colorado, VBM was broadly supported by both Democrats and Republicans in the state legislature. By 2018, each Utah county had opted into the program.

In 2019, Hawaii approved a law authorizing universal VBM in statewide elections beginning with the 2020 primary elections. The bill, which was estimated to save the state $750,000 per election cycle by hiring fewer poll workers, was also more broadly supported than the Colorado measure. It passed unanimously in the Hawaii Senate, while 60% of Republicans in the Hawaii House (and all Democrats) supported it (McAvoy 2019).

Beyond the five states with permanent VBM programs throughout the state, three additional states—California, Nebraska and North Dakota—permit counties to opt into all-mail elections. Unlike in Utah, all counties in these states have not (yet) chosen to adopt VBM on a permanent basis. In 2020, however, California did employ statewide VBM in light of the COVID-19 pandemic. Other statewide VBM programs were temporarily approved in the District of Columbia, New Jersey, Nevada, and Vermont, but each was limited to the 2020 election (Scanlan 2020).

EARLY VOTING GETS POLITICAL

In 2008, 31 states had early voting laws in effect. By this point, there were certainly some indications that convenience voting measures had become more partisan. Republican opposition to programs had stifled adoption in states such as Maryland, Michigan, and Missouri. However, new policies had still been approved by Republican governors in many other states, including politically competitive places like Florida and Ohio.

Republican resistance to early voting notably grew, however, after Barack Obama's victory in the 2008 presidential election. Many in the party believed that Obama benefitted from early voting laws in swing states such as Florida, North Carolina, and Ohio. Indeed, early voting had been an important part of Obama's strategy to mobilize his electoral base. In fact, Obama's national field director, Jon Carson, bluntly declared that "early voting didn't change our strategy. It was our strategy" (qtd. in Kenski et al. 2009). Unlike Democrats of the past, Obama had the finances to maintain a robust early vote operation throughout the weeks in which it was offered. A featured *New York Times* editorial commented that "Republican lawmakers have taken a good look at voting patterns, realized that early voting might have played a role in Mr. Obama's 2008 victory, and now want to reduce that possibility in 2012" (qtd. in "They Want to Make Voting Harder," 2011). Matt Taylor of *The National Memo* stated that "early voting has become a symbol of the Obama era, boosting minority and youth turnout to historic levels in 2008" (Taylor 2012). Cynthia Tucker of the *Atlanta-Journal Constitution* was blunter, arguing that "I remember a time when Republicans liked early voting. . . . When did they become unhappy with early voting? After 2008. The Obama campaign was extremely well-organized. And one of the things they did was to encourage their voters to come to the polls early. They did. After Obama took advantage of early voting, Republicans said 'oops,' we need to cut back that early voting" (qtd. in Tucker 2011).

Upon taking control of many state legislatures and gubernatorial offices after the 2010 elections, Republicans in many states pursued bills to limit (but not eliminate) early voting. They generally argued that doing so was necessary to cut costs. In May 2011, newly elected Florida Governor Rick Scott signed legislation that reduced the state's early voting period from 14 to eight days. Republicans argued that opening the polls for fewer days would aid crippled county budgets around the state. The bill made several other changes, including ending early voting on the Sunday before Election Day. Democrats and civic leaders felt that this action was politically motivated, arguing that Black Floridians would find it harder to get to the polls. Organizers had previously mobilized and transported Black voters to early voting sites as they exited church on Sunday mornings, events known as "Souls to the Polls." Buses would pick up parishioners at the church door and drive them to vote; pastors even led the parade to the polls on many occasions (Man 2010). The bill also included a provision preventing voters who had changed their address since the last election from updating their status at the polls. The address change restriction was expected to hurt university students in particular—a demographic that was integral to Obama's victory in 2008.

State Senator Mike Fasano was one of two Republican senators who voted against the final bill, arguing that Florida ought to expand early voting and encourage more voter registration activity. Fasano acknowledged that partisan considerations seemed to be behind the Republicans' actions, noting, "I'm a Republican, but I believe the only reason this bill was passed was to help one party over another" (qtd. in Whittenburg 2011). Senator Gwen Margolis, a Democrat from Aventura, said that the popularity of early voting across the state should mean more days and sites. She argued that the new law would "disenfranchise and really anger a lot of people" (qtd. in "Florida Republicans Push," 2011). After Florida suffered long lines during the 2012 elections, the legislature reversed itself somewhat, allowing counties to increase the early voting window to 14 days if they wished. In a victory for advocates, the legislature also restored early voting on the Sunday before Election Day (Cotterell 2013).

North Carolina Republicans also acted to limit early voting options. The party was angered in 2008, believing that some county officials altered their early voting programs to accommodate Obama campaign rallies. Specifically, Cumberland County (Fayetteville) had expanded the number of early voting sites open on Sunday, October 19, the date of a large Obama rally at the Crown Center Coliseum in Fayetteville. At the rally, Obama explicitly urged supporters to vote early, stating, "If you like what you hear today, and if you're ready for change, and if you haven't voted yet, don't wait until Nov. 4 . . . we want to get as many votes in as possible as early as possible" (qtd. in Baker 2008). Terri Robertson, director of Cumberland County's elections, defended the county's action, saying she was worried that a flood of voters after the rally would create too much stress for her staff. She stated, "We decided that the best thing to do for our staff was to open two more sites so they weren't up all night processing voters." Linda Daves, chairwoman of the state Republican Party, was not persuaded. She asserted that her party supported early voting, but that "[the county's] action makes the voting process an extension of a partisan political rally and that is clearly inappropriate" (qtd. in Baker 2008).

Over 60% of North Carolina votes were cast early in 2008, one of the highest rates in the nation. In early 2011, the Republican-controlled state assembly voted to cut the early voting period by a week, reducing it to 10 days before Election Day. The state senate passed a similar bill, arguing that cost savings were necessary. Jim Davis, a Macon County Republican, argued, "We were just trying to minimize the time early voting polls were open . . . so the expense is not so great for local election boards" (qtd. in Weiser and Norden 2012). But the North Carolina elections board and many county boards said the bill would actually cost more money because they would need to open more voting sites on Election Day. Michael Bitzer, a political scientist at Catawba College in Salisbury, said that if approved, the changes could have a big impact. He noted, "In today's world, people expect flexibility. They expect options, and that's one thing early voting gives them, being able to cast a ballot at their convenience" (qtd. in Morrill 2011). Ultimately, Democratic Governor Beverly Perdue received and vetoed a version of the law. After Republican Governor Pat McCrory was elected, the cuts to early voting were enacted in 2013.

In Ohio, a Republican-led legislature and Governor John Kasich approved a law reducing early voting from 30 days before an election to 21 days by mail and 17 in person—eliminating a "golden week" when citizens could register and vote on the same day. The bill also prohibited counties and others from continuing to mail unsolicited absentee ballot applications to all registered voters. Some counties, including Cuyahoga County, had adopted the practice because officials believed that the reduced hassle of requesting a ballot may improve turnout. Further, the legislation killed earlier efforts to expand early voting sites in Ohio, a state with few sites per capita.

Democrats in the state legislature said that the Republican-backed bill was aimed at suppressing the votes of poor and minority populations that tended to vote Democratic (Siegel 2011). Cuyahoga County officials also argued that pre-mailing absentee ballots to voters had effectively reduced the number of Election Day voters in 2008, thereby shortening lines and reducing administrative problems. Board of elections member Inajo Davis said, "We've had great success with the mailings. We do think it increases voter participation. . . . It also increases our ability to be efficient in tabulation and conducting all our election administration tasks" (qtd. in Guillen 2011).

Republican efforts to restrict voting access were not limited to early voting. After winning majorities in many state houses in 2010, Republicans passed 25 laws across 19 states making it harder to vote. Maine ended same-day registration (SDR), which has been found to increase turnout by several percentage points. Several states, including Florida, ended voter registration drives. A number of states required citizens to provide documentary proof of citizenship (e.g., a passport, birth certificate, or naturalization papers) in order to register to vote. Numerous states, including Texas, Mississippi, Alabama, Wisconsin, Tennessee, and Pennsylvania, adopted strict laws requiring photo identification in order to vote, despite the fact that up to 11% of eligible voters lack such identification (Brennan Center for Justice 2012).

A decade later, Republicans were still pushing restrictive voting measures. Efforts were seemingly reignited after Joe Biden defeated Donald Trump in the 2020 presidential election. In that contest, a record number of Americans—nearly two-thirds—had cast early ballots due to the COVID-19 pandemic. In the first three months of 2021 alone, over 250 restrictive voting measures were proposed across the states. Some quickly passed, including notable restrictions on absentee voting. Georgia shortened the window for requesting and returning absentee ballots, while also requiring that absentee voters possess a government-issued ID. The state also restricted people from providing food or water to those waiting in voting lines. Given that some Georgia voters faced lines over 10 hours in 2020, this latter provision was widely criticized (Corasaniti and Epstein 2021). Within months, Florida Republicans followed Georgia's lead in requiring identification to cast an absentee ballot. Governor Ron DeSantis also approved (1) cuts to ballot drop box hours, (2) restrictions on mailing ballots to those who did not request one, and (3) a more cumbersome application process for those applying for absentee ballots (Hassan 2021).

While Republicans have long cited budget considerations and the need to prevent voter fraud in justifying these measures, some have brazenly acknowledged a political motive. The majority leader of the Pennsylvania House, Mike Turzai, bragged in June 2012 that the state's new voter identification law was "gonna allow Governor [Mitt] Romney to win the state of

Pennsylvania, done" (qtd. in Waldman 2016). In Florida, former Republican Governor Charlie Crist told *The Palm Beach Post* in 2012 that the state's restrictive election laws had been devised to suppress Democratic votes (Kam 2012). The following year, a North Carolina Republican Party official said on Comedy Central's *The Daily Show* that his state's voter ID law would "kick the Democrats in the butt" (qtd. in Garcia 2013). In an academic study, Biggers and Hanmer (2017) find that a state's propensity to adopt strict photo ID laws increases when a Republican legislature and governor assume power and a state's Black and Latino populations (who tend to vote Democratic) are larger.

While Republican-led legislatures have often been able to pass voting restrictions by healthy margins, most must clear one final hurdle in order to become (or remain) law. That hurdle is the formidable Voting Rights Act.

THE VOTING RIGHTS ACT

The Voting Rights Act of 1965 has been hailed by many—including the U.S. Department of Justice—as the most effective civil rights law in U.S. history. Its full impact can only be understood by tracing the history that necessitated its passage. After the Civil War, three amendments were added to the U.S. Constitution. The 13th Amendment (1865) prohibits slavery. The 14th Amendment (1868) grants citizenship to anyone "born or naturalized in the United States" and guarantees every person due process and equal protection rights. Finally, the 15th Amendment (1870) provides that "the right of citizens of the United States to vote shall not be denied or abridged by the United States or by any State on account of race, color, or previous condition of servitude." In each case, these amendments empower Congress to enforce their provisions through "appropriate legislation."

During the Reconstruction period after the Civil War, Congress initially took aggressive action to ensure that voting rights for Blacks were upheld. The Enforcement Act of 1870 made it a federal crime to "deny the civil or political rights of any American." The law provided for federal supervision of the electoral process, including voter registration. Those who sought to block citizens from voting would be prosecuted in federal courts. By 1872, with Black citizens voting throughout the South, there were 320 elected Black legislators in the region serving in the federal and state governments, a figure unmatched even in the 1990s (Kousser 1999). The leaders of the South Carolina House and Senate, the governor of Louisiana, and a U.S. senator from Mississippi were all Black men. But as the passions of the Civil War faded and economic concerns increased in the 1870s, enthusiasm for enforcing voting rights in the South waned. In 1876, the Supreme Court limited the scope of the Enforcement Act, ruling (in *United States v. Reese*) that the 15th Amendment did not confer upon any individual the right to vote, but rather forbade states from giving any citizen preferential treatment. In other words, states could determine how voters were qualified and under what circumstances voting would be allowed. In doing so, the court effectively allowed states to design creative restrictions that could disproportionately prevent Blacks from voting.

With the blessing bestowed by *Reese*, Southern states adopted devices such as poll taxes, knowing that many poor Black sharecroppers were unable to pay. States administered literacy tests, many of which were designed to see citizens fail. In order to shield White voters from unaffordable taxes and difficult tests, many states adopted "grandfather clauses" exempting citizens whose grandfathers had been permitted to vote. For the most part, this exempted White voters, but not Black voters, whose grandfathers were slaves.

Between 1888 and 1908, every former Confederate state also initiated "White primaries." In the postwar South, the Democratic Party was dominant, meaning that the winner of primary elections typically won without much (if any) competition from the Republican Party. By restricting its' primaries to White voters, Southern Democrats effectively banned Blacks from voting in the most consequential elections. Parties argued that as private organizations, they had the right to determine nominees for office as they wished (Perman 2001).

For decades, the federal courts largely accepted these restrictive practices. In 1915, the Supreme Court did rule in *Guinn v. United States* that Oklahoma's grandfather clause (and those in many other states) was an unconstitutional violation of the 15th Amendment. But when Oklahoma and other states slyly rewrote their laws to continue disenfranchising Blacks, the Court looked the other way. In fact, it would not effectively end grandfather clauses until 1939 (in *Lane v. Wilson*). Five years later, the Court declared the White primary unconstitutional in *Smith v. Allwright* (1944). But Black participation in elections remained anemic, as violence, intimidation, and other forms of discrimination made registering and voting difficult. In many jurisdictions, despite the Court's ruling in *Lane*, White registrars only required Blacks to complete nearly impossible literacy tests.

At the height of the Civil Rights Movement in 1964, Congress passed and President Lyndon Johnson signed the Civil Rights Act. The law banned discrimination on the basis of "race, color, religion, sex, or national origin," ending racial discrimination and segregation in schools, employment, and public accommodations. Several months after the law's passage, civil rights organizations such as the Southern Christian Leadership Conference (SCLC) and the Student Nonviolent Coordinating Committee (SNCC) pushed for federal action to protect the voting rights of racial minorities. Voting protections had largely been omitted from the 1964 law. After peaceful marches in Selma, Alabama led to violent confrontations with police, momentum for action on voting rights increased. In August 1965, Congress passed and President Johnson signed the Voting Rights Act, a sweeping measure that would finally deliver the promise of the 15th Amendment nearly 100 years later (Waldman 2016).

The Voting Rights Act includes several sections designed to protect the ability of all persons—regardless of race—to vote. Notably, Section 2 prohibits any jurisdiction from implementing a "voting qualification or prerequisite to voting, or standard, practice, or procedure . . . in a manner which results in a denial or abridgement of the right . . . to vote on account of race, color, or language minority status." In 1982, Congress amended the law to add a "results" test, prohibiting any voting law that has a discriminatory *effect* regardless of whether the law was intentionally enacted or maintained for a discriminatory purpose. Section 4 of the law includes a coverage formula whereby certain jurisdictions with a history of discrimination are forced to comply with special provisions. The most recent coverage formula—updated in 1975—was applied to the entire states of Alaska, Arizona, Texas, Louisiana, Mississippi, Alabama, Georgia, South Carolina, and Virginia. Additionally, certain jurisdictions in California, South Dakota, Michigan, Florida, North Carolina, and New Hampshire were covered. While the federal government would enforce voting rights throughout the country, these jurisdictions—under Section 5 of the law—would be unable to make any changes to their voting laws without pre-clearance from the U.S. Justice Department.

The law was a quick success. While only 29.3% of Blacks were registered to vote in jurisdictions subject to the Section 4 coverage formula before the law, this number jumped to 52.1% within two years. Between 1965 and 1985, the number of Blacks elected as state legislators in the 11 former Confederate states increased from 3 to 176 (Fulwood 2016).

After Republican-led legislatures began restricting voting access in the early 2010s, the Voting Rights Act was the primary tool through which opponents—including the Obama administration—could challenge these measures in court. Challenging restrictions, however, became more difficult in Section 4 jurisdictions beginning in June 2013. In *Shelby Co. v. Holder* (2013), the Supreme Court invalidated the coverage formula, ruling that it was no longer justified given changes in the covered jurisdictions since 1975 (when the formula was last updated). Pre-clearance was still permitted, but only if a new formula was drafted and approved by Congress. With Congress gridlocked and unable to act, preclearance was effectively dead. Laws could be challenged only *after* they were adopted. The result has been a confusing cluster of court decisions allowing, ending, and delaying the implementation of laws. With the Supreme Court unable and unwilling to become involved in every specific case, lower federal courts have often had the final say regarding specific state laws, with varying results across the country.

Under the Voting Rights Act, states cannot adopt voting changes that disproportionately hurt racial and ethnic minority groups. Note, however, that states cannot be forced to adopt measures that make voting easier. For example, imagine that State A adopts early voting, but State B does not. If State A wishes to later cut its early voting offerings, it can only do so legally if federal courts determine that the changes do not disproportionately make voting harder for racial and ethnic minority citizens. If the cuts are deemed to have this effect, they can be struck down. In this example, State A is forced to continue its early voting program (without cuts), while State B is still permitted to have no early voting law. Under federal law, once you establish a new baseline of convenience, any changes cannot have a discriminatory impact on racial or ethnic minorities.

With these considerations in mind, federal courts by 2021 had allowed most new voting restrictions to stand, with some notable exceptions. Freed from the "pre-clearance" requirement by *Shelby*, southern states closed at least 1,200 polling locations between 2013 and 2019. Despite lawsuits, these closures were allowed to proceed (Sullivan 2019).

Courts did strike down (or at least force modifications to) voter ID laws in various states, including Texas, North Carolina, and Wisconsin. The 2011 Texas law required voters to produce one of seven photo IDs, such as a driver's license, military ID, or passport, before casting ballots. Evidence filed in a lawsuit indicated that as many as 600,000 eligible Texas voters had none of the acceptable IDs. After a district court invalidated the law, Texas came to a settlement whereby those without any of the IDs could still vote if they had a voter registration certificate, a birth certificate, a utility bill or bank statement, a government check, or any other government document with their name and address. In addition, voters would have to sign an affidavit stating that they were unable to easily procure any of the photo IDs (Wines 2016).

Early voting restrictions have also had mixed results in court. In Florida, a federal judge approved the state's early voting cuts in 2012, though the legislature gave counties the right to restore them in 2013. In 2014, Florida Governor Rick Scott issued a directive to county elections supervisors banning early voting sites on college campuses. The directive was challenged in court by the League of Women Voters of Florida and other plaintiffs. A federal district court issued a preliminary injunction, ruling that it was intentionally discriminatory on account of age, in violation of the 26th Amendment. The state relented in 2020 and counties were permitted to place sites on college campuses (Calvan 2020).

In 2016, the Fourth U.S. Circuit Court of Appeals ruled that North Carolina's 2013 state law that cut early voting by a week and ended SDR had targeted Blacks with "surgical precision." As a result, it was inconsistent with the Voting Rights Act. The legislature responded by mandating that all early voting sites in the state remain open on weekdays from 7 a.m. to 7 p.m. The requirement, which many localities found difficult to meet, required counties to shift resources and close nearly 20% of the state's early voting sites (Paterson 2018). The legislature also explicitly eliminated the popular last Saturday of early voting for all elections after 2018.

In 2016, the Sixth U.S. Circuit Court of Appeals permitted Ohio to implement a reduction in early voting days. In doing so, the state eliminated its "golden week," a seven-day period where voters could register and vote early at the same time (Graham 2016).

In 2016, a U.S. district judge blocked a Wisconsin law that cut early voting from 30 to 12 days, restricted early voting to weekdays, and permitted each jurisdiction to have only one early voting site. Ruling that Black and Latino voters were more likely to use early voting, District Judge James Peterson ruled that the law "intentionally discriminates on the basis of race" (qtd. in Levine 2018). In 2018, Wisconsin lawmakers passed an amended version of the law that cut early voting days, but allowed those days to include weekends. Peterson remained dissatisfied with the changes and quickly blocked the law (Levine 2019). However, the Seventh U.S. Circuit Court of Appeals restored the cuts in 2020, as well as a prohibition on sending absentee ballots to most voters by fax or email (Marley 2020).

As voting restrictions made their way through state legislatures and courtrooms, many states also quietly expanded voting rights. Since 2010, eight states—Maryland (2010), Massachusetts (2016), Minnesota (2016), Michigan (2018), New York (2019), Pennsylvania (2020), Rhode Island (2020), and Virginia (2020)—have implemented new permanent early voting laws (NCSL 2020a). Meanwhile, 12 states have adopted SDR laws since 2010, allowing any citizen to register on the same day that they cast a ballot (NCSL 2021b). Since 2015, 20 states and the District of Columbia have approved automatic voter registration (AVR) laws (NCSL 2021a). In these states, adult citizens are automatically registered whenever they interact with government agencies (though citizens can opt out if they choose). Those agencies then transfer voter registration information to election officials. Finally, while more than six million citizens were ineligible to vote in 2018 because of a felony conviction, this figure has dropped since 2010. In recent years, numerous states—including California (2016), Delaware (2016), Maryland (2016), Virginia (2016), Louisiana (2017), Wyoming (2017), Florida (2018), and New York (2018)—have loosened their laws regarding ex-felon voting rights (Mayes and Rabinowitz 2020).

CONCLUSIONS

The 2010s saw voting rights and access become a major political football. Republican-led legislatures became convinced that early voting, easing the registration process, and allowing those without identification to vote hurt them politically. Democrats rallied behind convenience programs, which they believed helped bring more voters (particularly more of *their* voters) to the polls. Despite this trend, however, early voting is hardly limited to "blue" states today. While programs are politically polarizing today, this was not the case when most states adopted them. Recall that Texas approved early in-person voting in the late 1980s through a noncontroversial voice vote. "Red" states like Idaho and Nebraska also approved programs with little controversy. While the politics in these states would make adoption of early voting less certain in 2021, the programs have now become embedded in their respective political systems. And importantly, their citizens almost universally like the ability to vote early.

In my conversations with county elections officials—to be discussed more in chapter 2—nearly all clerks reported that their voters appreciate early voting. One commented that citizens like that "they can vote . . . near work or errands, or on weekends" (Email to author, 2019). Another official noted that for some citizens, "the ease of traveling to the early vote location . . . is easier than to their own polling place" (Email to author, 2019). In Nevada, one official described early voting as very popular, highlighting that "our retail locations are by far the most popular, as people can vote and then do their shopping" (Email to author, 2019). Another added that with early voting, citizens can "plan voting around their day instead of their day around voting" (Email to author, 2019). Survey data supports the notion that early voting is popular with Americans. Two 2020 polls conducted by the American Bar Association found that over 70% of Americans support early voting (ABA 2020). A Pew Research Center survey showed that large majorities of early voters in 2020 had a positive experience casting their ballots (Pew 2020). In short, early voting is durable because it is extremely popular with voters. Furthermore, once an early voting program exists, cutting the program is difficult given the realities of the Voting Rights Act. Even when Republican-led states such as Florida, Georgia, and Texas approved new absentee voting restrictions in 2021, none sought to end their respective early voting programs. The Georgia law, in fact, expanded early in-person voting on weekends. Early voting, you might say, becomes too big to fail once it is adopted.

As I previously noted, many states temporarily expanded their early voting offerings in 2020 in light of the COVID-19 pandemic. Of the 15 states that still typically demand an excuse in order to receive an absentee ballot, three— Massachusetts, Delaware, and South Carolina—dropped the requirement.

An additional eight states—Alabama, Arkansas, Connecticut, Kentucky, Missouri, New Hampshire, New York, and West Virginia—allowed voters to cite the pandemic as a valid excuse to vote by mail. Only five states— Indiana, Louisiana, Mississippi, Tennessee, and Texas—continued to enforce their excuse requirements for absentee ballots. Meanwhile, several states that typically lack physical early voting sites, such as Alabama and Kentucky, provided the option in 2020. In fact, only Mississippi failed to provide all voters with the opportunity to either receive an absentee ballot or vote early in person (Scanlan 2020). While these changes were meant to be temporary, removing convenience measures that have been implemented is always difficult. Outrage at the aforementioned 2021 Georgia law was widespread, leading to condemnations from Georgia companies such as Delta and Coca-Cola. Major League Baseball even relocated its All-Star Game, which was slated to be played in Atlanta that summer. It is clear that voters become accustomed to convenience voting and react unkindly to its rescission. Republicans wishing to return to more restrictive early voting policies may ultimately find their efforts akin to closing the barn door after the horse has escaped. Only time will tell.

Even if early voting does revert to 2016 or 2018 levels, it remains worthy of our attention. More than one-third of the electorate now routinely casts early ballots. Election Day as we once knew it no longer exists in the United States. Distilling the aggregate effects of this massive change to our elections is a tricky enterprise. As I have discussed at length, early voting has not emerged (and does not exist) in a vacuum. As programs have developed, other changes to the electoral process and society have materialized. Voter identification laws have made voting harder in some places, but automatic and same-day voter registration have eased the process. Meanwhile, political polarization and tribalism have expanded, turning some voters away from politics, but making others more committed than ever to defeat the opposition. Early voting is only one small—but important—piece of American elections and democracy. Isolating its effects—both intended and unintended—on the political system is the ambitious goal of the chapters that follow.

NOTES

1. South Carolina was the final holdout, granting this right in 1860.
2. The Maryland Court of Appeals is the highest court in the state.

Chapter 2

Early Voting and County Turnout

Since the early 1990s, early voting has evolved from a novelty available in a handful of states to a staple of U.S. elections. Forty-two states and D.C. allow any registered citizen to either receive an absentee ballot or vote at a physical location somewhere in their county. Even before the COVID-19 pandemic led over 100 million voters to cast pre-Election Day ballots in 2020, early voting had become quite popular with voters. Since 2008, over 30% of the electorate has consistently voted early in presidential elections, including a strong majority of voters in several states. But while many voters participate in early voting, it is less clear if programs are encouraging *new voters* to cast ballots. In this chapter, I assess whether early voting increases turnout by making the process more convenient. Numerous researchers have investigated this question, though the verdict on early voting and turnout remains split. A number of initial studies, limited by the low number of states with programs at the time, reported a positive relationship (Dubin and Kalsow 1996; Oliver 1996; Stein and Garcia-Monet 1997; Stein 1998; Southwell and Burchett 2000; Berinsky et al. 2001; Neeley and Richardson 2001). More recent research, however, has been less promising. Examining state-level data, some studies have found early voting to have only a very limited effect on turnout (Gronke et al. 2007) or no effect at all (Fitzgerald 2005; Highton 2005; Primo et al. 2007; Scheele et al. 2008). One prominent study reported that early voting actually *reduces* turnout by limiting the civic excitement that traditionally surrounds Election Day (Burden et al. 2014). Another agreed that early in-person voting depresses turnout, but found that no-excuse absentee laws positively affect participation (Larocca and Klemanski 2011).

Before early voting is disregarded as a failed experiment (at least with regards to increasing turnout), the literature could benefit from new perspectives. Many studies have treated early voting as a binary variable, coding states simply on the basis of whether or not they have any policy in effect. Some, though not all, have assessed the turnout effects of early in-person voting versus no-excuse absentee voting. Very few studies, however, have considered variation in early voting implementation at the local level. When it comes to early in-person voting at least, county offerings often differ greatly even *within* early voting states. While some election clerks are committed to expansive early in-person voting programs, others offer the minimum services required by state law. Budgetary concerns also dictate the scope of early voting in many counties. While past research correctly posits that turnout should theoretically increase as voting becomes easier, it may overlook the variation with which early voting programs actually reduce participation costs in particular communities.

I develop a new model designed to more effectively account for the convenience offered to citizens through early voting. In most early voting states, counties (not states) have the freedom to determine the total number of sites offered. Therefore, my model applies county-level data from the U.S. Election Assistance Commission (EAC) to assess whether those with more sites per capita record higher levels of participation. I also measure the effects of universal vote-by-mail (VBM) and no-excuse absentee voting options, as well as the length of early voting periods. In all tests, I account for other known influences on participation such as lagged county turnout, registration laws, demographics, and political competitiveness.

Examining the 2012 and 2016 presidential elections, as well as the 2014 and 2018 midterm elections, I find that early voting sites have a significant and positive relationship with county turnout. Across many specifications, the relationship holds. Substantively, the findings suggest that adding 10 sites in a county of 10,000 voting-age residents increases turnout by several percentage points or more. In urban counties with large populations, the effect size is even larger, offering further confirmation that the findings are substantively meaningful. In most specifications, I report that liberalized absentee laws and longer early voting windows also lead to higher turnout. Contrary to the recent findings of others, early voting *can* increase participation. Its effect, however, is conditioned on the level of convenience it provides voters. These findings suggest that more attention must be paid to the specifics of early voting offerings (and all voter convenience policies) rather than simply the policy's adoption in a given state.

THE DECISION TO VOTE

A citizen's decision to vote has long confounded rational choice scholars. Assuming that individuals will vote when perceived benefits outweigh perceived costs, it is not obvious that it is a sensible decision. The odds of one vote affecting an election outcome are very long, while casting a vote requires effort in the form of learning about the candidates, driving to the polls, and waiting in (a sometimes long) line. Extending upon the seminal work of Downs (1957), Riker and Ordeshook (1968) argue that voting offers citizens a unique opportunity to affirm their allegiance to the political system and exercise support for candidates who share their beliefs. In this sense, voting provides benefits beyond the slim possibility that one's vote will affect an election outcome. Ashenfelter and Kelley (1975) introduce the notion that voting may not only be fulfilling, but fun. Election Day is a communal event that brings friends and neighbors together in a social setting. Participating in the process is therefore a form of entertainment.

Aldrich (1993) argues that the perceived benefits of voting are commonly manipulated. Citizens are subject to various messages from political campaigns, the media, and pressure groups that raise the perceived stakes of electoral contests. As lucrative benefits and dire consequences become tied to one's candidate choice, voting becomes seemingly more important, leading many to the polls.

Ferejohn and Fiorina (1974) focus on the cost side of the equation, offering a "minimax regret" explanation for voting. While failing to vote is unlikely to alter an outcome, it is a possibility. If we assume that risk-averse individuals act in a way that minimizes their maximum regret, voting becomes rational. Kenney and Rice (1989) offer support for this explanation through a study carried out in two different cities, finding that over one-third of respondents considered the possibility that failing to vote could cost their preferred candidate the election.

While efforts to define perceived costs and benefits have differed, academics and others have long applied rational choice logic to posit that making voting more convenient should increase the number of citizens choosing to do it (Wolfinger and Rosenstone 1980; Piven and Cloward 1989; Teixeira 1992; Rosenstone and Hansen 1993; Gronke and McDonald 2008; Fullmer 2015b). A large number of studies, for example, have both hypothesized and confirmed that same-day registration (SDR) laws increase turnout (Fenster 1994; Brians and Grofman 1999; Knack 2001; Burden et al. 2014; Leighley and Nagler 2014). Similarly, as early voting expanded in the 1990s and 2000s, numerous scholars began to examine its effects on participation. Initially, the results were promising. Oliver (1996) finds that early voting sites and no-excuse absentee laws aided turnout in 1992, at least when combined with mobilization efforts by candidates and parties. Dubin and Kalsow (1996) report small gains from early voting in California in the early 1990s, while Lyons and Scheb (1999) note that programs helped retain infrequent voters in one Tennessee county in 1996. Given that a relatively small number of votes were cast early in the mid-1990s, however, these findings have limited application today.

A number of early studies recognized the importance of early voting's implementation. Neeley and Richardson (1996) conclude that county turnout increases as the percentage of citizens living in a town with an early voting site rises, arguing that early in-person voting only increases convenience to a voter if a location is within a reasonable distance. Examining the 1992 elections in Texas, Stein and Garcia-Monet (1997) observe that counties that offer more nontraditional early voting stations (e.g., shopping malls) have higher levels of participation before Election Day and, most importantly, greater overall turnout.

A number of projects have applied aggregate data to the turnout question, examining the effect of early voting across the nation and, in some cases, across multiple years. These studies, however, have largely omitted any consideration of local implementation. Generally, they code states as simply having an early voting program or not, without regard to the degree to which it is accessible to citizens. Fitzgerald (2005) examines state-level turnout data from 1972 to 2002 and finds that while SDR is positively associated with higher turnout, early voting is not. Gronke et al. (2007) studies aggregate turnout trends from 1980 to 2004 and finds no positive relationship between early in-person voting and turnout. Only Oregon's universal VBM program—the only such program in the United States at the time—is reported to produce higher turnout (in presidential elections).[1] Giammo and Brox (2010) focus on a sample of counties across multiple presidential elections, reporting that early voting causes brief spikes in turnout, but not durable ones. The authors argue that early voting temporarily increases the perceived benefits associated with voting, but once it is no longer novel, these are not sustained.

Two recent studies have reported that early voting can negatively affect participation. Unlike Fitzgerald (2005) or Gronke et al. (2007), Burden et al. (2014) treat counties as their unit of analysis. County demographics are collected, while each locality is coded on the basis of whether it is located in a state with various reforms, including an early voting program and a SDR law. While the authors find that SDR increases turnout, early voting is not determined to have this independent effect. Instead, the effect is negative, leading the authors to argue that while early voting decreases the short-term costs of voting, it leads to interactive effects that reduce turnout. While creating more opportunities to vote, early voting also "rob(s) election day of its stimulating effects," reducing both the civic atmosphere surrounding Election Day and the intensity of get-out-the-vote (GOTV) efforts in the community. Concerns over early voting depressing the civic nature of Election Day have also been expressed by others (Thompson 2004; Fortier 2006).

Examining Current Population Survey (CPS) data from 2000, 2004, and 2008, Larocca and Klemanski (2011) find that while no-excuse absentee voting increases turnout, early in-person voting actually reduces it. The authors argue that early in-person programs do not increase convenience because they fail to cut the total number of "trips and tasks" required of voters, the most important measure of participation costs in their model. Further, they argue that early in-person voting is generally offered "at less numerous and often less conveniently located polling places." Nevertheless, the authors do not include any measure of early voting site placement or density in their model. Instead, they adopt the state-level indicators used by many aforementioned studies (Fitzgerald 2005; Gronke et al. 2007; Giammo and Brox 2010; Burden et al. 2014). As a result, they do not explore whether improving the number and location of early voting sites can make the programs effective at increasing turnout.

LOCAL IMPLEMENTATION

Many of the aforementioned studies have treated early voting as a binary variable, with states coded as adopters or nonadopters. But early voting varies both across and within states. While the decision to adopt early voting is made by state legislatures and governors, both state and county officials play an important role in implementing it. States typically determine eligibility for absentee ballots, as well as the number of days early in-person voting is available. States may also stipulate a minimum number of early voting locations that each county must offer, along with a minimum number of hours that each must be open (each day). But even in light of Republican-backed cuts in many states since 2010, local administrators often have considerable autonomy when implementing early in-person voting. In Florida, state law mandates that early in-person voting be offered at the office of each county's supervisor of elections. Each county, however, may also choose to designate any city hall or public library within its jurisdiction as a satellite early voting site. Nevada allows county officials to determine the number and location of sites without restrictions. In Clark County (Las Vegas), sites are often established in supermarkets and other areas with heavy commercial activity. The county regularly offers around 90 early voting locations to its voters. A county official stressed to me that this approach saves taxpayer money. He commented, "We are able to support 55 to 60 percent of our voters with 800 machines over 14 days. If not for [early voting] . . . we would need more machines to support turnout on Election Day" (Email to author, 2019).

California also provides counties with considerable freedom to determine site density, leading to some notable disparities within the state. In 2016,

Napa County established six early voting sites for its citizens. Meanwhile, nearly San Francisco—which has over six times more residents—offered just one. Texas sets a minimum standard for counties, requiring that at least one early voting site be designated within the borders of each state assembly district. Typically, counties offer more than the minimum number of sites. Harris County (Houston), for example, was required to provide 25 sites in 2008, but chose to offer 46. Hours of operation for early in-person voting may vary widely throughout the state's 254 counties, as each is free to set them as they wish.

A small number of states limit county freedom with regards to early in-person voting. Ohio generally permits only one early voting site per county, despite the fact that some have over one million residents (Cuyahoga and Franklin) and others have less than 15,000 residents (Monroe, Noble, and Vinton). Similarly, Maryland state law determines how many early voting centers each county must offer based on its number of registered voters. Counties with fewer than 150,000 registered voters must have one early voting center, those with between 150,000 and 300,000 registered voters must have three, and counties with more than 300,000 registered voters must have five locations. Counties are not permitted to add additional early voting sites.

In addition to determining the number of early voting sites available throughout the county, local officials are often responsible for promulgating and encouraging early voting to their citizens. Given their high level of autonomy, county officials have adopted unique strategies with regards to early voting site density and placement, as well as their advertising efforts. Through a series of conversations with county administrators in both 2011 and 2019, I am able to report some interesting insights regarding the decisions local officials make with regards to early in-person voting.

Lessons from the Clerks

In Buncombe County, North Carolina, one official stressed the importance of diversifying the sorts of sites offered. She commented, "We started off using only county libraries because the technology was available through the network system, and then, as early voting caught on, the State Board of Elections provided software that allowed us to use 'hybrid' and 'disconnected' sites" (Email to author, 2011). In 2008 and beyond, Buncombe County utilized libraries, additional county buildings, fire departments, churches, community centers, and one shopping mall for early voting.

Five factors are considered in determining site locations in Buncombe County. First, past turnout is studied. This helps the office determine which parts of the county are likely to have high demand, allowing for more sites in those areas. Second, registration records are used to identify areas that are growing in population from cycle to cycle, allowing necessary changes to be made. Third, convenience to the voters is weighed. Certain areas are more convenient for particularly dense neighborhoods or commuters. Sites on a main road, or those with sufficient parking, therefore take precedence. Fourth, all decisions must consider the county's budget. Sites cost money, in terms of equipment and manpower, and the county's budgets are often stretched. Finally, consistency is considered. While changes are made when necessary, too much experimenting from year to year can confuse voters and instill a sense that the system is too complicated. An elections official in Haywood County, North Carolina echoed this sentiment, stressing that the "key to successful early voting is stability and consistency; don't move sites or chaotically change operation times" (Email to author, 2019).

Cheatham County, Tennessee always offers early voting at the Election Commission Office, as is required by state law. The county, however, also offers satellite locations in all of its cities. Budget issues force tough decisions, but typically the county grants more sites to those areas that have concurrent city elections at a given time, as they will likely have more voters. This factor, officials said, "allows the scales to be tipped in their favor" (Email to author, 2011).

Officials in Watauga County, North Carolina have prioritized student convenience in determining sites. Early voting is always available at the county board of elections office, the Agricultural Extension Center, and at the Appalachian State University student union. Regarding the latter, the county seeks to make it easier for all voters, but "especially college students," as they are often numerous. In fact, during the 2008 election, the county opened up additional sites near the campus. It was this accommodation, combined with increased registration efforts on college campuses, which local officials believed was responsible for the county's increased turnout (Email to author, 2011). Similarly, in Cook County, Illinois (Chicago), officials offer 3-day early voting sites at multiple universities, including Northeastern Illinois University, the University of Illinois at Chicago, and Chicago State University. These sites complement additional sites in all 50 of the city's wards. The city believes that its robust early voting program typically reduces Election Day traffic by 30%. As a result, officials think that turnout has likely increased because "the number of voters who might have encountered a line . . . and possibly could have been discouraged" has been reduced (Email to author, 2019).

An elections clerk in Madison County, Illinois, cited the importance of site locations near other scheduled community events, including "Saturday side sales, parades, [and] block parties." These events, he believes, "have all boosted turnout" (Email to author, 2019).

Decisions about site placement are often complicated, as security, parking, Americans with Disabilities Act (ADA) compliance, cost, and even cell phone coverage must be considered. Additionally, site locations that are not convenient for voters—or that are not supported by those in the community—can create problems. Surely, some counties face larger obstacles than others when it comes to some of these considerations. A member of the Peoria County Election Commission in Illinois said officials must "get all stakeholders on board and involved in the discussion about locations, times and dates" (Email to author, 2019). An official in Washoe County, Nevada, where many sites are located in private establishments (e.g., shopping malls), agreed with this sentiment. She noted that counties are wise to "create strong partnerships with [their] early voting locations. A strong, positive relationship with . . . site management can ensure success; a bad one can lead to hardships and failure" (Email to author, 2019).

A lack of site density or wise site placement can have negative effects. In 2010, Washington County recorded one of the lowest early voting percentages in Maryland, as only 2.52% of eligible voters participated. Elections Director Kaye Robucci argued that this was because the only location in the county was an empty (former PNC Bank) building. She stated, "There's no reason to go there except to early vote" (Bond 2011).

Sites in remote locations are at odds with best practices, according to one Clark County, Nevada administrator. He stressed, "Go where the people are. . . . County or government facilities are not always the best locations. Consider using shopping malls, grocery stores. . . . We have had great success at three of our local malls." Backed by a lenient Nevada law regarding early voting, Clark County also employs innovative temporary sites, including trailers and convention tents, to provide voting where permanent facilities are unavailable (Email to author, 2019).

In addition to selecting sites, counties must take great steps to advertise their programs. Nearly all counties advertise their sites on their web pages, in local newspapers, and, increasingly, through social media sites such as Facebook and Twitter. In Union County, New Mexico, handouts are also delivered to local businesses so that "patrons have another avenue of learning about their elections" (Email to author, 2019). In Chaves County, New Mexico, officials also speak before civic organizations about early voting when given the opportunity (Email to author, 2019). In many locales, such as Clark County, voters can use a lookup tool online to find the nearest early voting sites. In addition, brochures are provided to community advocates who distribute information to voters. These are available in English, Spanish, and Filipino (Email to author, 2019). Similarly, in Lea County, New Mexico, officials "have cards printed in English and Spanish that [are] given out at all the city halls . . . as well as the Democratic and Republican headquarters" (Email to author, 2019). Regarding this latter comment, many counties find that working with candidates and parties is the most effective way to advertise early voting. After all, no one has more incentive to inform their supporters about opportunities to vote.

While counties have vastly different approaches, budgets, and views regarding early voting, most officials agree that programs both create and relieve stress for election officials. A common refrain from election clerks is that early voting requires additional staff, time, and attention. Voting sites must be continuously staffed and comply with all federal, state, and local laws regarding disability access, ballot security, and much more. One official lamented that "day to day you are dealing with all of the issues that can occur in a polling place on Election Day while trying to prepare for that election" (Email to author, 2019). Similarly, another commented that early voting "can really drain your staff, so finding ways to alleviate this is essential so that you can still make it through Election Day." One official added that "even with additional staff, early voting still takes two full-time employees away from other preparation needed for Election Day" (Email to author, 2019). One Illinois clerk described the scene in her office in 2016: "The entire staff was at the office until 10pm the night before the election and back at work at 4:30am on Election Day to conduct the election" (Email to author, 2019). Another clerk acknowledged that early voting increases administrative stress, but also noted that once "all the bugs are worked out," it gets easier (Email to author, 2019).

While early voting increases workloads, one clerk echoed a common sentiment, noting, "The benefit is we have more time to troubleshoot and make any changes we need over a two-week period" (Email to author, 2019). While officials are required to essentially run multiple Election Days, doing so allows for problems to be identified sooner so that they can be addressed before the largest crowds of voters arrive on the actual Election Day. And as I noted, officials frequently comment that early voting lessens lines on Election Day, which reduces stress at that stage.

EARLY VOTING AND TURNOUT: A NEW APPROACH

I offer a new framework for measuring the effects of early voting laws on voter turnout. In doing so, I account for the notable variation that exists in early in-person voting implementation both across and within states. Applying the rational choice perspective long advanced in the turnout litera-ture, reducing voting costs should bring more citizens to the polls. Therefore, I focus on the degree to which governments *truly reduce them*. Surely, longer early voting windows should ease the burdens of voting, as should universal and no-excuse absentee policies. But there are strong indications that many Americans prefer to cast in-person ballots. Even during the COVID-19 pandemic in 2020—when all but five states allowed no-excuse absentee voting—54% of Americans cast their ballots at an early or Election Day polling place. Some prefer the civic experience of voting in person, while others lack sufficient trust that their mail ballot will be received and counted. In some cases, citizens have no interest in navigating their state's procedures for procuring and submitting an absentee ballot. For these citizens who prefer to vote in person, simply offering early in-person voting does not necessarily lower the participation burden in a meaningful way. If a high-population county has one early voting site situated in a crowded, busy downtown, then this option hardly lowers costs for a marginally interested voter. This was the case in Los Angeles County, California in 2012, where one early voting site was tasked with serving over 10 million residents. Lines are likely to be very long at stations such as this, while the single site will probably be difficult to reach for many of the county's residents. Further, as Larocca and Klemanski (2011) and Burden et al. (2014) suggest, these programs may even have a perverse effect on turnout if voting simultaneously fails to become easier while mobilization efforts, civic attention, and media coverage surrounding Election Day decrease.

When abundant early voting sites are offered, there is greater reason to believe that costs are reduced. In these instances, it is far more likely that a site will be situated near a given individual voter's home, workplace, or shopping area. In aforementioned Clark County, Nevada, which has a substantially smaller population than Los Angeles County, 88 and 97 sites were provided in 2012 and 2016, respectively. In 2016, tiny Duval County, Texas (with less than 9,000 voting-age residents) had three early voting sites. Citizens had far more opportunities to cast early in-person ballots in these locales than in Los Angeles County or Cuyahoga County, Ohio, which also had just one site for over one million residents. Past research has found that voting sites (and their proximity to voters) indeed affect participation. Multiple academic studies report that the closer one lives to their polling location, the more likely they are to vote (Gimpel et al. 2003; Dyck and Gimpel 2005; Haspel and Knotts 2005). In several studies focused on Election Day Vote Centers (EDVCs), Stein and Vonnahme (2008, 2012) argue that voters prefer openness and centralization in the voting experience. Openness means that voters are able to cast ballots at any location throughout a county, while centralization refers to the convenience of polling places to one's home, workplace, or recreational setting. Early voting sites can provide similar conveniences to EDVCs (Fullmer 2015c). Citizens may vote at any established county site, while additional locations increase the likelihood that one is placed near one's dwelling, workplace, or social setting.

Similar to past reforms designed to lower voting costs, I do not believe additional early voting sites will inspire most non-voters in the United States to participate in elections. Gronke et al. (2007) are correct in asserting that early voting pales in comparison to "feelings of citizen empowerment, interest in and concern about the election, and political mobilization." The decision not to vote is rooted in both high costs *and* the perception of low benefits for some citizens. Abundant early voting sites, much like liberalized absentee rules or other convenience measures, likely cannot solve the latter. Nevertheless, I do expect robust pre-Election Day voting options to have some measurable and substantively significant impact on participation.

PRESIDENTIAL ELECTION MODEL

Because there are important differences between presidential and midterm elections, I examine the effect of early voting on turnout through separate (though similar) models. I first focus on the 2012 and 2016 presidential elections, then proceed to a discussion of the 2014 and 2018 midterm elections. While my presidential analysis does not include the more recent 2020 election, the four preceding elections are more likely to capture any typical relationship between early voting convenience and turnout. In 2020, the COVID-19 pandemic affected both the supply and demand of early voting opportunities in profound ways. The number of voters interested in casting absentee ballots soared from 2016 levels, as many worried about the health risks of visiting a physical polling site (Riccardi and Calvan 2020). Meanwhile, many jurisdictions—knowing that demand for in-person voting was lower and struggling to recruit poll volunteers—cut the number of (early and Election Day) physical sites offered to voters (Ahmed 2020). As I have noted, many states also changed their laws regarding voter convenience in 2020; many of these adjustments were temporary and may not extend to future elections. Because there are good reasons to believe that the circumstances surrounding 2020 were highly idiosyncratic, any findings from this cycle may have limited external validity. It is possible that 2020 more permanently altered the demand and supply of convenience voting options, but this cannot be known until post-COVID election cycles are complete. Assuming that citizens respond to early voting options *after the crisis* in a manner similar to *before the crisis*, the 2012–2018 elections should provide generalizable findings on any relationship between early voting offerings and voter participation.

In order to measure the relationship between early voting and turnout in the aforementioned years, I construct and run a series of ordinary least squares (OLS) regression models. In addition to determining whether a range of independent variables are associated with county turnout (my dependent variable).[2,3] OLS analyses allow me to estimate the size of any statistically significant relationships. I can assess, for example, the *extent* to which county turnout may increase or decrease (if at all) when a particular early voting option is available or additional polling locations are added.[4]

In this chapter, my primary independent variables are designed to capture the degree to which counties made voting convenient in the form of early voting options. In both 2012 and 2016, the U.S. EAC collected data from most U.S. counties on the number of early voting sites they offered. I use the site data to create a "sites per capita" variable, which measures the number of sites in each county per 1,000 voting-age residents.[5,6] If early voting indeed improves turnout, then we should expect this variable to have a positive relationship with the dependent variable (turnout) in each election year. I code the variable in this fashion because counties vary in population size. One site in Los Angeles County—where about 10 million people reside—represents weak early voting availability, though one site in Borden County, Texas— with a population of less than 1,000—should serve residents quite well.

While most counties reported their site data to the EAC, there are some cases in each year where this data is not available. In cases where I can credibly determine county sites from official state sources, I supplement the EAC data with this information. I have no reason to suspect systematic bias regarding the missing data points, and I therefore exclude counties with no site data from my various analyses. Furthermore, counties in Alaska are omitted because the state only reported early voting sites at the state level. Ultimately, 2,364 and 2,228 counties or independent cities—more than 70% of those in the United States—are included in the primary 2012 and 2016 models, respectively.

I also include a binary measure indicating whether no-excuse absentee voting was permitted in each respective county. Because states set absentee voting policies, all counties within a state are coded the same way. Recall that some states with early in-person voting, such as Texas, do not allow all voters to receive absentee ballots. I also account for the number of days that a county offered early voting. This, too, is set by states. Burden et al. (2014) find that days do not significantly increase participation, though Herron and Smith (2014) do report that Florida's 2012 early voting reductions may have diminished turnout among racial and ethnic minorities, registered Democrats, and independents.[7]

A handful of states employed some form of universal VBM in the elections analyzed. Uniquely among them, Colorado still provided both physical early and Election Day sites to voters. In order to account for these unique early voting programs, I include binary measures noting both universal VBM counties and, in the 2016 tests, Colorado counties.[8]

Finally, I include a binary measure noting simply whether a county is in a state that allows *any* sort of early voting, the primary independent variable in the Giammo and Brox (2010) and Burden et al. (2014) studies. This allows me to determine the role of site density, early voting days, and universal and no-excuse absentee voting while controlling for the effect of early voting itself.

The dependent variable in each analysis is a county's turnout rate among the voting-age population (VAP) in the respective election. All population data comes from the 2010 U.S. Census, which provides population estimates for each county. Raw vote totals from each county are provided by the EAC.

In designing my models, I am cognizant of potential endogeneity problems. Those states and counties that choose to offer more pre-Election Day voting options may be areas that place a higher value on turnout and civic participation. If this is so, then early voting is not a catalyst for higher turnout, but rather a proxy for it. In some cases, conventional controls may not capture a county's turnout norms for other reasons. For instance, a county may consist of small, rural communities where voting is a popular civic exercise for which nearly everyone engages. As such, I control for lagged turnout in each county. Therefore, if a county had high turnout (and perhaps a culture of civic participation) before early voting was adopted, then my models will not attribute high levels of participation in 2012 or 2016 to early voting sites or other voter convenience measures.

In order to account for these characteristics, I control for each county's average turnout rate in the 1992 and 1996 presidential elections. I use elections two decades prior to 2012 and 2016 because they represent years when early voting was in its infancy and the percentage of citizens taking advantage of it was very small. Therefore, this measure of lagged turnout largely precedes the treatment of my primary independent variables, while still capturing cultural characteristics of a county that would not typically change significantly in a decade or so.

In addition, my models control for administrative, political, and demographic influences on turnout. Regarding administration, I account for the number of polling places per capita on Election Day, as localities also differ with regard to these offerings. Election Day density should theoretically increase convenience and improve turnout, though Stein and Vonnahme (2008, 2012) argue that this is dependent on how well sites are staffed and equipped with voting devices.[9]

I control for whether or not a state required voters to present photo identification (ID) in order to vote in 2012 and 2016. As I discussed in chapter 1, many states have adopted voter ID laws since the early 2000s. The 2002 Help America Vote Act required that first-time voters who register through the mail show an ID before voting. Since this time, many states have taken additional steps. By the 2012 election, four states required photo ID at polling places in order for a registered citizen to vote. In 2016, the number doubled to eight.[10] Additional states request photo ID, but have provisions in place for those citizens lacking it.

While many political commentators have argued that ID requirements depress turnout—particularly among low-income and non-White citizens— research on this question remains split. Some early studies reported no notice-able drop in turnout due to ID laws (Mica et al. 2007; Primo et al. 2007; Erikson and Minnite 2009). Others, however, have reached different conclu-sions. Vercellotti and Anderson (2006) and Alvarez et al. (2008) each report that photo ID laws do significantly depress participation to some extent. In a more recent study, Bright and Lynch (2017) find that while voter ID require-ments may reduce turnout, this effect is reversible if sufficient information about obtaining an ID is made available to citizens. Examining county turn-out data from 2012 and 2016, Kuk and Hajnal (2020) disagree, finding that strict photo ID laws reduce turnout in racially diverse counties, regardless of efforts taken to help citizens obtain IDs.

I also account for whether a state had a SDR law on the books in 2012 and 2016, respectively. Many studies (Fenster 1994; Brians and Grofman 1999; Knack 2001; Burden et al. 2014; Leighley and Nagler 2014) have shown that eased registration requirements can boost turnout, though the degree of the effect varies among this research (see Hanmer 2009).[11] In addition, I control for counties in states with an automatic voter registration (AVR) program. In 2012, no states had yet adopted AVR, though North Dakota—which abol-ished voter registration in 1951—effectively had such a policy and is coded as such. By 2016, Oregon also had a fully implemented AVR program.

Turning to political considerations, I include a measure of campaign com-petitiveness in the 2012 and 2016 elections, noting whether or not the county is in a state where major party candidates for president or vice president vis-ited at least three times during the general election campaign.[12]

In terms of demographics, my primary early voting site density variable does not account for the physical size of counties, only their population. I sus-pect that population is a more important factor, as more voters should mean more traffic and longer lines at the polling place. It also suggests additional stress for election officials. While the physical distance in a rural county may be considerable, travel times may not be significantly different from those traveling a relatively short distance in a more urban area. Nevertheless, I include a measure of each county's percent rural to assess whether it is an important predictor of turnout. Furthermore, I include separate analyses for counties with populations (1) of at least 200,000 persons and (2) less than 200,000 persons. This allows me to assess whether the effects of site density and other measures are more pronounced in urban or more rural communities.

My models include numerous other demographic covariates, including each county's percent Black, percent Hispanic, percent over the age of 65, percent (over the age of 25) with a college degree, and mean household income. I also control for the percent of each county identifying as a non-U.S. citizen. I expect to find a county's percent noncitizen to be negatively associated with turnout, while percent rural, percent college-educated, and percent over 65, along with household income, should each have positive relationships with the dependent variable. Given the 2012 candidacy of President Barack Obama, I anticipate that a county's percent Black will also be positively associated with voting. In 2016, my expectation is that this effect will either disappear or notably weaken.

I also conduct some tests that examine only counties in those states that had early voting laws. This allows me to estimate the role of site density and other specific convenience measures once a state has made the decision to adopt some form of early voting. In addition, I include specifications that control for state-fixed effects to account for any unidentified state norms or traditions that affect all county cases within a state. Finally, in both 2012 and 2016, I run separate models assessing the cumulative effect of early voting site density and no-excuse absentee voting. This allows me to gauge the turnout effects of offering easier options to vote *both* through the mail and at physical sites before Election Day. With both options available, it is likely that more citizens will find a convenience measure that suits them. Furthermore, lines at both early and Election Day locations may conceivably be shorter when more citizens can vote through the mail.

PRESIDENTIAL ELECTION FINDINGS

Before delving into my analyses, I present two simple scatter plot graphs that demonstrate an apparent positive relationship between early voting site density and turnout in 2012 and 2016, respectively. While figures 2.1 and 2.2 do not consider any additional covariates, they offer a clear and useful starting point.

Table 2.1 displays a series of OLS regression specifications aimed at determining the effect of early voting site density and other convenience measures on 2012 and 2016 turnout. Across a range of tests, I find that site density is both a positive and significant predictor of county turnout. The effects are clear when controlling for a variety of voter convenience policies, as well as administrative, political, and demographic characteristics. The substantive effect of sites is between two and three percentage points in the primary specifications, implying that an additional early voting site per 1,000 voting-age residents is associated with 2.8 and 2.3 percentage-point increases in county turnout in 2012 and 2016, respectively. No-excuse absentee programs are also associated with higher turnout in the full models,

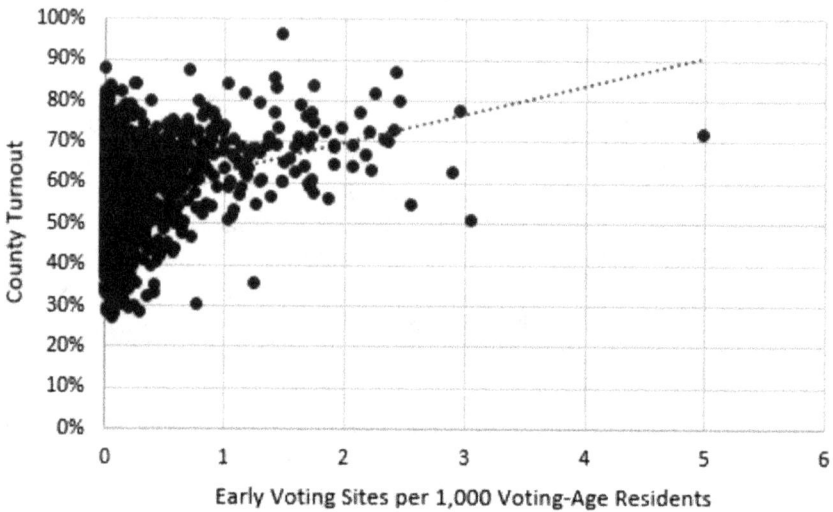

Figure 2.1 Early Voting Site Density and Turnout, 2012. *Source:* Created by Elliott Fullmer using data from the U.S. Census Bureau and the U.S. Election Assistance Commission's 2012 Election Administration and Voting Survey.

as counties with them are linked to 1.9 and 1.4 percentage-point turnout spikes in the respective years. In the limited number of universal VBM counties, the effect is even stronger, with 6 and 2.4 percentage-point turnout increases expected in 2012 and 2016, respectively. More early voting days do not predict higher turnout in 2016, though in 2012 an additional 10 days is associated with a modest 0.6-point increase in turnout. Notably, simply having an early voting program does not predict higher turnout in 2012 or 2016. In fact, the coefficient is significant and negative in both years. This finding is consistent with that reported by Burden et al. (2014). It appears that while the adoption of early voting does not equate to higher turnout, early voting programs that offer ample site density, liberalized absentee voting and (in 2012 at least) longer early voting windows do have this capability.

The remaining covariates in the model offer additional insights. Lagged turnout has a very strong and positive effect on turnout in both 2012 and 2016, confirming that a county's turnout can be heavily predicted by its past turnout. Election Day polling place density actually has a negative relationship with turnout in 2012, though the effect is very small. Counties in competitive presidential election states are associated with over four additional points of turnout in 2012 and 2016, respectively. In both years, counties with SDR laws are associated with higher levels of participation, a finding consistent with previous studies. The adoption of SDR is linked

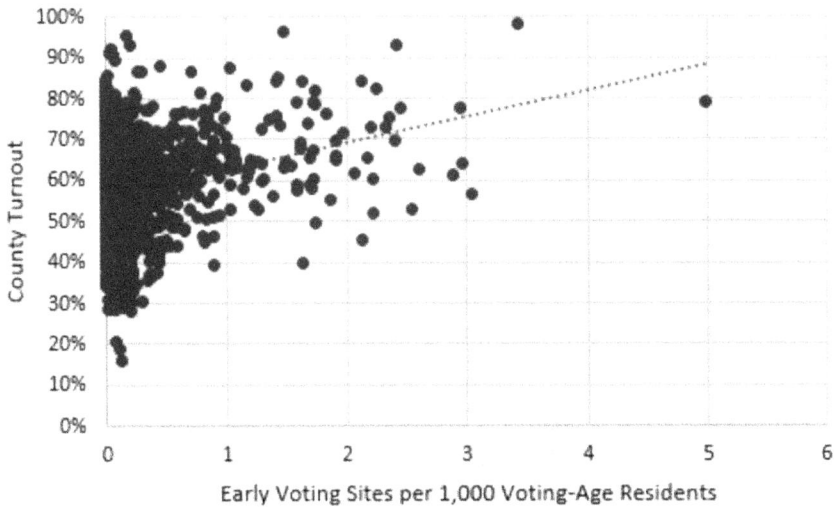

Figure 2.2 Early Voting Site Density and Turnout, 2016. *Source:* Created by Elliott Fullmer using data from the U.S. Census Bureau and the U.S. Election Assistance Commission's 2016 Election Administration and Voting Survey.

to an additional 2.6 and 2.8 percentage points of turnout in 2012 and 2016, respectively. While AVR is associated with higher turnout in 2012, the effect disappears in 2016. I caution that the AVR measure is effectively a dummy variable for North Dakota counties in 2012; in 2016, only Oregon counties are added. Interestingly, counties in states with strict voter ID laws did not have significantly lower turnout in either 2012 or 2016. In fact, the coefficient is significant and positive in 2016.

The demographic variables behave largely as expected. A county's percent noncitizen is a negative predictor of turnout, while a county's percent over 65, percent college-educated, percent rural, and mean household income are associated with higher turnout. A county's percent Black is a positive and significant predictor of turnout in both 2012 and 2016, though the effect size is expectedly lower in 2016. Notably, a county's percent Hispanic is a positive predictor of turnout in 2012, but a negative predictor in 2016.[13]

The third and fourth specifications in table 2.1 examine only counties located in early voting states. Here, I am able to examine the importance of sites and other convenience options once a state has made the decision to adopt some form of early voting. In these specifications, the effect of early voting site density is unchanged from the original models, predicting turnout gains of 2.8 points in 2012 and 2.3 points in 2016. No-excuse absentee policies are no longer significant turnout predictors in 2012, though in 2016 these laws are associated with a modest 0.7-point spike in turnout. Universal VBM

Table 2.1 Early Voting and County Turnout, 2012 and 2016

Variables	(1) 2012 turnout	(2) 2016 turnout	(3) 2012 turnout	(4) 2016 turnout	(5) 2012 turnout	(6) 2016 turnout
Lagged turnout	0.478***	0.424***	0.496***	0.464***	0.484***	0.447***
	(0.015)	(0.020)	(0.017)	(0.022)	(0.018)	(0.021)
Early voting state	−0.0526***	−0.0207***				
	(0.004)	(0.005)				
Early voting site density	0.0279***	0.0226***	0.0277***	0.0232***	0.0239***	0.0205***
	(0.003)	(0.004)	(0.004)	(0.004)	(0.004)	(0.003)
No-excuse absentee	0.0190***	0.0136***	0.00522	0.00680*		
	(0.003)	(0.004)	(0.003)	(0.004)		
Early voting days	0.000609***	1.35E-05	0.000731***	−8.48E-05		
	(0.000)	(0.000)	(0.000)	(0.000)		
Universal vote-by-mail	0.0597***	0.0236***	0.0648***	0.0297***		0.0473**
	(0.006)	(0.008)	(0.006)	(0.008)		(0.023)
Colorado		0.00907		−0.0107		
		(0.010)		(0.010)		
Election Day site density	−0.00260***	−0.000353	−0.00276***	−0.000421*	−0.00153*	−0.000231
	(0.001)	(0.000)	(0.001)	(0.000)	(0.001)	(0.000)
Same-day registration	0.0262***	0.0278***	0.0172***	0.0325***		
	(0.003)	(0.004)	(0.004)	(0.004)		
Automatic voter registration	0.0244***	0.00413	0.0312***	−0.00247		
	(0.007)	(0.008)	(0.007)	(0.008)		
Strict photo ID law	0.00399	0.0179***	0.00534	0.0317***		
	(0.003)	(0.004)	(0.004)	(0.005)		
Swing state	0.0407***	0.0421***	0.0672***	0.0573***		
	(0.003)	(0.004)	(0.004)	(0.004)		
Percent Black	0.228***	0.0641***	0.182***	0.0676***	0.159***	−0.0209*
	(0.009)	(0.011)	(0.012)	(0.013)	(0.011)	(0.012)
Percent Hispanic	0.0323***	−0.0509***	0.0326***	−0.0375**	0.0257*	−0.00316

	(0.012)	(0.016)	(0.012)	(0.015)	(0.014)	(0.017)
Percent noncitizen	-0.617***	-0.464***	-0.606***	-0.449***	-0.560***	-0.551***
	(0.044)	(0.057)	(0.046)	(0.057)	(0.043)	(0.052)
Percent over 65	0.299***	0.266***	0.342***	0.348***	0.340***	0.298***
	(0.030)	(0.039)	(0.033)	(0.040)	(0.030)	(0.037)
Percent college-educated	0.181***	0.146***	0.197***	0.161***	0.165***	0.158***
	(0.020)	(0.027)	(0.021)	(0.028)	(0.019)	(0.024)
Mean income	0.00243***	0.00267***	0.00245***	0.00310***	0.00249***	0.00317***
	(0.000)	(0.000)	(0.000)	(0.000)	(0.000)	(0.000)
Percent rural	0.0311***	0.0181***	0.0231***	0.0104	0.0200***	0.0111**
	(0.005)	(0.006)	(0.005)	(0.007)	(0.004)	(0.006)
Constant	0.0461***	0.0922***	-0.0195*	0.0104	0.0476***	0.0645***
	(0.010)	(0.013)	(0.012)	(0.015)	(0.010)	(0.012)
Observations	2,364	2,228	1,823	1,759	2,364	2,228
R-squared	0.78	0.648	0.796	0.708	0.667	0.623

Source: Created by Elliott Fullmer using data from the U.S. Census Bureau, the U.S. Election Assistance Commission's 2012 and 2016 Election Administration and Voting Surveys, the National Conference of State Legislatures (2012, 2016), and FairVote (2012, 2016).

Notes: *** $p < 0.01$, ** $p < 0.05$, * $p < 0.1$. Cell entries are OLS regression estimates with panel-adjusted standard errors in parentheses.

Table 2.2 Early Voting and County Turnout in Large vs. Smaller Counties, 2012 and 2016

Variables	(1) 2012 Turnout	(2) 2016 Turnout	(3) 2012 Turnout	(4) 2016 Turnout
Lagged turnout	0.461***	0.341***	0.472***	0.408***
	(0.044)	(0.075)	(0.016)	(0.020)
Early voting state	−0.0226**	0.0118	−0.0571***	−0.0304***
	(0.011)	(0.017)	(0.004)	(0.005)
Early voting site density	0.184*	0.771***	0.0295***	0.0237***
	(0.097)	(0.197)	(0.003)	(0.004)
No-excuse absentee	0.0462***	0.0243	0.0177***	0.0142***
	(0.008)	(0.015)	(0.003)	(0.004)
Early voting days	−0.000895**	−0.000965	0.000726***	4.48E-05
	(0.000)	(0.001)	(0.000)	(0.000)
Universal vote-by-mail	0.0467***	−0.00927	0.0601***	0.0311***
	(0.012)	(0.022)	(0.007)	(0.008)
Colorado		0.00348		0.00779
		(0.025)		(0.010)
Election Day site density	0.00358	0.0153	−0.00282***	−0.00029
	(0.014)	(0.022)	(0.001)	(0.000)
Same-day registration	0.0358***	0.0187	0.0260**	0.0317***
	(0.009)	(0.014)	(0.004)	(0.005)
Automatic voter registration		0.0267	0.0225***	−0.00119
		(0.028)	(0.007)	(0.008)
Strict photo ID law	0.0302**	0.0186	0.00338	0.0180***
	(0.012)	(0.017)	(0.004)	(0.004)
Swing state	0.0629***	0.0625***	0.0370***	0.0351***
	(0.007)	(0.011)	(0.003)	(0.004)
Percent Black	0.128***	−0.0486	0.237***	0.0773***
	(0.027)	(0.042)	(0.009)	(0.011)
Percent Hispanic	−0.0025	−0.135**	0.0259**	−0.0604***

	(0.035)	(0.057)	(0.013)	(0.016)
Percent noncitizen	-0.517***	-0.331**	-0.584***	-0.399***
	(0.095)	(0.160)	(0.049)	(0.062)
Percent over 65	-0.0903	-0.134	0.337***	0.345***
	(0.079)	(0.132)	(0.032)	(0.040)
Percent college-educated	0.188***	0.165**	0.174***	0.118***
	(0.047)	(0.080)	(0.022)	(0.028)
Mean income	0.00134***	0.000906**	0.00271***	0.00346***
	(0.000)	(0.000)	(0.000)	(0.000)
Percent rural	0.126***	0.088	0.0308***	0.0216***
	(0.035)	(0.055)	(0.005)	(0.006)
Constant	0.150***	0.288***	0.0315***	0.0517***
	(0.035)	(0.055)	(0.011)	(0.013)
Observations	211	232	2,153	1,996
R-squared	0.908	0.703	0.776	0.669

Source: Created by Elliott Fullmer using data from the U.S. Census Bureau, the U.S. Election Assistance Commission's 2012 and 2016 Election Administration and Voting Surveys, the National Conference of State Legislatures (2012, 2016), and FairVote (2012, 2016).

Notes: *** $p < 0.01$, ** $p < 0.05$, * $p < 0.1$. Cell entries are OLS regression estimates with panel-adjusted standard errors in parentheses.

is again linked to big turnout gains (6.5 points in 2012 and 3 points in 2016). Similar to the full models, early voting days have no significant relationship with turnout in 2016, though in 2012 an additional 10 days predicts a slight jump (0.7 points).

As a robustness check, I also include models that include state-fixed effects, recognizing that county variation in early voting sites may be indicative of state laws or traditions. In each specification, site density continues to positively predict higher county turnout in both 2012 (2.4 points) and 2016 (2.1 points). Because absentee rules and early voting windows do not vary by county within early voting states, these variables are omitted from these specifications.

Across multiple specifications, I have reported that an additional early voting site per 1,000 voting-age residents results in over two additional points of turnout in presidential years. Achieving this turnout increase, however, does require a significant investment in early voting sites. These locations come at a cost to local administrators, as they must be properly organized, advertised, and staffed. However, adding an additional site per 1,000 *is* achievable. In 2016, 79 counties already met this threshold, while 206 counties had at least one site for every 2,000 voting-age residents. While many of these counties are smaller, 54 counties with at least 20,000 voting-age residents met or exceeded this ratio in 2016.

It is not realistic, however, for very large counties to add an additional site per 1,000 or 2,000 potential voters. A county of 500,000 voting-age residents, for example, probably cannot afford to add 500 early voting sites. As a result, gaining 2–3 points of turnout for each site per 1,000 voting-age residents may have limited capacity to affect participation in these locales. In table 2.2, I split the analysis to gain insights into whether site density has different effects in large and smaller counties. I run separate tests in (1) counties with at least 200,000 residents and (2) those with fewer than this number of residents. In the first set of tests, with the largest counties isolated, sites remain a significant turnout predictor and the effect size soars. In 2012, the effect of adding one site per 1,000 voting-age residents equates to nearly 18.4 percentage points of turnout. In 2016, the effect spikes to an inconceivable 77.1 points. Again, however, counties of this size cannot realistically add an additional site per 1,000 voting-age residents. In many large cities, this would mean more than one site in some apartment buildings. However, it is realistic for a large county to invest in one site per 10,000 voting-age residents. In fact, of counties in early voting states with at least 200,000 persons in 2012, six already had this ratio. In 2016, the number jumped to eight counties. The above finding implies that even an additional site per 10,000 voting-age residents is associated with 1.8 and 7.7 additional points of turnout in 2012 and 2016, respectively. More aggressive investments are associated with even greater gains.

Table 2.3   Early Voting and County Turnout (with Interactions), 2012 and 2016

	(1)	(2)
Variables	*2012 Turnout*	*2016 Turnout*
Lagged turnout	0.471***	0.415***
	(0.015)	(0.020)
Early voting state	−0.0510***	−0.0186***
	(0.004)	(0.005)
Early voting site density × No-excuse absentee	0.0201***	0.0243***
	(0.006)	(0.008)
Early voting site density	0.0127**	0.0155***
	(0.006)	(0.004)
No-excuse absentee	0.0161***	0.00961**
	(0.003)	(0.004)
Early voting days	0.000623***	−3.08E-05
	(0.000)	(0.000)
Universal vote-by-mail	0.0632***	0.0275***
	(0.006)	(0.008)
Colorado		0.00683
		(0.010)
Election Day site density	−0.000265	−0.000283
	(0.001)	(0.000)
Same-day registration	0.0259***	0.0292***
	(0.003)	(0.004)
Automatic voter registration	0.0253***	0.00369
	(0.007)	(0.008)
Strict photo ID law	0.00395	0.0182***
	(0.003)	(0.004)
Swing state	0.0416***	0.0430***
	(0.003)	(0.004)
Percent Black	0.228***	0.0634***
	(0.009)	(0.011)
Percent Hispanic	0.0361***	−0.0480***
	(0.012)	(0.016)
Percent noncitizen	−0.624***	−0.482***
	(0.044)	(0.057)
Percent over 65	0.294***	0.259***
	(0.030)	(0.039)
Percent college-educated	0.182***	0.140***
	(0.020)	(0.027)
Mean income	0.00245***	0.00272***
	(0.000)	(0.000)
Percent rural	0.0292***	0.0157**
	(0.005)	(0.006)
Constant	0.0484***	0.0976***
	(0.010)	(0.013)
Observations	2,364	2,228
R-squared	0.781	0.65

Source: Created by Elliott Fullmer using data from the U.S. Census Bureau, the U.S. Election Assistance Commission's 2012 and 2016 Election Administration and Voting Surveys, the National Conference of State Legislatures (2012, 2016), and FairVote (2012, 2016).
Notes: *** $p < 0.01$, ** $p < 0.05$. Cell entries are OLS regression estimates with panel-adjusted standard errors in parentheses.

In the third test, I report that in the 2,153 smaller counties in 2012, an additional site per 1,000 voting-age residents is associated with a turnout increase of 2.95 points. In 2016, an additional site predicts an additional 2.37 points of turnout. Each of these tests offers further confidence that both large and smaller counties can expect a meaningful return on investment by adding early voting sites.

I also report strong evidence that both universal and no-excuse absentee laws improve turnout in counties of varying sizes. In 2012, universal VBM is associated with an additional 4.67 and 6 points of turnout in large and smaller counties, respectively. Meanwhile, no-excuse absentee voting predicts an extra 4.6 and 1.8 points of turnout in these two respective contexts. Both forms of liberalized absentee voting continue to show strong positive effects on turnout in smaller counties in 2016, though neither has a significant relationship with 2016 turnout in more populated counties. Meanwhile, the length of a state's early voting window only demonstrates a positive relationship with turnout in one of the four contexts analyzed—smaller counties in 2012.

Early voting site density consistently demonstrates a positive effect on turnout in 2012 and 2016 across a range of tests. While the reported effects are not as consistent, I generally find that no-excuse absentee laws—offered in 35 states—are also positively linked to participation. As a result, I run additional tests in Table 2.3 that examine—through interaction terms— whether the effect of sites on turnout is greater when a no-excuse absentee law is also present.[14]

In both 2012 and 2016, the interaction terms for no-excuse absentee laws and early voting site density are both positive and significant. While sites remain a significant predictor of higher turnout when no-excuse absentee policies are not present, the effect size grows considerably when they are. In 2012, an additional site per 1,000 voting-age residents predicts an additional 1.3 points of turnout in counties that lack a no-excuse absentee law. When such laws are present, an additional site per 1,000 residents is associated with 3.3 added points of turnout. In 2016, the effect is similar, as sites are linked to a 1.6 percentage-point spike in participation when an excuse is required to obtain an absentee ballot; in no-excuse counties, the effect of sites grows to 4 percentage points. Clearly, states and counties are more likely to boost participation by offering their citizens *both* the opportunity to obtain an absentee ballot and ample early in-person sites.

MIDTERM ELECTION MODEL

While the 2012 and 2016 findings suggest that early voting—when implemented aggressively—is an effective turnout catalyst, the analysis was limited to presidential elections. It is well-documented that presidential contests generate uniquely high interest in the electorate. In recent years, turnout has generally hovered around 60% of eligible voters in presidential races. In 2020, turnout was 66.7%, the highest figure since 1900. Midterm elections generate considerably less interest than presidential elections, though the last two elections (2014 and 2018) have seen unusually low and high turnout, respectively. In 2014, national turnout was estimated to be only 36.4% of eligible voters, marking the lowest total in 72 years. In 2018, with the country highly polarized around the presidency of Donald Trump, turnout jumped to 49.3%, the highest mark since 1914. Even in 2018, however, turnout was not high by international standards for a national election. As J. Campbell (1997) notes, midterm elections simply lack a "wow factor" for many citizens. Expanding on the work of A. Campbell (1966), he observes that presidential elections feature both "core voters" and "peripheral voters." The core voters follow politics more closely and have strong opinions about issues, parties, and candidates. By contrast, the peripheral voters are not as engaged, but the increased media attention, social discourse, and civic energy associated with presidential elections inspires them to vote. In the midterm elections that follow, the core voters remain, but the peripheral ones disappear, leading to a large turnout decrease. It is this tendency, Campbell argues, that typically leads the party of the successful presidential candidate to enjoy success in down-ballot races in presidential years (a "surge"), followed by losses when the peripheral voters disappear two years later (a "decline").

If Campbell and others are correct, the perceived benefits of participating are much lower in midterm cycles. While early voting convenience options can improve turnout by a few percentage points in presidential cycles, the same effects cannot be assumed in midterm years. It is possible that perceived benefits are sufficiently low in this context to prevent added convenience from having a measureable effect on turnout. Through similar OLS regression analyses of early voting and participation during the 2014 and 2018 midterms, I hope to provide some guidance on this question and subject my previous findings to additional scrutiny. By examining each of these particular cases, I am able to assess the role of sites and other offerings in unusually low and (relatively) high turnout midterm elections.

Once again, the dependent variable (turnout) is computed with EAC data on county votes and U.S. Census data on county VAP. The primary independent variable is the number of early voting sites available in a county per 1,000 voting-age residents. While most counties reported their site data to the EAC, there are again some cases in each year for which this data could not be included.[15] As I did in the presidential model, I again include binary metrics indicating the presence of an early voting program, a no-excuse absentee voting policy, and universal VBM. A continuous measure notes the number of early voting days allowed by the state. Finally, I again account for Colorado counties in order to capture the unique voter convenience circumstances in that state.

My model controls for each county's lagged turnout (in 1992 and 1996), as well as the same series of administrative, political, and demographic influences on turnout.

Because I am examining midterm cycles, the electoral context differs across states. I anticipate that states with competitive gubernatorial or Senate elections will have higher turnout in both 2014 and 2018. I therefore include a binary variable noting whether a state had either election in the respective year. Because my variable for competitiveness in the presidential election model (candidate visits) is inapplicable in a midterm year, I consider a state competitive if the top two candidates ultimately finished within 10 percentage points of one another in the popular vote.[16] While this measure could exclude some races that appeared competitive during some stage of the campaign, it should generally capture those races where campaigning was most intense and citizen interest was highest.

As I did in my presidential models, I include specifications limited to counties in states with an early voting program, as well as tests that account for state-fixed effects. Following my initial tests, I split the analysis between heavily and less-populated counties to again assess whether the scope of key relationships differs.

MIDTERM ELECTION FINDINGS

Figures 2.3 and 2.4 display the relationship between early voting site density and turnout. While these figures do not consider any covariates, they again suggest a possible relationship between the primary independent variable and turnout. Similar to the figures presented from presidential years, there appear to be positive associations in both midterm years between sites and turnout. The trend line does appear to be more notably positive in 2014 than 2018.

Table 2.4 presents my initial OLS regression findings for 2014 and 2018. Even with a broad array of controls in the model—including a very significant lagged turnout measure—early voting site density is positively and significantly associated with higher county turnout in both years. In the full model, an additional site per 1,000 voting-age residents leads to an additional 2.5 points of county turnout in 2014. For context, a 2.5 percentage-point increase in nationwide turnout in 2014 would have equated to nearly

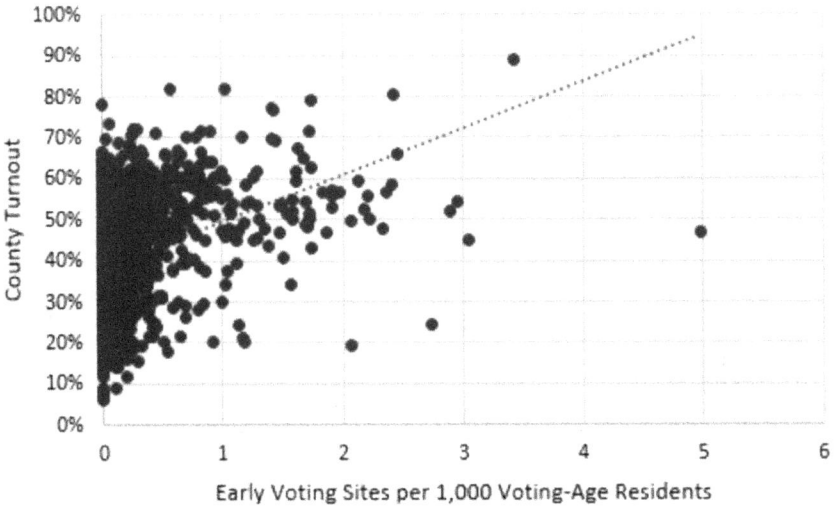

Figure 2.3 Early Voting Site Density and Turnout, 2014. *Source:* Created by Elliott Fullmer using data from the U.S. Census Bureau and the U.S. Election Assistance Commission's 2014 Election Administration and Voting Survey.

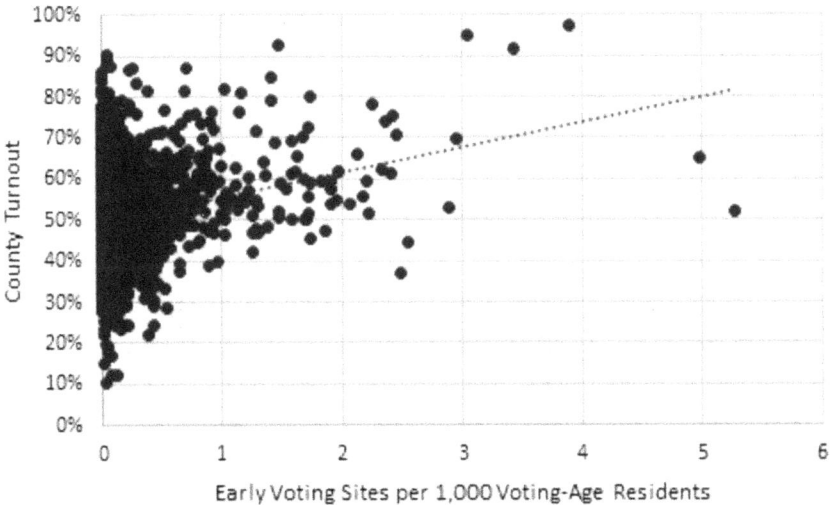

Figure 2.4 Early Voting Site Density and Turnout, 2018. *Source:* Created by Elliott Fullmer using data from the U.S. Census Bureau and the U.S. Election Assistance Commission's 2018 Election Administration and Voting Survey.

Table 2.4 Early Voting and County Turnout, 2014 and 2018

Variables	(1) 2014 Turnout	(2) 2018 Turnout	(3) 2014 Turnout	(4) 2018 Turnout	(5) 2014 Turnout	(6) 2018 Turnout
Lagged turnout	0.443*** (0.020)	0.290*** (0.019)	0.446*** (0.020)	0.252*** (0.022)	0.445*** (0.019)	0.418*** (0.021)
Early voting state	−0.0341*** (0.005)	−0.0479*** (0.005)				
Early voting site density	0.0250*** (0.004)	0.0152** (0.006)	0.0274*** (0.004)	0.0231*** (0.007)	0.00947*** (0.003)	0.0104* (0.006)
No-excuse absentee	0.0305*** (0.004)	0.0339*** (0.004)	0.0202*** (0.004)	0.0316*** (0.004)		
Early voting days	0.000468*** (0.000)	0.000407** (0.000)	0.000719*** (0.000)	0.000521*** (0.000)		
Universal vote-by-mail	0.0572*** (0.008)	0.0997*** (0.007)	0.0633*** (0.008)	0.101*** (0.008)		0.0153 (0.028)
Colorado	0.0996*** (0.009)	0.105*** (0.011)	0.0887*** (0.009)	0.0999*** (0.011)		
Election Day site density	−0.00227 (0.002)	0.00101 (0.002)	−0.00248 (0.002)	−9.60E-05 (0.002)	0.00305** (0.001)	0.00244 (0.002)
Same-day registration	−0.00419 (0.004)	−0.00241 (0.005)	−0.000196 (0.005)	0.00526 (0.005)		
Automatic voter registration	0.0467*** (0.010)	0.0118*** (0.004)	0.0551*** (0.009)	0.00931* (0.005)		
Strict photo ID law	−0.0499*** (0.004)	−0.00398 (0.004)	−0.0377*** (0.005)	0.00399 (0.005)		
Competitive Senate or governor race	0.0336*** (0.003)	0.0325*** (0.003)	0.0525*** (0.004)	0.0278*** (0.004)		
Percent Black	0.0575*** (0.011)	0.0420*** (0.010)	0.132*** (0.016)	0.0822*** (0.015)	0.0679*** (0.011)	0.00237 (0.012)

Percent Hispanic	-0.0585***	-0.00421	-0.0203	0.0106	0.0455***	0.0269
	(0.015)	(0.016)	(0.014)	(0.018)	(0.014)	(0.018)
Percent noncitizen	-0.345***	-0.546***	-0.397***	-0.539***	-0.409***	-0.584***
	(0.057)	(0.060)	(0.054)	(0.066)	(0.045)	(0.054)
Percent over 65	0.323***	0.354***	0.463***	0.462***	0.426***	0.284***
	(0.040)	(0.039)	(0.040)	(0.046)	(0.033)	(0.038)
Percent college-educated	0.111***	0.349***	0.130***	0.383***	0.131***	0.332***
	(0.026)	(0.027)	(0.026)	(0.031)	(0.020)	(0.024)
Mean income	0.00111***	0.00247***	0.00149***	0.00286***	0.00170***	0.00265***
	(0.000)	(0.000)	(0.000)	(0.000)	(0.000)	(0.000)
Percent rural	0.0430***	0.0552***	0.0364***	0.0518***	0.0452***	0.0360***
	(0.006)	(0.006)	(0.006)	(0.007)	(0.005)	(0.006)
Constant	-0.00753	0.0365***	-0.104***	-0.0424***	-0.0685***	-0.00813
	(0.013)	(0.012)	(0.014)	(0.016)	(0.011)	(0.012)
Observations	2,387	2,796	1,922	2,037	2,387	2,796
R-squared	0.685	0.609	0.749	0.627	0.596	0.571

Source: Created by Elliott Fullmer using data from the U.S. Census Bureau, the U.S. Election Assistance Commission's 2014 and 2018 Election Administration and Voting Surveys, and the National Conference of State Legislatures (2014, 2018).

Notes: *** $p < 0.01$, ** $p < 0.05$, * $p < 0.1$. Cell entries are OLS regression estimates with standard errors in parentheses.

six million additional voters. In 2018, the effect size is smaller, as an additional site is associated with nearly 1.5 additional points of turnout. Such an increase would have still meant over three million additional citizens casting ballots.

Meanwhile, counties in states that allowed no-excuse absentee voting are associated with turnout spikes of over three points in each year, a more robust finding than those reported in 2012 or 2016. Universal VBM, again limited to a very small number of states, is linked to considerably higher turnout in both 2014 (5.7 points) and 2018 (10 points). Colorado counties are associated with nearly 10 additional points of turnout in both 2014 and 2018, a notable finding given the unique mixture of early voting and universal VBM available in that state. This large effect differs from my 2016 models, when Colorado counties were not significantly associated with higher participation. The number of early voting days provided is also positive and significant in 2014 and 2018, though the effect is small. A state would have needed to add nearly 21 and 25 days of early voting in 2014 and 2018, respectively, in order for its counties to see one-point turnout increases.

The other covariates behave largely as expected. In the full models, lagged turnout has a very large, positive effect in each year, confirming again that the best predictor of a county's current turnout is its past turnout (even two decades prior).

While Election Day sites are not significant in either year, counties with a competitive Senate or gubernatorial race could expect a turnout rate about 3.4 and 3.3 points higher than those in noncompetitive states in 2014 and 2018, respectively. This finding is very similar to the one I reported for counties in presidential swing states in 2012 and 2016. Surprisingly, I find that SDR is not significantly related to turnout in 2014 or 2018. AVR, however, is associated with higher turnout in each year. This reform, of course, remains in its infancy and should continue increasing registration rates (and possibly turnout rates) in the years to come.

Interestingly, I find that strict voter ID states are associated with a turnout drop of nearly five percentage points in 2014, though the effect disappears in 2018. I had previously reported no negative effect in 2012 or 2016. This may suggest that high-enthusiasm elections—like presidential races and the uniquely engaging 2018 midterms—are better equipped to overcome the barriers associated with ID laws. In these elections, it is possible that affected voters (with the help of campaigns) are willing to bear more inconvenience in pursuit of acceptable IDs. In more typical midterm elections (like 2014), when perceived benefits are lower, the added burden of an ID card may be too great for a portion of the electorate.

In terms of demographics, a county's percent Hispanic is negatively associated with turnout in 2014, though this effect vanishes in 2018. In both years, percent noncitizen is a negative predictor of turnout, while a county's percent college-educated, percent rural, percent over 65, and mean household income are all linked to higher participation. A county's percent Black is also positively associated with turnout, though the effect size is lower than in the 2012 or 2016 presidential elections.

In the third and fourth specifications, I examine only cases in states with an early voting program. Doing so reduces the original sample size by 465 (in 2014) and 759 (in 2018) cases. In this model, sites remain a strongly positive predictor of turnout; in fact, the effect size actually grows in both 2014 and 2018. In early voting states, an additional site per 1,000 voting-age residents leads to 2.7 and 2.3 percentage-point bumps in county turnout in 2014 and 2018, respectively. The significant findings regarding no-excuse absentee laws, universal VBM, and early voting days also survive in both years.

In the fifth and sixth specifications, I run my full models with state-fixed effects. While the effect size of site density drops in both 2014 and 2018, it remains positive and significant. Even when state tendencies regarding sites are considered, county variation continues to be predictive of turnout. Because absentee rules and early voting windows do not vary within early voting states, these variables are dropped from the fixed effects tests.

In general, the effect sizes presented in table 2.4 are comparable to those reported in the 2012 and 2016 presidential elections. I am especially confident in the midterm findings given the diverse elections examined. Regardless of whether the electorate is unusually apathetic (like 2014) or unusually engaged (like 2018), site density and other early voting convenience measures appear to have a meaningful effect on turnout.

As I noted in the presidential analysis, it is again true that achieving a modest turnout increase does require a significant investment in early voting sites. These locations come at a cost to local administrators, as they must be properly organized, advertised, and staffed. However, adding sufficient sites to realize meaningful turnout gains is possible. Similar to 2012 and 2016, many counties are already meeting this threshold in midterm elections. In 2018, there were 82 counties with at least one site per 1,000 voting-age residents, while 207 had one site or more per 2,000 voting-age residents. Of these counties, 55 had at least 20,000 voting-age residents.

Because it is not realistic for very large counties to add an early voting site for every 1,000 or 2,000 potential voters, I again split the analysis between

Table 2.5 Early Voting and County Turnout in Large vs. Smaller Counties, 2014 and 2018

Variables	(1) 2014 Turnout	(2) 2018 Turnout	(3) 2014 Turnout	(4) 2018 Turnout
Lagged turnout	0.206***	0.323***	0.454***	0.274***
	(0.059)	(0.064)	(0.021)	(0.019)
Early voting state	0.026	−0.0111	−0.0412***	−0.0545***
	(0.018)	(0.019)	(0.005)	(0.005)
Early voting site density	0.423**	0.169*	0.0259***	0.0166***
	(0.169)	(0.090)	(0.004)	(0.006)
No-excuse absentee	0.00851	0.0702***	0.0312***	0.0295***
	(0.013)	(0.014)	(0.004)	(0.004)
Early voting days	0.000212	−0.00111*	0.000533***	0.000454***
	(0.001)	(0.001)	(0.000)	(0.000)
Universal vote-by-mail	0.0273	0.0729***	0.0656***	0.101***
	(0.019)	(0.019)	(0.009)	(0.008)
Colorado	0.0934***	0.188***	0.0949***	0.0849***
	(0.023)	(0.029)	(0.010)	(0.011)
Election Day site density	−0.0288	0.0181	−0.00234	0.00109
	(0.023)	(0.023)	(0.002)	(0.002)
Same-day registration	0.0117	−0.0104	−0.00444	0.00585
	(0.014)	(0.015)	(0.005)	(0.005)
Automatic voter registration		−0.0476***	0.0430***	0.0210***
		(0.014)	(0.010)	(0.004)
Strict photo ID law	−0.0623***	0.0483***	−0.0490***	−0.00552
	(0.018)	(0.015)	(0.004)	(0.004)
Competitive Senate or governor race	0.0643***	0.0532***	0.0307***	0.0317***
	(0.009)	(0.009)	(0.004)	(0.003)
Percent Black	−0.0298	−0.0649	0.0626***	0.0492***
	(0.040)	(0.041)	(0.012)	(0.011)
Percent Hispanic	−0.162***	−0.0294	−0.0587***	−0.0122

	(1)	(2)	(3)	(4)
	(0.050)	(0.057)	(0.015)	(0.016)
Percent noncitizen	−0.141	−0.364**	−0.345***	−0.464***
	(0.157)	(0.168)	(0.061)	(0.065)
Percent over 65	0.344***	−0.0277	0.333***	0.412***
	(0.125)	(0.138)	(0.042)	(0.041)
Percent college-educated	0.309***	0.432***	0.0903***	0.319***
	(0.072)	(0.079)	(0.028)	(0.028)
Mean income	−0.000416	0.00042	0.00137***	0.00309***
	(0.000)	(0.000)	(0.000)	(0.000)
Percent rural	0.116**	0.163***	0.0412***	0.0622***
	(0.049)	(0.054)	(0.007)	(0.006)
Constant	0.131***	0.162***	−0.0209	0.00304
	(0.047)	(0.051)	(0.014)	(0.013)
Observations	220	276	2,167	2,520
R-squared	0.777	0.669	0.686	0.628

Source: Created by Elliott Fullmer using data from the U.S. Census Bureau, the U.S. Election Assistance Commission's 2014 and 2018 Election Administration and Voting Surveys, and the National Conference of State Legislatures (2014, 2018).

Notes: *** $p < 0.01$, ** $p < 0.05$, * $p < 0.1$. Cell entries are OLS regression estimates with standard errors in parentheses.

large and smaller counties in table 2.5. The first two specifications examine only counties with at least 200,000 residents in 2014 and 2018, respectively, while the third and fourth include only those with fewer than this number of residents.

In 2014, with only the 220 largest counties included, sites remain a powerful predictor of county turnout. Notably, the effect size soars, as an additional site per 1,000 voting-age residents is associated with an additional 42.3 points of turnout. This coefficient, which is obviously unrealistic, speaks to the impossibility of a dense county adding one site for every 1,000 voting-age residents. While offering this level of site density is implausible, even offering an additional site per 10,000 voting-age residents is associated with 4.23 additional points of turnout. In the 2014 midterms, a 4.23-point spike in turnout would have resulted in about eight million additional votes nationwide. In 2018, the effect size is not quite as large, but remains substantively significant. An additional site per 10,000 voting-age residents is associated with an additional 1.69 points of turnout. Across the United States, an increase of this magnitude would have equated to nearly 4 million additional votes in 2018. This level of site density is certainly achievable. In both 2014 and 2018, 11 counties with at least 200,000 people already offered at least one site per 10,000 voting-age residents.

In the third and fourth tests, I report effects from counties with fewer than 200,000 people. In these 2,167 smaller counties in 2014, an additional site per 1,000 voting-age residents is associated with a turnout increase of 2.59 points, about the same as my original finding with all counties included. Adding a site per 1,000 residents is much more realistic in these smaller jurisdictions; in 2014, 102 of them already offered at least one site per 1,000 voting-age persons. In 2018, with only the 2,520 smallest counties included, an additional site per 1,000 voting-age residents is linked to an additional 1.66 points of turnout. Once again, the effect size is smaller in 2018, but meaningful nonetheless. Eighty-two counties with a population under 200,000 already offered at least one site per 1,000 voting-age residents in 2018.

Because both early voting sites and no-excuse absentee laws are significant and positive turnout predictors in 2014 and 2018, I again run specifications that interact these two variables. In table 2.6, I report a significant and positive interactive effect in 2014, as site density leads to 5.8 more points of turnout in no-excuse absentee counties than in those with more restrictive policies. In 2018, the interaction term remains positive, but it is no longer significant; unlike the other three elections analyzed, site density is not associated with greater turnout gains in 2018 when a no-excuse absentee law is present.

Table 2.6　Early Voting and County Turnout (with Interactions), 2014 and 2018

Variables	*(1)* *2014 Turnout*	*(2)* *2018 Turnout*
Lagged turnout	0.422***	0.285***
	(0.020)	(0.019)
Early voting state	−0.0309***	−0.0476***
	(0.005)	(0.005)
Early voting site density × No-excuse absentee	0.0578***	0.00529
	(0.007)	(0.009)
Early voting site density	−0.00651	0.0116
	(0.005)	(0.009)
No-excuse absentee	0.0203***	0.0331***
	(0.004)	(0.004)
Early voting days	0.000552***	0.000422**
	(0.000)	(0.000)
Universal vote-by-mail	0.0673***	0.0986***
	(0.008)	(0.008)
Colorado	0.104***	0.106***
	(0.009)	(0.011)
Election Day site density	0.00236	0.00174
	(0.002)	(0.002)
Same-day registration	−0.00616	−0.00276
	(0.004)	(0.005)
Automatic voter registration	0.0450***	0.0120***
	(0.010)	(0.004)
Strict photo ID law	−0.0506***	−0.00405
	(0.004)	(0.004)
Competitive Senate or governor race	0.0349***	0.0326***
	(0.003)	(0.003)
Percent Black	0.0583***	0.0417***
	(0.011)	(0.010)
Percent Hispanic	−0.0478***	−0.00458
	(0.015)	(0.016)
Percent noncitizen	−0.380***	−0.542***
	(0.056)	(0.060)
Percent over 65	0.302***	0.358***
	(0.040)	(0.040)
Percent college-educated	0.104***	0.350***
	(0.026)	(0.027)
Mean income	0.00121***	0.00247***
	(0.000)	(0.000)
Percent rural	0.0361***	0.0546***
	(0.006)	(0.006)
Constant	0.00218	0.0376***
	(0.013)	(0.013)
Observations	2,387	2,794
R-squared	0.695	0.608

Source: Created by Elliott Fullmer using data from the U.S. Census Bureau, the U.S. Election Assistance Commission's 2014 and 2018 Election Administration and Voting Surveys, and the National Conference of State Legislatures (2014, 2018).

Notes: *** $p < 0.01$, ** $p < 0.05$, * $p < 0.1$. Cell entries are OLS regression estimates with standard errors in parentheses.

CONCLUSIONS

In recent years, most academic research has concluded that early voting fails to meaningfully and durably increase turnout. Positive effects on participation, when they have been reported, have generally been limited to universal VBM and (occasionally) no-excuse absentee programs. Few have found that early in-person voting moves the turnout needle. After closely examining early in-person offerings at the county level across four recent national elections, I reach a different conclusion. I can confidently report that early voting site density has a consistent, significant, and positive relationship with county turnout.

With most U.S. counties included in the primary models, an additional site per 1,000 voting-age residents is associated with several additional points of voter turnout in both presidential (2012, 2016) and national midterm elections (2014, 2018). This finding survives the inclusion of many significant covariates, including a highly predictive lagged turnout measure. Splitting the analysis by county size, I find substantively significant findings in both large and smaller jurisdictions. In the 2016 presidential election, the effect of site density on turnout is exceptionally large in counties with at least 200,000 persons, suggesting that the addition of just one site per 10,000 voting-age residents is associated with nearly eight additional points of turnout.

In most cases, I also report positive findings regarding liberalized absentee laws and turnout. Universal VBM, practiced in all or part of just six states in the years analyzed, is consistently associated with turnout increases between two and six percentage points. No-excuse absentee laws also appear to boost turnout by several percentage points, though the findings are a bit less consistent than those reported for early voting site density or universal VBM. Notably, in three of the elections analyzed, I report positive interactive effects between no-excuse absentee policies and site density. In short, early voting sites seem to produce larger turnout gains when no-excuse absentee voting is also an option. This offers strong evidence that states and counties offering a variety of early voting options are more likely to see positive turnout dividends. Finally, in three of the four elections analyzed (2012, 2014, and 2018), longer early voting windows appear to boost turnout, though the effect sizes are small. In 2012, an additional 10 days is associated with just 0.6 turnout points, while the effects are even smaller in 2014 and 2018.

My findings offer insights about other covariates in the models. SDR is associated with higher turnout in the presidential years, but (surprisingly) the effect is not repeated in the midterm years. AVR has a positive and significant effect on turnout in each election, though the effect size dropped in 2018 when more states became adoptees. This makes sense, as many of the AVR states were at the early stages of implementing their programs in 2018.

With time, programs should produce more registrants and, perhaps, higher turnout. Colorado counties, where voters are automatically mailed ballots and provided access to early in-person sites, are linked to nearly 10 points of added turnout in midterm years, though no effect is found in 2016. Voter ID laws, suspected to decrease participation, are only linked to turnout drops in 2014. As I explained earlier, this may suggest that ID laws are more likely to depress turnout when citizen enthusiasm is low. In high-enthusiasm elections, such as 2016, 2018, and 2020, voters and campaigns may be more equipped to overcome challenges posed by these restrictive policies.

It is worth noting that the elections examined in this chapter were each quite distinctive. The first presidential election (2012) was the second contest won by President Barack Obama. As the first Black president, Obama certainly galvanized segments of the electorate in unique ways. In fact, 2012 was the first U.S. election where Black turnout exceeded White turnout. In 2016, Secretary Hillary Clinton was the first woman to be nominated by a major political party for president. Clinton and her opponent, Donald Trump, were also uniquely polarizing figures in American politics. The passions generated in these elections are liable to raise external validity concerns about my conclusions. But this should not be an issue, as any particular effects of Obama, Clinton, or Trump's candidacies were national. In other words, each was relevant across counties regardless of whether or not they had early voting or, when applicable, a dense number of sites. For example, my 2012 findings suggest that, all things equal, counties mobilized by Obama *with more sites* were still likely to have higher turnout than counties mobilized by Obama *with less sites*. Because Obama was a candidate in all counties, his effect was controlled.

Regarding the midterm analysis, the cases examined featured unusually low (2014) and unusually high (2018) voter turnout. As discussed, the 2014 cycle had the lowest participation rate for a midterm election in 72 years. Meanwhile, the 2018 midterms saw the highest rate in 104 years. The difference in turnout between the two cycles was nearly 15 percentage points. Given that early voting site density actually *declined* slightly between 2014 and 2018, it is clear that the positive change in participation was mostly driven by other factors. Applying the rational choice model dominant in the turnout literature since Downs (1957), it is important to remember that both perceived benefits and costs affect the decision to vote. In 2018, many citizens were much more engaged and motivated to vote than in 2014. President Trump's election led to considerable activism and engagement among progressives across the country, while his supporters were also unusually mobilized to support Republican candidates. If citizens are disinterested in an election, then SDR, AVR, the option to vote by mail, and additional early voting sites will probably not be sufficient to move them to the polls.

Conversely, if they are determined to vote, waiting in line on Election Day or traveling a long distance to an early voting site will likely not deter them. My findings simply suggest that when the cost-benefit difference is otherwise marginal, early voting site density and liberalized absentee policies can move a meaningful number of additional citizens to the polls. In an election like 2014, this may mean 36% turnout rather than 34% turnout in counties with better options. In 2018, it may mean 49% instead of 47% turnout. The baseline potential for turnout is driven by many factors, but early voting can move the needle in a notable way.

Finally, in both the presidential and midterm cases, my results lend strong support to the notion that the efficacy of electoral reform depends— to some extent at least—on local implementation. Many scholars have reported that the adoption of early in-person voting fails to raise participation rates (Fitzgerald 2005; Highton 2005; Primo et al. 2007; Scheele et al. 2008; Giammo and Brox 2010; Burden et al. 2014). Others have found that while no-excuse absentee laws can boost turnout, in-person programs do not (Gronke et al. 2007; Larocca and Klemanski 2011). These studies, however, have generally paid little attention to differences in early voting implementation at the local level. Disparities are indeed drastic *within* early voting states and must be examined. Counties that have been able to make the option more readily available *are* witnessing notable increases in turnout.

Of course, site density is not the only decision that local administrators make with regard to early voting. As I discussed, site placement also varies considerably. While many counties limit sites to elections offices, others (like those in Nevada) have innovated by placing them outside shopping malls, supermarkets, and other areas that citizens frequent. In some jurisdictions, administrators have intentionally placed sites near college campuses. Counties in at least 13 states now regularly offer drop-box locations or places where voters can drop completed absentee ballots.[17] While these locations are distinct from traditional early voting sites, there is cause to believe that they could also increase convenience and turnout. Given that the nuances of early voting implementation appear to matter, I encourage scholars to explore whether both placement decisions and drop-box offerings also affect voter participation.

NOTES

1. While Gronke et al. (2007) report that universal VBM is linked to higher turnout in presidential elections, the effect size is less than half of that previously reported by Southwell and Burchett (2000).

2. Variables are associated when they effectively "move" together. For example, scientists have determined that the more someone smokes cigarettes, the greater their risk for certain health problems becomes. In this example, smoking is an independent variable; as it varies, health outcomes (the dependent variable) can be expected to change as well. In this chapter, I generate regression output indicating whether a series of independent variables lead to increases or decreases in voter turnout (the dependent variable). By convention, variables are said to be *significantly* related to one another if a relationship can be established with 90%, 95%, or 99% confidence.

3. In an OLS regression model, statistical significance is determined by calculating a p-value. A p-value estimates the possibility that a significant relationship would be observed between variables if one did not truly exist. When this number is sufficiently small, confidence increases that an observed relationship is real. When a p-value is less than 0.10, a researcher can determine that variables are related with 90% confidence. When a p-value is less than 0.05, confidence rises to 95%. Finally, a p-value less than 0.01 generates a confidence level of 99%.

4. Each of my regression models include a series of independent variables. By including multiple independent variables in my tests, I am able to estimate the independent effect of each variable, while holding the effects of the others constant. For example, suppose I believe that *both* the presence of plentiful early voting sites and high rates of college education may improve a county's voter turnout. By including both variables in my models, I am able to estimate the independent effect of *each* variable on turnout while controlling for any effects of the other.

5. In some states, independent cities—not located within a county—administer their own elections. The EAC also provides site data for most of these cities, allowing them to be included alongside counties in the dataset.

6. In some states (e.g., New England states, Wisconsin), elections are administered by towns. In these cases, the EAC provides site data for towns instead of counties. Because towns sit within county borders, I simply add the total number of town sites within a county to create the numerator for my site density measure.

7. In 2011, Florida cut early voting days from 14 to eight and eliminated the final Sunday of early voting.

8. Colorado had not yet adopted universal VBM in 2012.

9. I hoped to include metrics for both staff and equipment density in my models. The EAC provides the number of poll workers employed in each county, but does not identify whether they participated in both early voting and Election Day administration. As a result, it is difficult to determine how many actual workers were at each early and Election Day site. Regarding equipment, the EAC provides the number of voting apparatuses used in each county, but does not include information on how many were used during early voting and on Election Day, respectively. As a result, I do not include these variables in my models.

10. This data is provided by the National Conference of State Legislatures (NCSL 2021c). In 2012, four states—Georgia, Indiana, Kansas, and Tennessee—had enforceable strict photo identification laws. In 2016, four additional states—Mississippi, North Dakota, Virginia, and Wisconsin—also had enforceable laws.

11. According to the NCSL (2021b), 11 states—Connecticut, Idaho, Iowa, Maine, Minnesota, Montana, Ohio, New Hampshire, North Carolina, Wisconsin, and Wyoming—allowed citizens to register and vote on the same day in 2012. In 2016, four additional states—Colorado, Illinois, Maryland, and Vermont—had laws in place. Ohio, however, had discontinued its SDR law by this time.

12. I consider any candidate visit in August through November of the election year to be a general election campaign visit. According to FairVote, the candidates made at least three visits to 12 states in 2012—Colorado, Florida, Iowa, Michigan, Minnesota, Nevada, New Hampshire, North Carolina, Ohio, Pennsylvania, Virginia, and Wisconsin. In 2016, most of the competitive states remained the same. Arizona and New Mexico were added to the list, while Minnesota was dropped from it.

13. When a county's noncitizen percentage is omitted from the model, percent Hispanic is negatively associated with turnout in both elections.

14. While universal VBM programs are also consistently linked to higher turnout, I do not include the variable in my interaction terms. Only a small handful of states offered such policies in 2012 or 2016. Furthermore, I cannot generate interaction terms that include early voting sites and universal VBM programs because the two offerings are mutually exclusive (except in Colorado).

15. I exclude all cases in Alaska and (in 2014 only) Georgia. Alaska only reported total sites at the state level in both 2014 and 2018. Georgia's 2014 reported sites are filled with apparent errors. Fulton County, for example, claimed to have 275 early voting sites, while Gwinnett County claimed to have 175. Other counties had unusually high totals as well. I confirmed that these figures were inaccurate, but could not obtain exact figures regarding the correct number of sites. The mistakes appear to have been corrected in 2018, as figures were more typical. I therefore exclude Georgia counties from my analysis in 2014, but include them in 2018.

16. In 2014, competitive states included Colorado, Connecticut, Florida, Georgia, Illinois, Iowa, Kansas, Maine, Maryland, Massachusetts, Michigan, Minnesota, New Hampshire, North Carolina, Oregon, Pennsylvania, Rhode Island, Virginia, Vermont, and Wisconsin. In 2018, competitive states included Arizona, California, Connecticut, Florida, Georgia, Indiana, Iowa, Kansas, Maine, Michigan, Missouri, Montana, Nevada, New Hampshire, Ohio, Oregon, South Carolina, South Dakota, Texas, West Virginia, and Wisconsin.

17. In 2020, with an unprecedented number of voters requesting absentee ballots in light of the COVID-19 pandemic, 38 states provided drop-box locations. It remains unclear if many of these states will retain this option after the pandemic (Rakich 2020).

Chapter 3

Early Voting and Individual Turnout

The findings reported in chapter 2 lend confidence to the idea that early voting site density, along with other convenience measures, produces at least modestly higher levels of turnout. The survival of the central finding despite numerous controls—including a highly significant lagged turnout variable—suggests that early voting can be an effective tool for increasing voter participation. The models presented in chapter 2, however, relied exclusively on county and state-level data. This is common for electoral reform studies, as individual effects are often difficult to both observe and measure. In this brief chapter, I build on my county-level findings with an individual-level model of sites and turnout. Applying data from the two middle cases from chapter 2—the 2014 midterm election and the 2016 presidential election—I estimate if the likelihood that individuals will choose to vote varies depending on the early voting options available in their respective counties. These tests offer a powerful robustness check on my previously reported findings.

Across a range of specifications covering two elections, I ultimately confirm that early voting site density has a strong, positive effect on one's likelihood of voting. I find that universal vote-by-mail (VBM) programs continue to be associated with greater participation as well. I reach less consistent results concerning no-excuse absentee laws, as such policies do not always make a citizen more likely to cast a ballot. Finally, I report that the length of a state's early voting window does not increase one's likelihood of voting in either midterm or presidential elections.

DATA AND METHODS

In order to extend my analysis, I use Current Population Survey (CPS) data from both November 2014 and November 2016. The CPS is a monthly survey of about 60,000 U.S. households conducted by the U.S. Census Bureau. The Census, more specifically its Bureau of Labor Statistics (BLS), uses the data to gain knowledge about employment in the United States. Since 1964, the CPS has also included a Voting and Registration Supplement in the November of even-numbered years. In addition to demographic information, respondents are asked if they are registered to vote and, if so, whether they voted in the recent national election. The state of residence is always included for each respondent in the supplement. The county of residence is included for some, but not all, respondents. Counties cannot be identified for some respondents because of confidentiality restrictions on public data. More specifically, counties that are particularly small lack the necessary number of households to preserve confidentiality under law. Therefore, those respondents who come with county identifiers are skewed in the sense that they never come from the smallest U.S. counties. Other than the size of their respective counties, however, the sample carries no further systematic biases.

In 2014 and 2016, the available samples of voting-age citizens with county identifiers in the survey are quite large—35,534 in 2014 and 29,134 in 2016. These cases represent 37.3% and 31.5% of all qualified CPS respondents in 2014 and 2016, respectively. Because the CPS asks about voting behavior, I am able to capture individual-level data that includes both county of residence and turnout information for this very large sample of U.S. residents. I then merge the Election Assistance Commission (EAC) site density data used in chapter 2 with each individual observation in the CPS, creating a measure of *individual* site convenience for all persons in the sample. This allows me to observe whether those living in more site-dense counties were more likely to vote in the 2014 and 2016 elections. Because my dependent variable is now binary (vote/did not vote), I run Probit regression analyses to identify whether site density (and other variables) affects one's decision to participate. Probit regression is similar to OLS regression, but the interpretation of variables is a bit different. Through a Probit regression, I can determine whether changes in my independent variables significantly increase or decrease the likelihood that my dependent variable will be 1 rather than 0 (i.e., someone choosing to *vote*, rather than *not vote*). For example, I can assess whether a citizen with access to more early voting sites is significantly more likely to vote than those without such access.

I also account for other early voting options in each respondent's respective state. I create binary measures noting whether one resides in an early voting state, a state with a universal VBM program, or a no-excuse absentee state. The number of early voting days in each respondent's state is also included. As I did in chapter 2, I include a binary measure for citizens residing in Colorado, as the state offered a unique blend of universal VBM and early voting options in both 2014 and 2016. Beyond early voting, I account for strict photo ID laws, same-day registration (SDR), automatic voter registration (AVR), and electoral competitiveness in each respective year. In 2014, I again consider a state competitive if either a Senate or gubernatorial race in the state was decided by 10 percentage points or less. In 2016, I note whether the individual lived in a swing state, measured again as a state where major party presidential or vice presidential candidates made at least three visits during the general election campaign. Similar to chapter 2, no respondents from Alaska are included in either year, as county site data was not provided to the EAC. Respondents from Georgia are also excluded in 2014 because of the aforementioned issues with the state's EAC data that year.

Thankfully, the CPS asks a series of demographic questions that allow me to reproduce much of the turnout model presented in chapter 2. The survey includes individual data on each respondents' age, gender, race, ethnicity, education, and income. In the primary model, I therefore control for age, as well as the following demographic identifiers: Woman, Black, Hispanic, Income below $50,000, Income above $100,000, and College-educated.

MIDTERM ELECTION FINDINGS

I first examine the 2014 CPS, which was conducted shortly after that year's national midterm election. In order to test the relationship between early voting and turnout, I run a series of Probit analyses. The first includes my full model with all covariates. The second assesses the role of site density and other variables on turnout only in states that had early voting programs. Each Probit regression helps identify whether particular options available to an individual, as well as a series of other demographic and political covariates, made them more (or less) likely to cast a vote in the 2014 elections. While these results will indicate whether significant relationships exist, I rely on margins tests to decipher the size of any significant effects.

Across both 2014 specifications in Table 3.1, I can report that early voting site density is a positive and significant predictor of individual voter turnout. The coefficients are highly significant in both specifications, surviving the inclusion of numerous demographic and political covariates in each case. Additionally, I report that residing in Colorado or a state with universal VBM is associated with a higher likelihood of voting in each test. Unlike the county-level analysis in chapter 2, however, neither the length of a state's early voting window nor no-excuse absentee voting predicts a higher likelihood of voting in 2014.

Chapter 3

Table 3.1 Early Voting and Individual Turnout, 2014

Variables	(1) 2014 Voter	(2) 2014 Voter
Early voting state	−0.0454	
	(0.044)	
Early voting site density	0.688***	0.698***
	(0.200)	(0.203)
No-excuse absentee	0.00934	0.0138
	(0.038)	(0.041)
Early voting days	−0.00363***	−0.00459***
	(0.001)	(0.001)
Universal vote-by-mail	0.372***	0.433***
	(0.063)	(0.066)
Colorado	0.410***	0.449***
	(0.064)	(0.068)
Election Day site density	−0.141**	0.000578
	(0.057)	(0.076)
Same-day registration	0.108***	0.112***
	(0.027)	(0.031)
Automatic voter registration	0.467***	0.503***
	(0.117)	(0.119)
Strict photo ID law	−0.119***	−0.106**
	(0.046)	(0.046)
Competitive Senate or governor race	0.159***	0.167***
	(0.028)	(0.035)
Black	0.265***	0.239***
	(0.030)	(0.036)
Hispanic	−0.174***	−0.168***
	(0.029)	(0.031)
Age	0.0237***	0.0237***
	(0.001)	(0.001)
Woman	0.0460**	0.0404*
	(0.019)	(0.022)
College-educated	0.502***	0.478***
	(0.022)	(0.025)
High income	0.117***	0.137***
	(0.026)	(0.030)
Low income	−0.307***	−0.289***
	(0.022)	(0.026)
Constant	−1.244***	−1.335***
	(0.050)	(0.059)
Observations	24,440	18,330

Source: Created by Elliott Fullmer using data from the 2014 Current Population Survey and the U.S. Election Assistance Commission's 2014 Election Administration and Voting Survey.

Notes: *** $p < 0.01$, ** $p < 0.05$, * $p < 0.1$. Cell entries are OLS regression estimates with standard errors in parentheses.

The additional covariates contain no surprises. SDR and AVR are linked to higher turnout, while voter ID laws make respondents less likely to vote. Women, Blacks, those with college degrees, those with high family incomes, and older voters are more likely to vote, while Hispanics and those with low family incomes are less likely to vote.

Table 3.2 reports the margins for various levels of site density. Because the highest level of county site density found in the dataset is slightly higher than 0.6 sites per 1,000 voting-age residents, I measure the likelihood of voting for those living in counties with 0 sites per capita, then display additional likelihoods for those with 0.1, 0.2, 0.3, 0.4, 0.5 and 0.6 sites per capita available, respectively.

In each test, the predicted likelihood of an individual choosing to vote in 2014 rises as the level of site density increases. In the full model, with all covariates included, a citizen has a 50.29% likelihood of voting if no sites are available in his or her county. This likelihood then gradually rises, as those in counties with 0.6 sites available per 1,000 voting-age residents are 64.15% likely to cast a vote, a nearly 14-point increase over those with no sites. In the second test, with only respondents in early voting states considered, the effect is comparable. The increase in likelihood of voting from a citizen with no sites to one with the highest density observed is slightly over 14 points.[1]

Figure 3.1 displays one's likelihood of voting in the full model as their exposure to site density increases. While some of the confidence intervals are rather large, the lowest levels of site density have no overlapping area with the highest level, reinforcing the significant finding between site density and turnout.

This analysis also provides an opportunity to observe the effects of other covariates in the model. Because these covariates are mainly binary variables, it is useful to measure any marginal effects on the dependent variable. Figure 3.2 displays the marginal effects for all significant binary variables in the

Table 3.2   Margins Analysis of Early Voting Site Density and Turnout, 2014

Early Voting Sites per 1,000 Voting-Age Residents	*Probability of Voting (Full Model) (%)*	*Probability of Voting (Early Voting States Only) (%)*
0	50.29	49.50
0.1	52.65	51.89
0.2	55.00	54.27
0.3	57.33	56.63
0.4	59.64	58.97
0.5	61.92	61.28
0.6	64.15	63.55

Source: Created by Elliott Fullmer using data from the 2014 Current Population Survey and the U.S. Election Assistance Commission's 2014 Election Administration and Voting Survey.

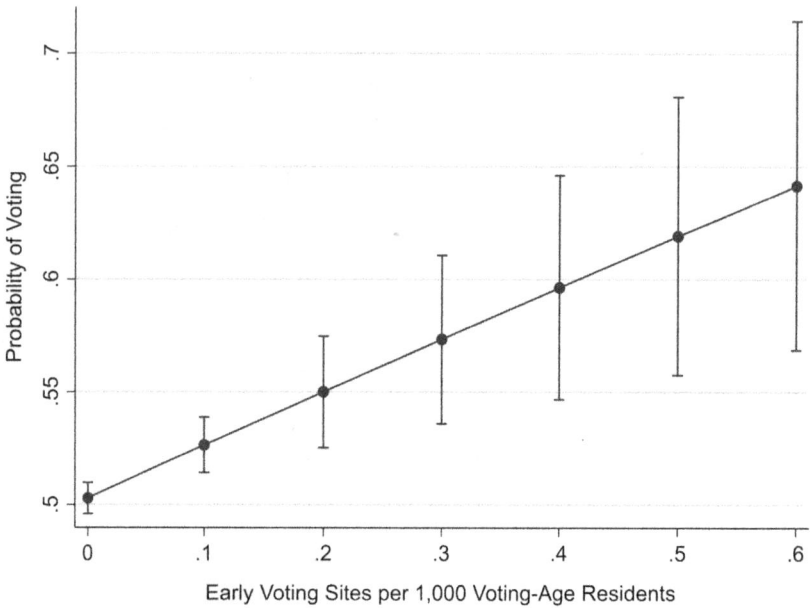

Figure 3.1   Early Voting Site Density and Probability of Voting, 2014 (Full Model). *Source:* Created by Elliott Fullmer using data from the 2014 Current Population Survey and the U.S. Election Assistance Commission's 2014 Election Administration and Voting Survey.

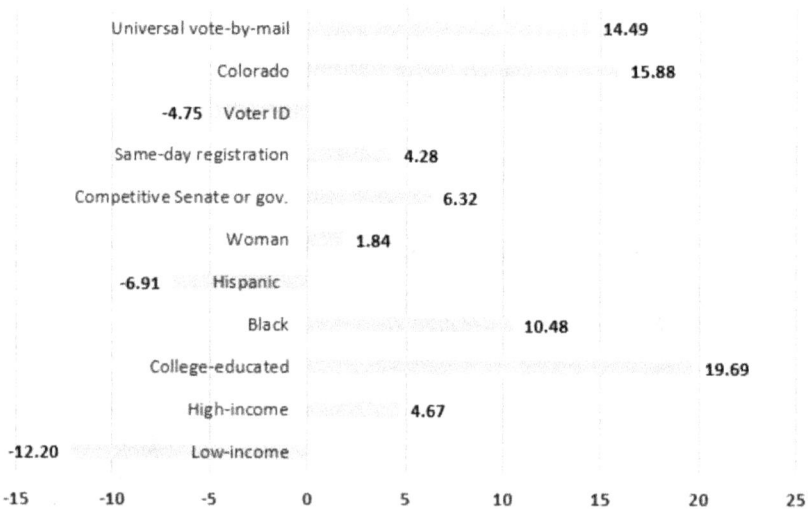

Figure 3.2   Marginal Effects on Turnout (in Percentage Points), 2014. *Source:* Created by Elliott Fullmer using data from the 2014 Current Population Survey and the National Conference of State Legislatures (2014).

primary (first) specification. The numbers displayed indicate the percentage-point increase in likelihood of an individual choosing to vote in 2014 if they fit the corresponding characteristic.

Figure 3.2 confirms that numerous administrative, political, and demographic covariates have a meaningful effect on an individual's decision to vote. Regarding early voting options, a citizen is 14.49 percentage points more likely to vote if they reside in a state with a universal VBM program. Those residing in Colorado—with both universal VBM and physical voting sites at their disposal—are 15.88 points more likely to cast a ballot. Other covariates have powerful effects on participation. A citizen is 4.75 percentage points less likely to vote if their state had a strict photo identification law. Living in a state with a competitive Senate or gubernatorial race is associated with a 6.32 percentage-point bump in the likelihood of voting. Women (1.84 points), Blacks (10.48), those with college degrees (19.69), and those with high family incomes (4.67) are significantly more likely to vote as well. Finally, Hispanics (−6.91) and those with family incomes below $50,000 (−12.20) are significantly less likely to vote. Each of these findings is consistent with previous research and confirms my own conclusions from chapter 2. One difference from my county-level findings surrounds SDR. While I reported no significant relationship between SDR and turnout in chapter 2 (in 2014), I do find that citizens living in states with this option are 4.28 percentage points more likely to vote in the CPS analysis.

PRESIDENTIAL ELECTION FINDINGS

The 2016 analysis explores the role of county site density and other convenience options on an individual's decision to vote in a presidential election. Table 3.3 displays the findings from two Probit regressions. Identical to the midterm models, the first test includes all covariates, while the second includes only observations in early voting states. Across both specifications, early voting sites per capita again have a positive and significant relationship with voting. The presence of universal VBM is also a significant predictor of voting, as is living in Colorado. Unlike the 2014 analysis, the likelihood of voting in 2016 also rises when one resides in a no-excuse absentee voting state. Early voting days are negatively associated with voting, though the effect size is again small. Meanwhile, voter ID laws, SDR, and AVR have no significant effect on voting. My findings regarding voter ID laws mirror those reported in chapter 2, when I also found significant turnout effects in 2014, but not 2016. As for registration, my findings differ, as significant effects were reported in chapter 2 for both SDR and AVR laws in 2016.

Table 3.3   Early Voting and Individual Turnout, 2016

Variables	(1) 2016 Voter	(2) 2016 Voter
Early voting state	−0.0272	
	(0.049)	
Early voting site density	0.342**	0.332**
	(0.162)	(0.167)
No-excuse absentee	0.106**	0.134***
	(0.047)	(0.051)
Early voting days	−0.00320*	−0.00423**
	(0.002)	(0.002)
Universal vote-by-mail	0.225**	0.308***
	(0.102)	(0.111)
Colorado	0.311***	0.426***
	(0.089)	(0.094)
Election Day site density	0.0384	0.344***
	(0.046)	(0.095)
Same-day registration	0.0534	−0.0103
	(0.035)	(0.042)
Automatic voter registration	0.0578	0.0493
	(0.128)	(0.128)
Strict photo ID law	0.0215	0.02
	(0.052)	(0.053)
Competitive Senate or governor race	0.0921***	0.0992**
	(0.027)	(0.041)
Black	0.216***	0.141***
	(0.033)	(0.042)
Hispanic	−0.128***	−0.143***
	(0.029)	(0.033)
Age	0.0132***	0.0138***
	(0.001)	(0.001)
Woman	0.142***	0.157***
	(0.020)	(0.025)
College-educated	0.561***	0.543***
	(0.024)	(0.029)
High income	0.247***	0.258***
	(0.028)	(0.034)
Low income	−0.290***	−0.279***
	(0.024)	(0.029)
Constant	−0.304***	−0.450***
	(0.046)	(0.071)
Observations	22,295	14,954

Source: Created by Elliott Fullmer using data from the 2016 Current Population Survey and the U.S. Election Assistance Commission's 2016 Election Administration and Voting Survey.

Notes: *** $p < 0.01$, ** $p < 0.05$, * $p < 0.1$. Cell entries are OLS regression estimates with standard errors in parentheses.

Living in a presidential swing state leads to a greater likelihood of casting a ballot in 2016, while the demographic covariates behave as they did in the midterm models. Women, Blacks, those with college degrees, those with high family incomes, and older voters are more likely to vote, while Hispanics and those with low family incomes are less likely to vote.

In order to assess the substantive effects of the site density measure, I again run a margins analysis with the full model. Because the highest level of county site density found in the 2016 dataset is slightly higher than 0.7 sites per 1,000 voting-age residents, I measure the likelihood of voting for those with 0 sites per capita, then display additional likelihoods for those with 0.1, 0.2, 0.3, 0.4, 0.5, 0.6, and 0.7 sites per capita available, respectively. Table 3.4 displays these results. In each case, the probability of voting rises notably as site density increases, though the effect sizes are smaller than those observed in 2014. With all controls included, a citizen in a county with no early voting sites has a 72.24% probability of voting; this rises over six points to 78.98% for those living in a county with 0.7 sites per 1,000 voting-age residents.[2] While this is a smaller disparity than I observed in the midterm model, it remains a substantively large difference. The effect sizes are similar in the second test, with only respondents in early voting states included.

The margins plot in figure 3.3 displays the positive relationship between site density and probability of voting in the full model. The 95% confidence intervals included for each level of density confirm the significance of the relationship. However, because the effect is somewhat weaker than in the midterm model, the bars overlap more than in 2014.

In order to determine the substantive effects of the binary covariates in the model, I again run a marginal effects analysis on the full model (see Figure 3.4). The effect sizes remain substantively meaningful for each of the significant political covariates, though—as with early voting site density—they are smaller than those reported in 2014. Living in a no-excuse absentee voting

Table 3.4   Margins Analysis of Early Voting Site Density and Turnout, 2016

Early Voting Sites per 1,000 Voting-Age Residents	*Probability of Voting (Full Model) (%)*	*Probability of Voting (Early Voting States Only) (%)*
0	72.24	72.03
0.1	73.27	73.02
0.2	74.27	73.99
0.3	75.25	74.95
0.4	76.22	75.88
0.5	77.16	76.80
0.6	78.08	77.70
0.7	78.98	78.58

Source: Created by Elliott Fullmer using data from the 2016 Current Population Survey and the U.S. Election Assistance Commission's 2016 Election Administration and Voting Survey.

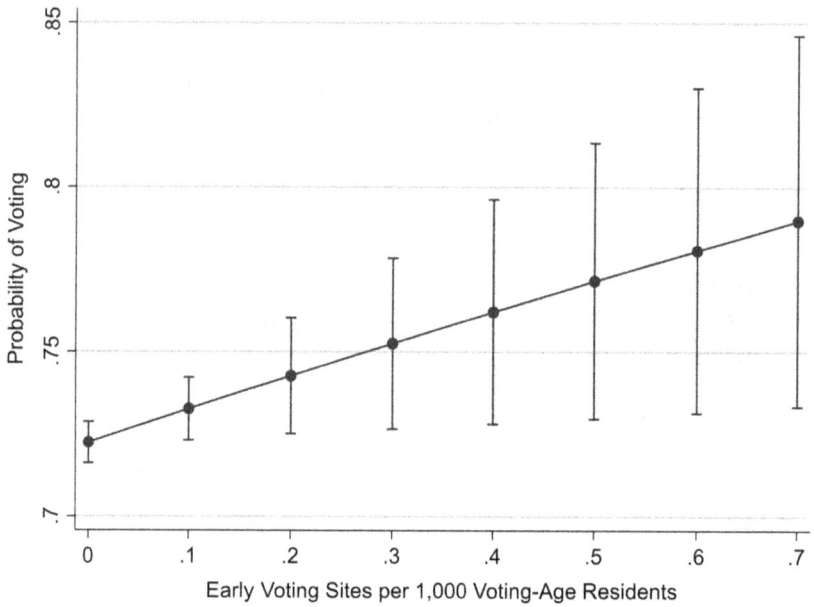

Figure 3.3 Early Voting Site Density and Probability of Voting, 2016 (Full Model). *Source:* Created by Elliott Fullmer using data from the 2016 Current Population Survey and the U.S. Election Assistance Commission's 2016 Election Administration and Voting Survey.

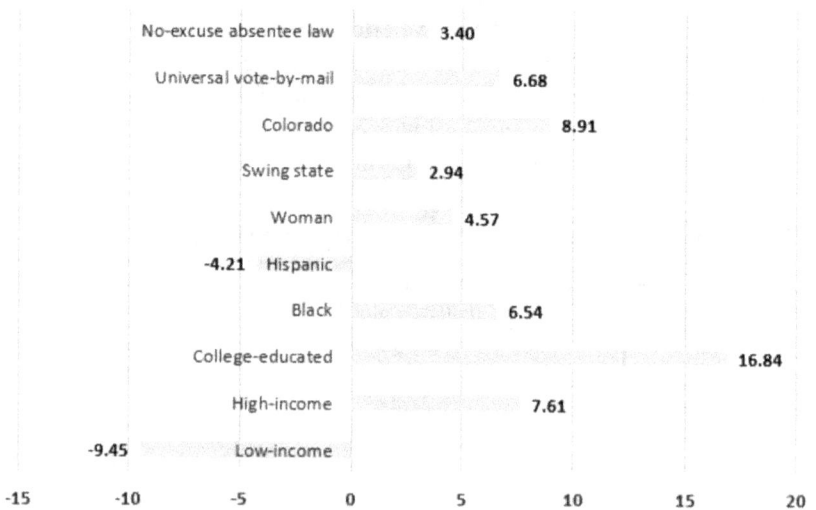

Figure 3.4 Marginal Effects on Turnout (in Percentage Points), 2016. *Source:* Created by Elliott Fullmer using data from the 2016 Current Population Survey and the National Conference of State Legislatures (2016).

state is associated with a 3.4 percentage-point increase in one's likelihood of voting, a smaller effect than that reported for early in-person site density. Meanwhile, universal VBM (6.68), Colorado (8.91), and swing state (2.94) residents are also associated with higher voting probabilities.

Several of the demographic covariates have a stronger effect on voting in 2016 than they did in 2014, including women (4.57) and those with high incomes (7.61). Others, including Hispanics (−4.21), Blacks (6.54), those with college degrees (16.84), and those with low incomes (−9.45), have smaller effects on voting than in 2014.

CONCLUSIONS

The findings in this short chapter confirm that early voting site density is associated with higher turnout in midterm and presidential election cycles. Across several specifications, individual citizens demonstrate higher likelihoods of voting when their respective counties offer more sites per capita. The findings are substantively strong despite the inclusion of many covariates that are linked to voting. In the 2014 analysis, the likelihood of voting varies by up to 14 percentage points depending on the availability of early voting locations. The substantive effect was smaller in 2016, but still varies over six percentage points depending on site availability. While my chapter 2 findings were promising, the unit of analysis (counties) raised valid ecological inference concerns. The findings in this chapter, however, largely confirm the county analysis in both midterm and presidential election contexts through individual models. In doing so, they provide an important robustness check on my primary conclusions.

The Probit analyses also confirm a strong relationship between universal VBM and turnout, while the findings regarding no-excuse absentee voting are more mixed. No significant effect is reported for 2014, though in 2016 a modest relationship between no-excuse absentee policies and turnout does emerge. The length of an early voting window (measured in days), a positive but small predictor of higher turnout in chapter 2, is associated with *less* turnout in the individual analysis. This finding lends some doubt regarding the efficacy of long early voting periods. It appears that site density and absentee options bring more voters to the polls than lengthy early voting windows.

Neither the county nor individual analyses suggest that early voting sites, like any convenience reform, can bring the United States to the top of the international leaderboard in turnout. As I have discussed in earlier chapters, making voting more convenient is not a panacea. Rather, this chapter (and the one preceding it) suggests that modest increases are possible with ambitious, but not unrealistic, state and local efforts. Given the relatively stubborn nature of voter participation in the United States, any public policy found to have a positive and substantively significant relationship with turnout should be taken seriously.

The findings in chapters 2 and 3 also demonstrate that early voting differs considerably both across and within states, something for which research must account. In assessing whether reducing the costs of voting brings new voters to the polls, scholars must properly identify how—and to what degree—costs are truly being lowered. This approach is a prudent one when investigating all types of election administration, as well as other public policies.

NOTES

1. National turnout in 2014 is estimated to have been 36.4% of eligible voters. As is often the case, the reported turnout rate in the CPS survey is clearly higher than observed turnout. I do not believe this poses a serious problem for my findings, as there is no reason to suspect that respondents are more likely to be dishonest about voting if they live in counties with more (or less) early voting site density.

2. The reported turnout rate in the CPS again exceeds the observed turnout rate (60.1%) in the 2016 election. Again, I have no reason to suspect that those living in high site density counties were more likely to be dishonest about voting (or not voting).

Chapter 4

Early Voting and Down-Ballot Roll-Off

Innovative public policies invariably produce unintended consequences. As I have documented in previous chapters, early voting was created to increase participation, boost citizen convenience, and ease the election administration process. In chapter 2, I reported that many county administrators have indeed found that early voting reduces Election Day stress, while increasing staff demands in the weeks preceding it. In chapters 2 and 3, I found that early voting does achieve its goal of increasing turnout when broadly available to citizens. It is unrealistic, however, to expect these outcomes to be exhaustive. Rather, fundamentally altering the electoral process with early voting may bring unforeseen (and perhaps undesirable) effects as well.

Merton (1936) originally coined the term "unintended consequences," arguing that several factors limit an actor's ability to anticipate all outcomes of "purposive action." Not only are human assumptions about the future naturally imperfect, but often the desire for beneficial consequences, or "the impervious immediacy of interest," blinds reformers to other potential outcomes of an action. Excitement over reducing the costs of voting may, for example, prevent lawmakers and others from recognizing new challenges or problems introduced by early voting policies.

Political scientists have studied unintended consequences across a vast array of public policies. As I noted in the introductory chapter, changes to the presidential nomination system in the 1970s created advantages for particular candidates and their supporting factions (Joslyn 1976; Lengle and Shafer 1976; Maisel and Lieberman 1977; Marshall 1979; Hammond 1980; Geer 1986, 1989; Ansolabehere and King 1990), increased party factionalism (Kamarck 1987), and disadvantaged the Democratic Party (Cavala 1974; Kamarck 1987; Wattenberg 1991).

Unintended consequences have also stemmed from congressional reforms. The 2002 Bipartisan Campaign Reform Act (BCRA) banned "soft-money" contributions, resulting in the rise of 527 groups or tax-exempt organizations able to raise and spend unlimited sums for political advocacy purposes (Valdemoro 2005). The decentralization of welfare programs across the industrialized world has had unfavorable effects on single mothers' health and well-being (Bitler et al. 2005; Grogger and Karoly 2005; Brewer 2007; Francesconi and van der Klaauw 2007; Baker et al. 2008), while there is some evidence that the 1996 U.S. reform measure led to a "race to the bottom" in benefits among individual states (Rom et al. 1998; Figlio et al. 1999, Volden 2002; Bailey and Rom 2004). With regards to voting reforms, Clayton (2012) reports that the adoption of direct recording electronic devices (voting machines) created new problems at polling places. While these machines were popularized in the early 2000s to simplify the voting process, some municipalities found that the lack of a paper trail led to new headaches. In fact, malfunctions led to the loss of thousands of votes in a 2006 Florida congressional election.

Most research on early voting has measured its effectiveness in boosting turnout. This research—including that presented in earlier chapters of this book—typically measures turnout for top-ticket races, such as the presidency and high-level state positions. In this chapter, I assess turnout for less publicized, but often powerful, political offices. It has been speculated by some that the rapid growth of early voting may decrease participation for down-ballot races, or those found after presidential, gubernatorial, or senatorial contests on a ballot. Early voters, the theory suggests, are making their choices weeks before Election Day, often before down-ballot campaigning has commenced. As a result, some voters have little knowledge of these races and may choose not to cast a vote in them—creating "roll-off."

While roll-off has been studied in the academic literature, research has mostly neglected the possibility that early voting has the unintended consequence of increasing it. I shed light on this question through several OLS regression analyses. In the interest of conducting a focused analysis, I concentrate on the case of Ohio, a state that adopted early voting after the 2004 election and has seen it explode in popularity in recent years. Ultimately, I find that early voting has produced modestly higher levels of ballot roll-off in both partisan and (especially) nonpartisan Ohio elections.

BALLOT ROLL-OFF

Down-ballot roll-off occurs when citizens cast a vote for offices listed at the top of their respective ballots, but fail to vote for offices (one or many) further down the ballot. Some degree of roll-off is relatively common in the United States, as campaigns for offices such as president and governor typically generate more citizen interest than less highlighted offices such as state treasurer or county commissioner. Researchers have studied ballot roll-off for several decades, though the literature is not particularly dense. Roll-off has been attributed to a number of predictable factors, including the information environment regarding respective political races (Nicholson 2003, 2005) and the media coverage devoted to campaigns (Bowler and Donovan 1994). Simply put, the more information voters have about campaigns, often from the news media or candidates themselves, the more likely they are to vote in down-ballot races.

In addition, the racial composition of an electorate can influence roll-off, with Blacks traditionally more likely to roll off than non-Hispanic Whites (Magleby 1985; Vanderleeuw and Engstrom 1987; Darcy and Schneider 1989). A study commissioned by Emily's List, a group committed to helping elect pro-choice Democratic women, claims that younger and less-educated voters, as well as those living in poverty, roll off at higher rates ("Why People Don't Vote," 2009). The length of a ballot in a particular jurisdiction also increases roll-off (Walker 1966; Taebel 1975; Brockington 2003), as longer ballots may cause voters to skip races (intentionally or not). Nonpartisan elections (such as referenda and judicial elections) typically have a higher percentage of roll-off as well (Hall 1999; Schaffner et al. 2001). Scholars have attributed this effect to the removal of a partisan cue, which often guides voters when they know little about candidates on the ballot. Relatedly, an option to vote a straight-party ticket (available in six states) reduces roll-off in partisan contests (Walker 1966; Kimball et al. 1996; Nichols 1998).[1] Lastly, scholars note that the complexity of referenda language can have an impact on roll-off, as more complicated descriptions lead to greater levels of it (Bowler and Donovan 1994; Reilly and Richey 2011).

Little attention has been paid to early voting's implications for ballot roll-off. A handful of articles have reported that universal vote-by-mail (VBM) *reduces* roll-off by allowing voters to complete ballots on their own time (Southwell 2009b, Marble 2017; Menger et al. 2018). Alvarez et al. (2011), however, disagrees, finding that VBM programs actually increase roll-off. Not only does the debate remain unsettled, but these studies have been limited to states with universal VBM programs. Most early voting states are not VBM states, making it less clear whether these findings are applicable in places where voting occurs both in-person and through the mail.

Many political operatives and journalists have voiced concerns that some early voters are participating before they have full information about candidates. If voters participate before campaigning for some offices has peaked or even begun, then they may be more inclined to skip those races when filling out a ballot. In particular, roll-off may occur more for nonpartisan races where a partisan voting cue is missing.

A high-level Democratic Party operative who worked in Ohio during the 2010 midterm cycle reported that increased levels of early voting in the state led to concerns about down-ballot roll-off (Email to author, 2011). In response, the party emphasized the inclusion of down-ballot races on campaign mailers that it sent to prospective voters. In addition, party-sponsored phone calls often reminded people to "vote for Democrats all the way down the ballot." For many candidates for these offices, this was indeed the only exposure that they would receive before the early voting period, as their campaigns had not yet begun advertising a month before Election Day. Anticipating roll-off problems in light of increased early voting across the nation, the AFL-CIO, the nation's largest federation of labor unions, also launched additional efforts to inform early voters about down-ballot candidates in 2010. They feared that those participating early would "skip casting a vote in those contests because they don't know anything about them" ("Early Bird Gets the Vote," 2010).

Concerns were particularly high for Ohio Supreme Court races, a nonpartisan office in the state. In August 2010, a federal district court upheld Ohio's ban on listing political party labels for judicial candidates. Ohio Democratic Party chairman Chris Redfern acknowledged that supreme court races are always difficult to mobilize due to the lack of a party label. Responding to a comment that Democratic-oriented judges did poorly in Ohio despite Barack Obama's victory there in 2008, Redfern responded, "That's what we are trying to prevent (in 2010)." In light of early voting's expansion, he authorized three million pieces of mail to be sent to voters referencing supreme court candidates backed by the party (Wilkinson 2010). The majority were sent before the early voting period began or at least reached its peak participation.

The possibility of down-ballot roll-off has important implications for the success of early voting. If the practice increases turnout for top-ticket offices, but reduces or fails to improve participation in down-ballot races, then its positive effects on democracy are potentially compromised. It has long been argued in both theoretical (Tocqueville 1838) and empirical (Macedo and Karpowitz 2006; Swanstrom 2008) works that down-ballot offices in the United States are often those closest to voters, as they are responsible for many of the day-to-day issues that people face.

DATA AND METHODS

I examine the effects of a new early voting policy on ballot roll-off. Specifically, I am interested in determining whether the adoption and expansion of early voting lead more voters to ignore races that appear toward the bottom of their ballots. I focus on the state of Ohio for several reasons. First, Ohio did not have an early voting program prior to 2006. Absentee ballots were available to those with an accepted excuse, but others were forced to vote on Election Day. Ohio chose to adopt early voting in 2005 (it took effect in 2006) in the wake of long lines and heavy participation in 2004. Both no-excuse absentee voting and early in-person voting were approved (Ohio General Assembly 2005). Early voting, many believed, would limit wait times, offer more convenience to voters, and increase flexibility for those who worked on Election Day.

Second, Ohio, like most states, does not offer voters the option to cast a "straight-ticket" ballot, or one where votes are automatically cast for all candidates on the ballot from a particular party. As a result, voters must choose to vote for each office on the ballot. In Ohio, some offices feature candidates with party labels, while a few do not. Therefore, I am able to assess not only the prevalence of ballot roll-off but also whether this varies depending on the type of race. Third, early voting in Ohio has quickly increased since its adoption. While 2006 was the first year in which early voting was legal in the state, over a quarter of Ohioans have voted early in each national election cycle since 2008. Since the program led to quick and significant changes in the way citizens participate, Ohio is a convenient place to assess a potential effect. Finally, Ohio is eminently testable because it features numerous statewide down-ballot offices up for election in national midterm cycles, allowing for convenient pre- and post-treatment comparisons of roll-off.

I utilize OLS regression techniques to assess whether an Ohio county's early voting rate predicts higher levels of county roll-off. While an individual-level analysis would be ideal, the Ohio state voter file does not indicate whether a citizen voted in each individual race. Ohio is not unique in this regard, as this information is rarely made available to researchers. In addition, the Ohio file fails to note whether one voted early. Research (Reilly and Richey 2011) has acknowledged the methodological limits of studying roll-off and accepted that aggregate-level regression analyses remain the best approach.

Treating Ohio's 88 counties as the unit of analysis, my primary model focuses on 2010, the first midterm cycle where a sizable share of Ohio voters cast early ballots. While early voting was available is 2006, it remained new and sparsely used. In fact, the percentage of voters participating early jumped less than five percentage points in 2006 despite the fact that all voters became eligible to do so. As a result of greater advertising by election administrators and campaigns, the percentage of voters casting early ballots rose quickly in the years that followed. In 2008, 29.7% of Ohio voters cast early ballots; the rate has stayed above 25% in each election since.

The primary independent variable is the percentage of voters participating before Election Day in a particular county. In 2010, Ohio allowed its voters to complete a ballot 35 days before Election Day at a designated site(s) in their respective counties. Despite the state's high rate of early participation, county early voting rates varied considerably. While some counties had early voting rates below 20% (the lowest was Fulton County at 14.8%), several counties saw nearly half of their ballots cast early (the highest was Cuyahoga County at 49.6%).

The dependent variable is the level of ballot roll-off in a particular county. Roll-off is measured as the percentage decrease in total votes for a given office when compared to the top office on the ballot. The Ohio gubernatorial race is considered the top-ticket race across each of the state's 88 counties in 2010.

In addition to my primary independent variable (early voting rate), I control for each county's lagged roll-off rate in 2002, the final midterm cycle before early voting was adopted. Because 2006 was the first year of early voting in Ohio, I use 2002 as the lagged variable. I anticipate that a county's 2002 roll-off will be highly predictive of its 2010 roll-off, as the former should capture any idiosyncratic features that may affect a county's roll-off rate across election cycles.

I obtain election results and early voting statistics from the Ohio Secretary of State's webpage, while data on county demographics is collected from the 2010 U.S. Census. As I noted, I examine down-ballot roll-off in both partisan and nonpartisan offices in Ohio. The partisan offices include state auditor, secretary of state, state treasurer, and attorney general. Each of the four offices featured a contested race between a Democratic and a Republican candidate in 2010. The level of competition for the partisan offices was relatively similar to that in 2002 (the lagged year in my model) in both the secretary of state and state treasurer races, which should imply comparable levels of citizen interest. In 2002, Republican Ken Blackwell won 59% of the vote in the secretary of state election, while eight years later, Republican Jon Husted won 54% while seeking the same office. Republican Joseph Deters won the state treasurer race in 2002 with 53% of the vote, while Josh Mandel won with support from nearly 55% of voters in 2010.

While both the state auditor and attorney general races were contested in 2002 and 2010, the margins of victory differed across election cycles. In 2010, Republican Dave Yost won with 51% of the vote. This was much more competitive than Republican Betty Montgomery's successful campaign in 2002, when she received 64% of the vote. While the 2002 race for attorney general resulted in a lopsided victory for Republican Jim Petro (he received 64% of the vote), Mike DeWine won a tight contest in 2010 over Richard Cordray by less than two percentage points. It is worth noting that DeWine was also not a typical down-ballot candidate in 2010, as he had previously served in the U.S. House, U.S. Senate, and as the state's lieutenant governor.[2] As a result, it is conceivable that his name recognition could have reduced both roll-off and any likelihood that early voters would be more inclined to engage in it.

The nonpartisan offices included in my analysis are contests for seats on the Ohio Supreme Court. In both 2002 and 2010, Ohio voters cast ballots for two contested seats on the court. The races were never particularly close, though the margins of victory varied somewhat. In 2002, Maureen O'Connor and Evelyn Stratton won these races with 57% and 55% percent of the vote, respectively. Stratton was an incumbent judge seeking reelection, while O'Connor was seeking a seat for the first time. In 2010, O'Connor and incumbent Judith Lanzinger won with 68% and 57% of the vote, respectively. In determining each county's roll-off rate in Ohio Supreme Court races in both 2002 and 2010, I average the rate across the two contests held in the respective years.

My model also includes several demographic variables that past research suggests may affect roll-off. I account for each county's percent Black, percent Hispanic, percent living below the poverty line, percent college-educated, and percent over 65.

FINDINGS

Each Ohio office recorded a positive roll-off rate in 2010, suggesting that the gubernatorial election received more total votes that year than each down-ballot race. In Ohio Supreme Court races, the roll-off rate was easily the highest, as an average of one in six (17%) county voters did not cast a vote in these elections. The roll-off rate was much lower in the four partisan statewide offices. This is consistent with past research, as the fact that no party label appears on the ballot for judicial races arguably removes an important cue for voters without knowledge of the race or candidates. In the state auditor, state treasurer, and secretary of state contests, the average county roll-off rate was quite similar, ranging from 2.4% to 2.6%. Notably, roll-off was much lower (less than 1 percent) for the attorney general race. Again, I suspect that this may be due to the candidacy of former U.S. senator Mike DeWine, a well-known figure in the state.

My regression analyses assess whether the variation in county roll-off rates is affected by the share of a county choosing to vote before Election Day. Table 4.1 examines the relationship in nonpartisan Ohio Supreme Court races. With all controls included, the effect of early voting is both positive and statistically significant. The size of the relationship is substantively

Table 4.1   Early Voting and Ballot Roll-Off in Ohio Supreme Court Races, 2010

	(1)
	2010 County Roll-Off Rate
2002 county roll-off rate	0.742***
	(0.220)
County percent voting early	0.307***
	(0.116)
County percent Black	−0.209
	(0.131)
County percent below poverty	0.0829
	(0.160)
County percent Hispanic	−0.505
	(0.305)
County percent college-educated	0.15
	(0.112)
County percent over 65	−0.526
	(0.323)
Constant	0.183**
	(0.073)
Observations	88
R-squared	0.349

Source: Created by Elliott Fullmer using data from the Ohio Secretary of State's Office (2002, 2010) and the U.S. Census Bureau.
Notes: *** $p < 0.01$, ** $p < 0.05$. Cell entries are OLS regression estimates with standard errors in parentheses.

meaningful as well. In interpreting the effect size, I focus on the effect (on roll-off) of a 20 percentage-point change in a county's early voting rate. In 2010, a 20-point increase in a county's early voting rate is associated with a 6.14 percentage-point increase in ballot roll-off. For some context, in a county of 50,000 voters, this would imply that an additional 3,070 voters failed to cast a vote in supreme court races. In a larger county of 300,000 voters, this level of roll-off would imply that 18,420 additional gubernatorial voters failed to cast a vote in these races. [3]

A county's 2002 roll-off rate is an expectedly powerful predictor of its roll-off rate in 2010, as the lagged measure is designed to capture any idiosyncratic county qualities that are not explained by the demographic covariates in the analysis. The demographic covariates themselves, however, are insignificant in the supreme court model.

Table 4.2 displays the relationship in the four partisan statewide offices held in 2010. Early voting rates continue to predict higher levels of roll-off in the state auditor, secretary of state, and state treasurer races, as the coefficient is positive and significant in each of these cases. The effect sizes, however, are smaller than those found in Ohio Supreme Court races. Given that these elections include a party identifier on the ballot, this might be expected. In

Table 4.2   Early Voting and Ballot Roll-Off in Ohio Partisan Races, 2010

	(1)	(2)	(3)	(4)
	2010 County Roll-Off Rate (Attorney General)	2010 county Roll-Off Rate (State Auditor)	2010 County Roll-Off Rate (Secretary of State)	2010 County Roll-Off Rate (State Treasurer)
2002 county roll-off rate	0.147*	0.217**	0.233***	0.220***
	(0.074)	(0.088)	(0.064)	(0.068)
County percent voting early	0.0106	0.0686**	0.0604**	0.0450*
	(0.022)	(0.030)	(0.027)	(0.023)
County percent Black	−0.0379	−0.0606*	−0.0595*	−0.0476*
	(0.025)	(0.035)	(0.030)	(0.027)
County percent below poverty	0.0679**	0.0644	0.109***	0.0838**
	(0.030)	(0.042)	(0.037)	(0.033)
County percent Hispanic	−0.00235	0.0903	0.0595	0.0336
	(0.060)	(0.082)	(0.072)	(0.065)
County percent college-educated	0.0288	0.0144	0.0265	0.0177
	(0.022)	(0.030)	(0.026)	(0.023)
County percent over 65	0.0126	0.0286	0.0627	−0.0302
	(0.063)	(0.088)	(0.077)	(0.068)
Constant	−0.0159	−0.00943	−0.0263	−0.00203
	(0.014)	(0.020)	(0.017)	(0.015)
Observations	88	88	88	88
R-squared	0.12	0.176	0.31	0.252

Source: Created by Elliott Fullmer using data from the Ohio Secretary of State's Office (2002, 2010) and the U.S. Census Bureau.
Notes: *** $p < 0.01$, ** $p < 0.05$, * $p < 0.1$. Cell entries are OLS regression estimates with standard errors in parentheses.

the state auditor and secretary of state contests, an additional 20 percentage points of early voting in a county is associated with over one additional point of roll-off.[4] In the state treasurer race, the effect size is smaller, but significant nonetheless. An additional 20 points of early voting is associated with nearly one point of added roll-off.[5] In chapters 2 and 3, I reported that early voting can increase overall turnout by a few percentage points under certain conditions. But if heightened early voting also increases roll-off by a point or more, then some of these turnout gains may not fully extend to down-ballot races.

A county's early voting rate did not predict higher roll-off in the 2010 Ohio attorney general race. Roll-off was extremely low (0.5%) in the highly competitive election between Republican Mike DeWine and Democrat Richard Cordray. Given DeWine's substantial name recognition owing to his long service in the U.S. House and Senate, I am not surprised that my general findings are not reflected in this anomalous case. The theory holds that early voters may be more likely to roll off because they have received little or no information about the candidates seeking down-ballot office. There is little reason to believe that this would be a concern in this particular case.

Several covariates are found to have a significant effect on roll-off across the partisan races. A county's lagged roll-off rate is easily the most significant predictor of its 2010 roll-off rate in each case, while poverty predicts higher roll-off in each race except the state auditor contest. Meanwhile, a county's percent Black is associated with lower levels of roll-off in each election except the race for attorney general. This finding differs from that reported in a series of 1980s publications (Magleby 1985; Vanderleeuw and Engstrom 1987; Darcy and Schneider 1989). As was the case in the supreme court model, I continue to find no significant relationship between a county's percent Hispanic, percent college-educated, or percent over 65 and its roll-off rate.

ROLL-OFF IN 2018

I initially focused on the 2010 elections because Ohio had recently adopted early voting and watched it quickly grow. As a result, there was reason to believe that candidates, parties, and voters may not have fully adapted to the new political environment. While some campaigns and groups actively sought to prevent roll-off among early voters in 2010, it was unclear that these efforts would be sufficient. With campaigning for down-ballot races often beginning late in the election cycle, some voters could have cast ballots before being exposed to information about these races. My findings suggest that early voting did indeed produce heightened roll-off across a variety of Ohio contests in 2010.

I next run identical models in 2018 to assess whether early voting continued to have similar effects on roll-off in a more recent midterm election. It is possible that eight years later—once early voting became fully embedded in Ohio's political culture—candidates and parties had sufficiently adapted their campaigns in ways that made roll-off less likely.[6]

Early voting participation was again high in Ohio in 2018, as 29.7% of voters cast early ballots (McDonald 2018). Once again, early voting rates varied widely by county. Columbiana County had the smallest share of votes cast early (19.8%), while Belmont County led the way with 45.2%. The early voting window was shorter in 2018, as the state cut the number of early voting days in 2013. Controversially, the Republican-led state legislature also eliminated "golden week," a period where Ohio voters could register and vote early in the same visit.

In 2018, Ohio again had two contested state supreme court elections, one of which featured an incumbent and one in which the seat was open. Incumbent

Justice Mary DeGenaro was defeated by challenger Melody Stewart, who captured 52.6% of the vote. In the open contest, Michael Donnelly defeated Craig Baldwin decisively, winning 61% of the vote. Similar to 2010, each of the state's partisan statewide offices was contested in 2018. Each race was an open seat that was ultimately won by a Republican in a close contest. Dave Yost was elected attorney general with 52% of the vote, while Keith Faber defeated former Congressman Zach Space with nearly 50% of the vote to secure the state auditor position. Frank LaRose won nearly 51% of the vote to defeat a Democratic challenger for secretary of state, while Robert Sprague secured over 53% of the vote in the state treasurer contest.

Roll-off rates varied quite a bit in 2018. The average roll-off rate in the two supreme court races was over 27%, much higher than the 17% recorded in 2010. The roll-off rates for the partisan statewide races were comparable to those seen in 2010, though the attorney general race—no longer featuring a well-known former U.S. senator—increased to 1.7%, similar to the other contests. The presence of roll-off, of course, does not necessarily imply a role for early voting. Roll-off can result from many factors, including the effectiveness (or ineffectiveness) of campaigns. OLS regression tests again help identify whether higher levels of early voting are responsible for greater levels of ballot roll-off.

The findings in table 4.3 suggest that early voting continued to affect roll-off in both Ohio Supreme Court and two partisan statewide races in 2018. While I do not report a significant effect in either the attorney general (again) or state auditor races, early voting rates remain a positive and significant predictor of roll-off in both the secretary of state and state treasurer contests.

In the Ohio Supreme Court races, a 20 percentage-point increase in a county's early voting rate is associated with a four-point increase in its roll-off rate. This figure is less than the six percentage-point increase observed in 2010, but large nonetheless. The effect sizes for the secretary of state and state treasurer races are notably smaller. In the former, an additional 35 points of a county's electorate voting early is associated with an additional point of roll-off. Notably, the largest gap between Ohio counties regarding early voting rates was about 25 points in 2018. In the state treasurer election, the effect remains small, as almost 31 points of early voting would be needed to produce an additional point of roll-off.

In general, early voting still appears to have affected roll-off in 2018, but the relationship is a bit weaker. Significance is no longer reported in the state auditor contest, while the degree to which early voting is associated with heightened roll-off is less than 2010 in all three races where relationships are reported (supreme court, secretary of state, and state treasurer). It is possible that these findings suggest a learning effect, whereby Ohio candidates, campaign operatives, and citizens have adjusted a bit to the new realities of

Table 4.3 Early Voting and Ballot Roll-Off in Ohio Races, 2018

	(1) 2018 County Roll-Off Rate (Supreme Court)	(2) 2018 County Roll-Off Rate (Attorney General)	(3) 2018 County Roll-Off Rate (State Auditor)	(4) 2018 County Roll-Off Rate (Secretary of State)	(5) 2018 County Roll-Off Rate (State Treasurer)
2002 county roll-off rate	0.496***	0.0284	0.109**	0.0605	0.126**
	(0.182)	(0.0628)	(0.0547)	(0.0368)	(0.0489)
County percent voting early	0.202*	0.0106	0.00787	0.0286*	0.0327*
	(0.102)	(0.0196)	(0.0199)	(0.0163)	(0.0179)
County percent Black	-0.207**	-0.0420**	-0.00534	-0.0224	-0.00197
	(0.103)	(0.0201)	(0.0204)	(0.0165)	(0.0181)
County percent below poverty	-0.0569	0.0804***	0.0452*	0.0539**	0.0344
	(0.137)	(0.0258)	(0.0261)	(0.0213)	(0.0236)
County percent Hispanic	0.591**	0.0938*	0.182***	0.100**	0.0638
	(0.262)	(0.0508)	(0.0516)	(0.0422)	(0.0471)
County percent college-educated	-0.0864	0.0227	0.0408**	0.00548	0.00863
	(0.0973)	(0.0187)	(0.0191)	(0.0156)	(0.0172)
County percent over 65	-0.760***	0.0122	0.0248	0.0110	0.0131
	(0.278)	(0.0545)	(0.0559)	(0.0452)	(0.0500)
Constant	0.297***	-0.00486	-0.00934	-0.00774	-0.000996
Observations	88	88	88	88	88
R-squared	0.260	0.139	0.299	0.177	0.176

Source: Created by Elliott Fullmer using data from the Ohio Secretary of State's Office (2002, 2018) and the U.S. Census Bureau.
Notes: *** $p < 0.01$, ** $p < 0.05$, * $p < 0.1$. Cell entries are OLS regression estimates with standard errors in parentheses.

early voting. This would not be surprising, given that campaigns have been concerned about early voting and roll-off for at least a decade. The continued existence of a relationship (even a reduced one) between early voting and roll-off does suggest, however, that these efforts have not fully corrected the issue.

CONCLUSIONS

Research on early voting has largely neglected the possibility that the practice increases down-ballot roll-off. With more citizens visiting the polls weeks before Election Day, campaign operatives have expressed concern that some may be casting votes before down-ballot candidates have had a sufficient opportunity to promulgate their candidacies (and ideas). While many voters often know little about down-ballot candidacies even on Election Day, even a modest increase in those unaware of lower-tier races could result in higher levels of roll-off. The risk is particularly notable in nonpartisan races, which lack an important information cue used by many voters when little is known about a candidate(s).

Examining both partisan and nonpartisan races in Ohio in 2010, I find evidence that the quick development of early voting indeed led to heightened levels of ballot roll-off. The results are both statistically and substantively significant, even with the inclusion of a highly significant lagged roll-off variable included in the model. In nonpartisan Ohio Supreme Court races, a very realistic 20 percentage-point spike in a county's early voting rate is associated with a six percentage-point increase in roll-off. Given that the most optimistic studies—including mine!—about the turnout gains produced by early voting are generally limited to a handful of points, this finding is notable. In partisan statewide offices, the effects are smaller, though they remain meaningful. A 20 percentage-point increase in early voting often predicts an additional point of roll-off. Effects of early voting on roll-off are still present in 2018, though they are a bit less prevalent and substantively smaller. This may suggest that early voters were a bit more prepared by 2018 to cast votes for down-ballot offices.

I encourage further attention and innovation on this important research question, which has thus far been understudied. Future analyses would be wise to examine states beyond Ohio, including those with higher early voting rates (e.g., Arizona, Nevada, and North Carolina). An analysis of multiple states may examine whether effects differ depending on when an early voting program begins each year. Iowa, which begins early voting in late September, may be more susceptible to heightened roll-off than Oklahoma, where early voting is limited to only a handful of days before Election Day.

Additional down-ballot offices should be studied as well. In particular, ballot referenda—prevalent in many states—offer another opportunity to examine the effects of early voting on roll-off in a nonpartisan context. Eventually, should the data become available, an individual-level analysis (rather than a county-level one) of this question would also be an important contribution to the literature.

NOTES

1. The states that allow straight-ticket voting are Alabama, Indiana, Michigan, Kentucky, Oklahoma, and South Carolina (NCSL 2020b).

2. DeWine would later serve as governor of Ohio, taking office in 2019.

3. The coefficient indicates that as early voting increases by one percentage-point in Ohio counties, roll-off increases by 0.307%. Therefore, a county that goes from having 5% to 25% of its voters participate early could expect to see a 6.14 percentage-point increase in ballot roll-off. In a county of 50,000 top-ticket voters, this is equivalent to 3,070 fewer voters.

4. The coefficient of 0.0686 in the state auditor specification suggests that as a county goes from 5% to 25% of its voters participating early, roll-off increases by 1.372 percentage points. The coefficient of 0.0604 in the secretary of state test suggests that the same jump in early voting is associated with an additional 1.208 points.

5. The coefficient of 0.0450 suggests that as a county goes from 5% to 25% of its voters casting early ballots, roll-off increases by 0.9 percentage points.

6. I considered analyzing roll-off in 2014 as well, though I decided against it because of the unusual circumstances of the 2014 Ohio gubernatorial election. Incumbent Governor John Kasich easily defeated his Democratic challenger, Ed Fitzgerald, by over 30 points. This unusually lopsided race in Ohio was affected by revelations that Fitzgerald was found with a woman—who was not his wife—at 4:30 am in a parking lot several years prior. Because the race was not competitive, I suspect that citizen interest in the gubernatorial race was lower than usual in 2014. If this is true, then the gap in attention between the top-ticket race and the remaining Ohio statewide races was likely much smaller than usual.

Chapter 5

Early Voting and Racial Inequity

Chapter 4 identified down-ballot roll-off as a potential unintended consequence of early voting. In this chapter, I explore another potential side effect of the popular reform—the extent to which early voting may exacerbate inequality with regard to electoral convenience. More specifically, I am interested in whether early voting sites are disproportionately available in counties with larger non-Hispanic White populations.

Chapters 2 and 3 confirmed that site density appears to be an important catalyst in early voting's success. Chapter 2 found that counties with ample sites saw notable increases in turnout in recent elections, while chapter 3 confirmed this finding through an individual-level analysis of Current Population Survey (CPS) data. Given the importance of sites, it is worthwhile to examine their distribution with additional scrutiny. Sites are not randomly assigned, but rather result from decisions by state and local officials. In this chapter, I am interested in observing if the racial and ethnic composition of a county predicts high (or low) levels of site density. This question was originally motivated in part by a specific challenge issued by Gronke and McDonald (2008). The authors observed that states with permissive early voting laws (before 2008) tended to have electorates with a higher proportion of non-Hispanic Whites. At the time, they speculated that early voting options may not "be implemented in a consistent manner across all racial communities." Gronke and McDonald did not directly test their hypothesis, but instead challenged the field to address the question.

If they indeed exist, racial and ethnic site disparities have important ramifications. As I discussed in chapter 1, Section 2 of the Voting Rights Act (1965) declares that electoral laws cannot be altered in a way that dilutes minority voting strength.[1] These provisions apply even if the policies leading to a disparity were unintentional. If heavily non-Hispanic White counties are enjoying a reform that is largely denied in heavily non-White counties, then such a dilution may be present and a case for federal intervention becomes plausible.

In this chapter, I accept Gronke and McDonald's (2008) challenge by exploring whether early voting sites are disproportionately available to particular racial or ethnic groups. Examining each national election between 2012 and 2018—the same cycles analyzed in chapter 2—I report that counties with larger Black populations offer significantly fewer early voting sites to citizens. A county whose percent Black is 20 percentage points higher than another similarly sized county can expect to have several fewer early voting sites in both presidential and midterm election years. This finding is present in both urban and more lightly populated counties. Conversely, heavily Hispanic counties have significantly *more* early voting sites per capita, perhaps owing to their high numbers in states with long early voting traditions.

DATA AND METHODS

Unlike earlier chapters, site density now serves as my dependent variable. In crafting this variable, I again use Election Assistance Commission (EAC) data on the number of early voting sites in a county per 1,000 voting-age residents. Because this analysis examines the site choices made by state and local governments, I only examine counties in states that have chosen to adopt early voting. Obviously, the number of sites in counties in non-early voting states is 0.

My independent variables include demographic, political, and administrative factors that may affect the dependent variable. For county demographic data, I again use 2010 U.S. Census estimates. I include variables on the percentage of each county's population that is Black, Hispanic, noncitizen, college-educated, and over 65. I also include a variable noting each county's mean household income. Given the role of budget considerations in site decisions, one may expect wealthier communities to offer more early voting locations. I also control for each county's population per square mile because I suspect that more sparsely populated communities will offer more sites per capita, as fewer individuals generally reside in these communities. One site serves the 6,086 voting-age residents of Greenlee County, Illinois, but a similar ratio of residents per site would require 652 sites in Cook County, Illinois (Chicago), a figure that is not particularly practical. Furthermore, while most early voting states allow counties to determine the number of sites they wish to offer, some do not. These limits have the effect of hurting site density in heavily populated counties. For example, Ohio limits each of its 88 counties to one site. While this appears equitable at first glance, population varies considerably across the state's counties. Cuyahoga County has over 1.2 million residents, while Vinton County has a population around 13,000 people. Across the state, site density is therefore much higher in lightly populated communities. As I did in chapter 2, I include specifications that isolate those living in counties with (1) at least 200,000 residents and (2) fewer than 200,000 residents. This allows me to identify whether site discrepancies on the basis of race and ethnicity—if they exist—are prevalent in both sorts of communities.

In the midterm years, I include a variable for states that had a competitive Senate or gubernatorial election, as expected turnout (and perhaps sites provided) should be higher. As I did in previous chapters, I consider a state competitive if either a Senate or gubernatorial race saw the top two candidates finish within 10 percentage points of one another. In the presidential years, I also account for competitiveness; I consider a state politically competitive if candidates for president or vice president visited at least three times during the general election campaign.

Regarding election administration, I include a binary measure indicating whether the state allowed no-excuse absentee voting. In these states, a smaller share of voters may be expected to cast ballots in person, perhaps lessening the need for sites. Relatedly, I include a binary variable for counties in Colorado. The state's hybrid system of universal vote-by-mail (VBM) and early voting led to less emphasis on sites (beginning in 2014) because of the large number of voters casting ballots through the mail. Finally, I account for the number of early voting days provided by each county's state in each cycle. It is possible that states choosing to invest in longer early voting windows have done so at the expense of early voting sites.

PRESIDENTIAL FINDINGS

Descriptive statistics offer clues regarding the relationship between race, ethnicity, and site density. In 2012, 189 counties in the dataset had both an early voting program and at least 20% of residents identifying as Black. Of these counties, not a single one had at least one early voting site per 1,000 voting-age residents. In fact, only one county had one site per 2,000 residents. In 2016, the figures were very similar. Of 290 counties with an early voting program and at least 20% of residents identifying as Black, only one had a site per 1,000 residents. Five had at least one site per 2,000 residents. Meanwhile, of the 292 counties with at least 20% of citizens identifying as Hispanic in 2012, 10 had at least one early voting site per 1,000 voting-age residents and 29 had a site for every 2,000 residents. In 2016, the numbers dropped a bit. Eight reported at least one site per 1,000 voting-age residents, while 21 had at least one site per 2,000 residents. At first glance, it certainly appears that site density is much greater in heavily Hispanic communities than heavily Black ones.

Table 5.1 reports my findings across several OLS regression models. In both 2012 and 2016, there is overwhelming evidence that a county's percent Black is negatively associated with site density. The first two specifications include the full models for each respective presidential election year. In an effort to clearly interpret the findings in an applicable way, I capture the difference (in sites offered) between counties of comparable sizes whose percent Black differs by 20 percentage points. In 2012, with all controls included, a county of just 10,040 people (a relatively small county) in which 40% of the residents are Black can expect to have one fewer early voting site than a county of the same size in which 20% of persons are Black.[2] In 2016, the effect size is slightly smaller, but remains substantively meaningful. A county of 12,376 people in which 40% of the residents are Black can expect to have one fewer site than a comparable county where 20% of all residents are Black. Meanwhile, a county's percent Hispanic is linked to more site density in both 2012 and 2016. In counties of 13,550 and 14,327 persons, respectively, a 20 percentage-point change in percent Hispanic is associated with one additional early voting site in each year. Many of the states with the largest Hispanic populations—in the West and Southwest—were among the first to adopt early voting in the late 1980s and early 1990s. Counties in these states—which include Arizona, California, Colorado, New Mexico, and Texas—typically offer a healthy number of early voting sites.

Several other covariates in the primary models are significant. While a county's noncitizen percentage predicts fewer sites per capita, its percent over 65 is linked to more sites. Neither finding is surprising. Counties with large noncitizen populations may be expected to have less robust local services. In addition, officials likely know that a larger share of their residents are not eligible to vote. Meanwhile, elderly communities may have higher levels of civic activity and more intense pressure for additional sites.

Interestingly, counties in no-excuse absentee states have significantly *more* sites in each year, meaning that liberalized absentee policies are not coming at the expense of physical early voting locations. Early voting days are negatively associated with sites, suggesting that counties do compensate for longer early voting periods by opening fewer sites. This is consistent with the feedback provided by county clerks in chapter 2, as county resources—especially staff—are often quite limited. The effect sizes, however, are quite small. In 2012, 60 days of early voting—an impractical number—is associated with one fewer site; in 2016, the effect grows, as an additional 34 days are linked to one fewer early voting location. Surprisingly, Colorado counties are not linked to fewer sites in 2016, suggesting that even when the state

Table 5.1 Demographics and Early Voting Site Density, 2012 and 2016

Variables	(1) 2012 Early Voting Site Density	(2) 2016 Early Voting Site Density	(3) 2012 Early Voting Site Density	(4) 2016 Early Voting Site Density	(5) 2012 Early Voting Site Density	(6) 2016 Early Voting Site Density
Percent Black	-0.498***	-0.404***	-0.0437*	-0.0426**	-0.540***	-0.438***
	(0.111)	(0.088)	(0.024)	(0.021)	(0.124)	(0.097)
Percent Hispanic	0.369***	0.349***	0.0879***	0.0264	0.416***	0.392***
	(0.107)	(0.108)	(0.030)	(0.031)	(0.116)	(0.116)
Percent noncitizen	-1.224***	-1.307***	-0.197*	-0.0689	-1.254***	-1.393***
	(0.425)	(0.408)	(0.091)	(0.091)	(0.479)	(0.457)
Percent over 65	1.821***	1.732***	-0.0781	-0.114	1.912***	1.836***
	(0.270)	(0.252)	(0.071)	(0.070)	(0.293)	(0.274)
Percent college-educated	0.154	0.225	0.0688	0.105**	0.174	0.239
	(0.187)	(0.183)	(0.044)	(0.042)	(0.211)	(0.205)
Mean income	-0.00156	-0.00208*	-0.000214	-0.000525**	-0.00159	-0.00215
	(0.001)	(0.001)	(0.000)	(0.000)	(0.001)	(0.001)
Pop. per sq. mile	-2.32E-05	-2.05E-05				
	(0.000)	(0.000)				
No-excuse absentee	0.0512*	0.0525*	-0.0180***	-0.0151**	0.0578*	0.0581**
	(0.027)	(0.027)	(0.007)	(0.007)	(0.030)	(0.030)
Early voting days	-0.00166*	-0.00295***	-0.00076***	-0.000133	-0.00191*	-0.00332***
	(0.001)	(0.001)	(0.000)	(0.000)	(0.001)	(0.001)
Colorado		-0.0257		-0.00162		-0.0404
		(0.061)		(0.011)		(0.069)
Swing state	0.0151	-0.00901	0.0153**	0.00955	0.0277	0.00556
	(0.026)	(0.025)	(0.006)	(0.007)	(0.029)	(0.028)
Constant	0.0131	0.0834	0.0550**	0.0679***	-0.0038	0.073
	(0.091)	(0.084)	(0.024)	(0.022)	(0.102)	(0.094)
Observations	1,902	2,081	162	172	1,740	1,909
R-squared	0.075	0.072	0.261	0.164	0.068	0.065

Source: Created by Elliott Fullmer using data from the U.S. Census Bureau, the U.S. Election Assistance Commission's 2012 and 2016 Election Administration and Voting Surveys, the National Conference of State Legislatures (2012, 2016), and FairVote (2012, 2016).

Notes: *** $p < 0.01$, ** $p < 0.05$, * $p < 0.1$. Cell entries are OLS regression estimates with standard errors in parentheses.

adopted universal VBM, it did not lag behind other early voting states in site density. A county's percent college-educated, mean income, population density, and political competitiveness also have no significant effect on site density in either 2012 or 2016.

The third and fourth specifications assess the role of sites in counties with at least 200,000 residents. I include this analysis to ensure that the significant findings I reported in the initial tests are not simply the result of county demographic trends. Non-Whites are more likely to live in densely populated communities, making it perhaps more likely that they reside in counties with fewer sites per capita. But if the reported effects remain present when highly populated counties are isolated, then I can be more confident in the conclusions.

In both 2012 and 2016, I can confirm that a county's percent Black continues to be associated with fewer early voting sites per capita in the 162 (2012) and 172 (2016) largest U.S. counties in the dataset, respectively. In 2012, a large county of 228,832 persons where 40% of the population is Black can be expected to have two fewer early voting sites than a comparable county where 20% of residents are Black. The effect is slightly smaller in 2016, as this difference would be expected in counties with 234,742 persons. A county's percent Hispanic continues to be predictive of greater site density in highly populated counties in 2012, but the effect disappears in 2016. In 2012, a county of 227,532 people would be expected to have four additional sites as its Hispanic share rises by 20 percentage points. Unlike the full models, no-excuse absentee voting is associated with fewer sites in heavily populated counties in both 2012 and 2016. Early voting days continue to be a negative predictor of sites in 2016, though the coefficient is not significant in 2012.

In counties with smaller populations, both a county's percent Black and Hispanic continue to be negatively and positively associated with site density, respectively. In fact, in both 2012 and 2016, the effects are the largest yet observed. In 2012, a county of just 9,259 persons can be expected to have one fewer early voting site if its percent Black is 20 percentage points higher than a comparable county. In 2016, the same can be said for counties of just 11,416 persons. When less populated counties are isolated, the positive effects regarding a county's percent Hispanic are also powerful. In both 2012 and 2016, counties of 12,019 and 12,755 residents, respectively, can be expected to have an additional site if Hispanics constitute 20 percentage points more of their population. No-excuse absentee programs are heavily predictive of sites in more sparsely populated communities, as such a policy is associated with an additional site for every 17,000 residents. The number of early voting days offered is again linked to fewer sites in these counties.

MIDTERM FINDINGS

I next examine the role between county demographics and site density in two midterm elections—2014 and 2018. Descriptive statistics again confirm the difference in site density between heavily Black and Hispanic counties. Of the 102 examined counties with an early voting program and at least 20% of the residents identifying as Black in 2014, none had an early voting site per 1,000 voting-age residents. Only one county reported one site per 2,000 residents. Of the 82 such counties in 2018, none had an early site per 1,000 voting-age residents, while just two had at least one site per 2,000 residents. Meanwhile, of the 304 counties with at least 20% of citizens identifying as Hispanic in 2014, 13 reported at least one site per 1,000 residents. Twenty-nine counties reported at least one site per 2,000 residents. In 2018, the figures were similar, as 14 such counties had at least one site per 1,000 residents and 37 had at least one per 2,000 residents.

The findings in table 5.2 are more illuminating. With all controls included, counties with higher Black populations again have fewer early voting sites per capita in both 2014 and 2018. The substantive effects are comparable to those reported in the 2012 and 2016 presidential cycles. In 2014, a county of 9,488 people in which 40% of the residents are Black can be expected to have one fewer early voting site than a county of the same size in which 20% of persons are Black. In 2018, the effect is only slightly smaller, as comparable differences are expected in two counties with only 11,765 persons. Once again, a county's percent Hispanic is associated with more early voting site density. In 2014, a county of 15,924 persons in which 40% of residents are Hispanic can be expected to have one more early voting site than a county of the same size where only 20% of residents are Hispanic. In 2018, the effect is even larger, as comparable differences are expected in two counties with about 13,699 residents.

While there is no significant effect in 2014, no-excuse absentee laws are linked to more sites in 2018. Counties with these laws are expected to have an additional site per 17,153 voting-age residents in 2018, a similar finding to those reported in presidential years. Early voting days are again associated with fewer sites, a finding that has been consistent across all four elections analyzed. I report several other notable relationships regarding site density. While counties with higher shares of noncitizens and higher incomes (surprisingly) have fewer sites per capita in 2014 and 2018, those with greater 65 and older populations again have more sites in each year. Competitive Senate or gubernatorial races are predictive of more sites in 2018, but not 2014.

Similar to the analysis in presidential years, the following specifications isolate heavily populated and less populated counties. In the third and fourth tests, I isolate counties with at least 200,000 residents. In these counties, I

Table 5.2 Demographics and Early Voting Site Density, 2014 and 2018

Variables	(1) 2014 Early Voting Site Density	(2) 2018 Early Voting Site Density	(3) 2014 Early Voting Site Density	(4) 2018 Early Voting Site Density	(5) 2014 Early Voting Site Density	(6) 2018 Early Voting Site Density
Percent Black	-0.527***	-0.425***	-0.0527***	-0.120***	-0.577***	-0.447***
	(0.108)	(0.096)	(0.019)	(0.042)	(0.122)	(0.106)
Percent Hispanic	0.314***	0.365***	0.0315	-0.0812	0.355***	0.413***
	(0.100)	(0.104)	(0.024)	(0.057)	(0.108)	(0.112)
Percent noncitizen	-0.802**	-1.057**	-0.147*	0.169	-0.784**	-1.084**
	(0.400)	(0.418)	(0.075)	(0.175)	(0.452)	(0.472)
Percent over 65	1.679***	1.452***	-0.0553	-0.236*	1.745***	1.576***
	(0.259)	(0.265)	(0.061)	(0.139)	(0.284)	(0.288)
Percent college-educated	0.177	0.246	0.0776**	-0.0415	0.203	0.274
	(0.183)	(0.191)	(0.035)	(0.081)	(0.207)	(0.216)
Mean income	-0.00247**	-0.00274**	-0.000353*	-0.00023	-0.00266*	-0.00270*
	(0.001)	(0.001)	(0.000)	(0.000)	(0.001)	(0.001)
Population per square mile	-1.15E-05	-2.08E-05				
	(0.000)	(0.000)				
No-excuse absentee	0.0385	0.0583**	-0.0119**	-0.0320***	0.0513*	0.0738***
	(0.025)	(0.025)	(0.005)	(0.012)	(0.027)	(0.027)
Early voting days	-0.00225**	-0.00369***	-0.000057***	-0.000824*	-0.00273***	-0.00425***
	(0.001)	(0.001)	(0.000)	(0.000)	(0.001)	(0.001)
Colorado	-0.0208	-0.0527	-0.00274	0.0031	-0.0295	-0.063
	(0.060)	(0.062)	(0.010)	(0.022)	(0.067)	(0.069)
Competitive Senate or gov.	-0.0249	0.0700*	0.0383**	0.0137	-0.0245	0.0762*
	(0.053)	(0.041)	(0.019)	(0.017)	(0.057)	(0.045)
Constant	-0.682	-0.954**	-0.118	0.315	-0.664	-1.012**
	(0.418)	(0.430)	(0.084)	(0.195)	(0.465)	(0.477)
Observations	1,998	2,017	183	179	1,815	1,838
R-squared	0.07	0.07	0.226	0.119	0.061	0.065

Source: Created by Elliott Fullmer using data from the U.S. Census Bureau, the U.S. Election Assistance Commission's 2014 and 2018 Election Administration and Voting Surveys, and the National Conference of State Legislatures (2014, 2018).
Notes: *** $p<0.01$, ** $p<0.05$, * $p<0.1$. Cell entries are OLS regression estimates with standard errors in parentheses.

again confirm that site density is considerably lower as a county's percent Black increases. In 2014, a county of 284,630 voting-age residents can expect three fewer sites if its share of Black citizens is 20 percentage points higher. In 2018, the effect is even stronger. A county of just 208,333 voting-age residents is expected to have *five* fewer sites as its Black share rises by 20 percentage points. As I observed in presidential years, there is no significant relationship between a county's percent Hispanic and its site density in the largest 183 (in 2014) and 179 (in 2018) counties, respectively. In these more populated counties, both no-excuse absentee voting and early voting days are associated with fewer sites, a similar finding to that reported in 2012 and 2016.

The results in the final two specifications—which examine counties with fewer than 200,000 persons in 2014 and 2018—are comparable to those in my primary models. A county's percent Black is associated with fewer sites per capita, while its percent Hispanic is linked to greater site density. The effect sizes are even greater than those reported in presidential years. A county of just 8,666 voting-age residents can expect one fewer site in 2014 as its percent Black increases by 20 points; in 2018, a county of 11,186 such residents can expect the same. A county of 14,085 voting-age residents is associated with one additional site as its percent Hispanic grows by 20 points; in 2018, a county of 12,107 voting-age residents sees the same effect. Once again, counties in no-excuse absentee states are associated with more sites, while extra early voting days are linked to less site density.

FIXED EFFECTS MODELS

In both the presidential and midterm years, I run models with state-fixed effects, recognizing that some county variation is dependent on state-level policies, norms, or traditions. Ohio and Maryland, for example, each mandate a certain number of sites for each county, allowing no flexibility for local clerks. Some states, such as Massachusetts, provide ample funding to counties for early voting, while others do not. In some states, a long tradition of early voting may mean more plentiful sites in its respective counties. Interestingly, when fixed effects are included, a county's percent Black and percent Hispanic are no longer predictive of site density in the presidential years (see table 5.3). The coefficients are in the expected directions, but each narrowly misses significance.[3] This suggests that state factors, rather than county considerations, may be somewhat responsible for racial and ethnic discrepancies regarding site availability. This does not necessarily mean that state policies have been created or modified with race or ethnicity in mind, but simply that the lower levels of site density in heavily Black counties (and higher levels in heavily Hispanic counties) appear to be predominately the result of these state differences.

Table 5.3   Demographics and Early Voting Site Density (with State-Fixed Effects), 2012–2018

Variables	(1) 2012 Early Voting Site Density	(2) 2016 Early Voting Site Density	(3) 2014 Early Voting Site Density	(4) 2018 Early Voting Site Density
Percent Black	−0.205	−0.124	−0.264**	−0.202*
	(0.128)	(0.106)	(0.125)	(0.110)
Percent Hispanic	0.204	0.151	0.102	0.0537
	(0.126)	(0.127)	(0.119)	(0.125)
Percent noncitizen	−0.643	−0.694*	−0.26	−0.158
	(0.414)	(0.399)	(0.392)	(0.411)
Percent over 65	1.621***	1.502***	1.328***	1.331***
	(0.269)	(0.250)	(0.258)	(0.264)
Percent college-educated	−0.21	−0.142	−0.0849	−0.182
	(0.183)	(0.176)	(0.176)	(0.186)
Mean income	−0.00155	−0.00196	−0.00298**	−0.00226*
	(0.001)	(0.001)	(0.001)	(0.001)
Population per square mile	−5.66E-06	−4.76E-06	−3.99E-06	−7.34E-06
	(0.000)	(0.000)	(0.000)	(0.000)
Constant	0.0989	0.126	−0.0604	0.0276
	(0.092)	(0.086)	(0.405)	(0.423)
Observations	1,902	2,081	1,998	2,017
R-squared	0.049	0.047	0.044	0.038

Source: Created by Elliott Fullmer using data from the U.S. Census Bureau, the U.S. Election Assistance Commission's 2012, 2014, 2016, and 2018 Election Administration and Voting Surveys, and the National Conference of State Legislatures (2012–2018).
Notes: *** $p < 0.01$, ** $p < 0.05$, * $p < 0.1$. Cell entries are OLS regression estimates with standard errors in parentheses.

In the midterm years, a county's percent Hispanic continues to have no significant relationship with site density once state-fixed effects are added. A county's percent Black, however, is again a significant and negative predictor of site density. In these cases, even when state tendencies are considered, county site offerings are weaker when Blacks comprise a larger share of a county. In other words, even within the same state, one can expect counties with larger Black populations to have fewer early voting sites per capita.

CONCLUSIONS

Given that site density helps determine whether early voting programs are able to increase turnout, it is important to assess the nature of its distribution.

Through a series of specifications across four elections, I report that site availability differs considerably along racial and ethnic lines. Heavily Black counties, in both large and smaller counties, have significantly fewer sites per capita available to them. The effect sizes are quite large. In a heavily populated county of 300,000 voting-age residents in an early voting state, a difference in the Black population of about 20 percentage points is consistently linked to two or three fewer sites. In a smaller county of about 20,000 residents, we can expect about two fewer sites if the percent Black is 40% rather than 20%. Meanwhile, heavily Hispanic counties have significantly more early voting sites per capita, perhaps owing to their high numbers in states with long early voting traditions. Recall that Arizona, Colorado, Nevada, New Mexico, and Texas—all heavily Hispanic states—were all early adopters of early voting. Each state established robust programs that have continued to this day. Given that the relationship between a county's percent Hispanic and sites disappears in all four elections when state-fixed effects are included, it is possible that statewide early voting features explain the high levels of site density found in counties with large Hispanic populations.

Inequality is nothing new with regard to voting laws in the United States. As I discussed in chapter 1, the decentralized nature of American elections often means considerable differences across states. States also have varying policies with regard to voter identification at the polls, registration laws, and much more. Regarding early voting, the greatest inequality remains the fact that eight states continue to disallow most citizens from voting before Election Day. Nevertheless, site inequality in early voting states deserves scholarly attention for several reasons. First, Section 2 of the Voting Rights Act is rather clear in affirming that electoral reforms cannot dilute the voting strength of minority groups. It is therefore quite reasonable that site inequality (on the basis of race) could receive judicial attention. Second, because I have demonstrated that early voting sites increase turnout, these findings suggest that early voting has yet to reach its full potential. Heavily Black counties can reasonably expect further turnout gains if they are able—through government investments or court orders—to add additional sites.

Moving forward, I encourage scholars to explore the root causes of low site density in heavily Black counties. Site discrepancies may be partially due to restrictive state laws that require site uniformity across counties regardless of their geographic or population size. They could also be the result of funding constraints at the local level, or perhaps discrimination by officials on the basis of race or partisanship. In-depth qualitative analyses, including interviews with state and local officials where discrepancies are notable, could help shed light on this important question.

NOTES

1. Section 2 of the Voting Rights Act applies to all states. It was not affected by the *Shelby Co. v. Holder* (2013) Supreme Court decision.

2. The coefficient of −0.498 suggests that as a county goes from being 0% Black to 100% Black, it offers 0.498 fewer early voting sites per 1,000 voting-age residents. Therefore, as a county goes from being 20% Black to 40% Black, it can be expected to offer 0.0996 fewer sites per 1,000 voting-age residents. This is equivalent to offering one fewer site per 10,040 voting-age residents.

3. In 2012, the *p*-value ($p = 0.109$) for percent Black is especially close to the threshold for statistical significance.

Chapter 6

Early Voting and Presidential Nominations

In addition to consequences for down-ballot elections and racial equality, early voting may alter the information environment in campaigns in unintended ways. Those who vote early may do so before important information becomes available in the final days and weeks of a campaign. As a result, some may cast votes that they regret by Election Day. Many have speculated that early voting may particularly affect presidential nomination contests, as support for candidates tends to be more unstable and voting often commences before candidates fully launch campaigns in respective states. I suspect that early voting should benefit early front-runners in these contests, as voters may cast early votes for these candidates before considering their less-known opponents. Examining exit poll data from the 2008 and 2016 Democratic primaries, I find that Hillary Clinton indeed benefited from early voting across several early primary states in both years.

INFORMATION ASYMMETRIES

When voters submit ballots early, they complete their civic duties ahead of schedule. With votes already cast, political campaigns essentially conclude weeks early for these citizens. There is no mechanism by which one can change a submitted vote; early voters can only wait and observe whether election outcomes (reported on Election Night or primary day) match their preferences. Of course, campaigns themselves do *not* end early. Candidates continue to fund television and digital ads, send direct mail, participate in debates, and grant interviews and news conferences. The news media investigates voting records and past associations. Parties and outside groups remain active as well. Lacking any knowledge of late campaign developments, those who choose to vote early ultimately do so without the same information as Election Day voters.

Late information comes in many forms during political campaigns. The term "October Surprise" has become synonymous with a news event holding the potential to influence an election's outcome. Examples can be found throughout American political history. In the days leading up to the 1968 presidential election, President Lyndon Johnson (for whom Hubert Humphrey, the Democratic candidate, was vice president) announced a halt of the bombing campaign in North Vietnam; Humphrey quickly gained in the polls, though Republican Richard Nixon ultimately prevailed (Tucker 2011). In late September 2008, as Americans were beginning to vote early in the presidential campaign, the country watched closely as Barack Obama and John McCain navigated the collapse of Lehman Brothers and an ensuing financial panic. Obama was widely credited for his response, even by Republican president George W. Bush (2010). McCain, however, was criticized for seeming erratic and reactionary (Henninger 2008).

The more recent 2016 and 2020 elections featured a number of late developments. In October 2016, a video was released showing Republican nominee Donald Trump brag about groping women to an *Access Hollywood* reporter. Weeks later, the FBI announced that it was reopening an investigation into Democratic nominee Hillary Clinton's use of a private email server during her tenure as Secretary of State. In 2020, Trump (now running for reelection) was hospitalized with a COVID-19 infection in early October. That same month, following Justice Ruth Bader Ginsburg's death, Trump and Senate Republicans moved forward with the Supreme Court appointment of Amy Coney Barrett. The move was controversial because Senate Republicans had refused to consider President Barack Obama's Supreme Court appointment of Merrick Garland in 2016—claiming that because it was an election year, the winner should make the appointment. In 2020, more than half of all votes were cast by the time Barrett was confirmed in late October.

Debates have long been considered an important factor in vote selection and a major conveyor of candidate differences in presidential campaigns (Schroeder 2001). In 2020, the three debates did not commence until October 3.[1] By this point, 32 states had already begun accepting early ballots through the mail and at designated sites (Higgins and Rattner 2020). At least 50 million votes (nearly a third of the ultimate total) had been cast by the time President Trump and Vice President Joe Biden debated for the second and final time on October 22.

Researchers have found that early voters tend to be more politically astute and partisan (Patterson and Caldeira 1985; Dubin and Kalsow 1996; Stein 1998; Stein et al. 2004; Baretto et al. 2006), leading some to suggest that additional information may not alter their preferences. But a deep literature also shows that people tend to be overconfident in their decision-making (Svenson 1981; Camerer and Lovallo, 1999; Barber and Odean 2001). More specifically, voters routinely underestimate the likelihood that their preferences will shift (Meredith and Malhotra 2011), and do become more likely to support a candidate once the media determines that they are viable (Abramowitz 1989; Polsby and Vildavsky 2008).

Late information is also prevalent during presidential nominating campaigns. Modern nomination races feature over 50 primaries and caucuses held sequentially in states and territories between January (or early February) and June of presidential election years. Candidate fields are typically large in the early stages of a contest, though poor performances and insufficient fundraising inevitably cause candidates to withdraw from the race before all state contests have concluded (Mathews 1978; Brams 1978; Aldrich 1980; Bartels 1988; Norrander 1996; Jewitt 2019). As a result, early voters may cast votes for candidates who ultimately quit before the state's respective primary day even occurs. Analyzing the 2008 California presidential primary, Meredith and Malhotra (2011) find that precincts with more early voters gave a significantly greater share of their vote to John Edwards, Rudy Giuliani, and Fred Thompson, three candidates who were actively seeking the nomination when the early voting period began (on January 7), but dropped out before the primary date (February 5).

Further, important information can emerge about nomination candidates who remain in the race. In 1992, Bill Clinton was accused of having a 12-year extramarital affair in the weeks before the New Hampshire primary (Sabato 1998). In 2008, Barack Obama was forced to address controversial comments made by his pastor, Jeremiah Wright, during his campaign against Hillary Clinton (Ross and El-Buri 2008). More generally, presidential nominations are fluid contests, as candidates are often relatively unknown to large chunks of voters until the final days and weeks before a state's primary or caucus. With the exception of Iowa and New Hampshire, where campaigning begins as much as one year before the contests, most states see high levels of campaign activity only in the week or so before their respective primary or caucus. Candidates can only be in one place at a time, while other campaign resources (e.g., money, staffers) are also limited. Traditionally, winning (or exceeding expectations) in "the next" primary or caucus produces momentum in the form of positive media coverage and, perhaps most importantly, financial contributions (Aldrich 1980; Bartels 1985, 1988; Lichter et al. 1988; Geer 1989; Abramowitz 1989; Kamarck 2018; Jewitt 2019). The ability to win a state contest and slowly generate momentum and resources is seen to benefit poorly funded, low name-recognition candidates. However, if a voter has already cast an early ballot, then new information about candidates cannot be incorporated into one's vote choice.

Many political operatives, journalists, and academics have suggested that early voting produces information asymmetries that may affect primary outcomes. Political analyst Craig Wilson believes early voting can easily produce voter regret, stating, "One downside to early voting is that once you cast that vote, there's still two weeks or a month to go and what happens if something eventful happens with a campaign or a candidate during that period and you change your mind" (qtd. in Domurat 2008). Patt Morrison of the *Oakland Tribune* agreed, stating, "Casting an absentee ballot so far ahead of Election Day is like picking a Super Bowl winner based on who's ahead at halftime. It's like recommending a book you've only halfway read. It's like getting married on the first date" (qtd. in "Early Voting," 2008). Paul Gronke, director of the Early Voting Information Center at Reed College, has argued that early voters may miss information that could affect their votes ("Early Voting Grows," 2008). Robert Stein, a longtime early voting researcher, offered a similar perspective, suggesting that Hillary Clinton did better among early voters in some 2008 primaries because "her polling numbers were higher" when early voting began (qtd. in Hylton-Austin 2008).

I posit that early voting produces information asymmetries that can affect voting behavior in presidential primaries and caucuses, as well as the strategies campaigns pursue in their quest to win these contests. In particular, I believe that early voters should be more likely than primary day voters to support early front-runners and those with high levels of name recognition. Those who wait until primary day will have more exposure to less well-known candidates, thereby increasing the odds that their preferences will shift away from an established party figure(s). Further, I suggest that front-running candidates (and their campaigns) may view early voting as an opportunity to target and accumulate votes in favorable states while their popularity is high, thereby blunting the effects of negative momentum that may develop later in the nomination season.

In addition to addressing an important implication of early voting, this analysis contributes to a long literature on how the rules of the nominating process affect the types of candidates that ultimately succeed and compete to serve as president. Studies have previously reported that early front-runners already enjoy numerous advantages throughout the process, including disproportionate media coverage (King 1990; Redlawsk et al. 2010) and the increased front-loading of primaries and caucuses (Mayer and Busch 2004). Given that early voting now plays a prominent role in presidential nominating contests, it is useful to examine its potential effects as well.

CASE SELECTION

I anticipate that the effects of early voting on candidate support should be greatest when a presidential nomination contest features a clear front-runner and a challenger(s) with less exposure to the electorate. This type of dynamic has been relatively common over the past several decades. The 1984 Democratic nomination contest featured a close competition between former vice president Walter Mondale and Senator Gary Hart of Colorado, who was not well-known until his surprise victory in the New Hampshire primary (Gallup 2004). In 2000, Vice President Al Gore was the clear favorite for the Democratic nomination, while his principal challenger, Senator Bill Bradley, remained unknown to 57% of the electorate two months before the Iowa Caucus ("Poll," 1999). In the Republican contest that same year, surveys showed that John McCain was considerably less well-known than his front-running opponent, George W. Bush ("N.H. Voters," 2000).

The 2008 and 2016 Democratic campaigns provide useful opportunities to examine the effect of early voting on candidate choice. In both cases, Hillary Clinton was a clear, early front-runner who was principally challenged by a lesser-known senator. In 2008, Clinton was challenged by then first-term Senator Barack Obama of Illinois. In 2016, she was challenged by Senator Bernie Sanders of Vermont, a self-proclaimed democratic socialist largely anonymous to most Americans at the time. Each senator's path to the nomination would require them to generate momentum through strong performances in early states. Doing so would establish them as credible challengers to Clinton. Then, as the nomination schedule progressed, the candidates would need to campaign in states in the days and weeks leading up to each respective contest. Both Obama and Sanders hoped that after truly introducing themselves to a state's electorate (e.g., through door knocks, visits, ads, etc.), they would be able to persuade enough voters to switch their allegiance away from Clinton.

Both candidates enjoyed early success against Clinton. In 2008, Obama scored victories in the Iowa Caucuses and the South Carolina primary (by a large margin) in January. In 2016, Sanders won the New Hampshire primary in convincing fashion. Sanders' victory, however, was seen by some as less impressive because it came in the Vermont senator's neighboring state. Arguably, his most notable early victory came in the Michigan primary on March 8, a large state he won after trailing in the polls by over 20 points. After early victories, the next challenge for Obama and Sanders would be converting this momentum into new support in the states whose contests followed. One potential roadblock would be that Clinton was able to secure early votes in many states before Obama or Sanders had generated momentum through early victories or begun aggressive efforts in those respective states.

THE CLINTON EARLY VOTE STRATEGIES

In both 2008 and 2016, Clinton's campaign was acutely aware of its advantage and actively sought to benefit from early voting programs. In 2008, Clinton was a former first lady and a sitting two-term senator from New York. Few Americans (let alone politicians) rivaled her name recognition in the years preceding the campaign. Anticipation about a presidential run was present for years, even before her 2006 reelection to the Senate. Clinton announced her candidacy in January 2007, declaring "I'm in it to win it" (qtd. in Roberts 2007). She led a field of eight challengers, including Obama, by double digits throughout 2007 and at times looked like the inevitable nominee.

Despite her strong position, Clinton never felt confident about the Iowa Caucuses and even considered withdrawing her campaign from the state in May 2007. Unlike many other states, her husband (former president Bill Clinton) had never run a caucus campaign in Iowa.[2] Further, John Edwards, the 2004 Democratic vice presidential nominee, had an established base in the state from his 32% vote share in the 2004 caucuses. Lastly, Barack Obama polled better in the state than in some later primary and caucus states. Numerous November 2007 polls showed Obama trailing Clinton by only a handful of points in Iowa, a sharp contrast from the nearly 20-point lead she held in national polls. By skipping the caucuses, she could delegitimize them and force New Hampshire (a state where she appeared stronger) to be the first true Democratic battlefield.

In May 2007, Clinton's deputy campaign manager, Mike Henry, issued a memo urging the campaign to ignore Iowa and instead direct the candidate's limited time and resources to contests in larger states such as Florida, Arizona, California, Georgia, and Texas. Henry noted that all of those states, along with several others whose primaries were to be held in early February, would be allowing early voting in the weeks before Iowans gathered for their caucuses. Henry wrote, "Iowans will not be the first to vote. . . . Hundreds of thousands of voters will be voting in California, Florida and Texas. We must fund an expensive paid communications and vote by mail/early vote program in these mega-states" (qtd. in Broder 2007).

While Henry's memo did not convince Clinton to ignore Iowa, the campaign did launch an aggressive early voting campaign. The strategy mirrored the conventional approach to mobilizing early voters, using data to target Clinton's strongest supporters in the weeks before each state's primary day (Stein 2008). Aware that Iowa may produce negative momentum for Clinton, the campaign hoped to secure tens of thousands of votes before that event occurred. It targeted voters in early voting states with direct mail, radio advertisements, and door-to-door canvassing. Figuring that Iowa "would come out, at best, a muddle," Clinton's New Hampshire state director, Nick Clemons, planned for this contingency, actively mobilizing her supporters to vote via absentee ballots beginning in December. The idea was "to get their votes in before Iowa even happened" (qtd. in Tumulty 2008). Clemons sought to mitigate the effects of Obama's post-Iowa momentum by securing Clinton votes before people could change their minds. As New Hampshire is not a no-excuse early voting state, the pool of individuals for which this was possible was limited, but nonetheless potentially decisive. Clemons focused his absentee mobilization efforts on both college students and Boston commuters committed to Clinton (Tumulty 2008). Both were sizable groups that had legitimate excuses to receive absentee ballots in New Hampshire. Both, the campaign believed, could conceivably shift from Clinton to Obama supporters after the Iowa Caucuses. In the end, Clinton defeated Obama 39%–36%, a margin of only 7,500 votes. It is unclear whether Clemons' early voting strategy made the difference between winning and losing, but the campaign believed it helped.

Clinton employed this strategy in other states during the 2008 campaign. In the weeks before Super Tuesday (February 5), her campaign worked to secure early votes before the South Carolina primary, where they knew Obama could perform well (Balz et al. 2008).[3] "Absentee and early voting are votes in the bank. The more votes we can get in the bank before Election Day, the better off we are," said campaign spokeswoman Ana Cruz (qtd. in "Early Voting Key to Victory," 2008).

In California, more than one million of the nearly five million votes cast occurred before Obama gained new momentum after winning in South Carolina (on January 26) by almost 30 percentage points. By then, Clinton had successfully mobilized many of her supporters, particularly women and Hispanics, to vote early. Ace Smith, director of Clinton's California campaign, spent months acting as though there was "an election every day here for 29 days" (qtd. in Benac 2008). Those deemed most likely to support Clinton were sent three mailings over the course of the early voting period. In addition, when early voting began in early January, Clinton campaigned throughout the state and spent time with campaign workers in San Diego calling potential early participants.

Barack Obama also had the campaign funds to mobilize early voters in the weeks before Super Tuesday. His campaign placed over 500,000 calls in an attempt to secure early voters in California and Arizona. Further, his canvassers also knocked on doors in these states, as well as in Georgia, Tennessee, and Utah, to mobilize supporters to cast early ballots. Obama spokesman Ben LaBolt was confident that these efforts would yield dividends, stating, "All Obama supporters have been reminded about early voting and been given the tools to do so" (qtd. in Benac 2008).

But while Obama could mobilize his early supporters, polls suggested that he simply had fewer of them than Clinton in the weeks leading up to the

Super Tuesday contests. Perhaps both Clinton and Obama were simply securing votes from those whose minds could never be changed. But if voters do indeed underestimate the likelihood that their preferences will shift (Svenson 1981; Camerer and Lovallo, 1999; Barber and Odean 2001; Meredith and Malhotra 2011), then perhaps Clinton's early advantage translated into votes that may have shifted to Obama if early voting was not an option. Anecdotally, Clinton's effort to "take advantage of her name recognition" seemingly worked. In Long Beach, California, where Clinton had mobilized many elderly Latinas, some Clinton voters later admitted to reporters that they would have voted for Obama if they had waited until primary day (Newton-Small 2008). Further, in California, exit polls indicated that Clinton had a narrow advantage over Obama, 49%–46%, among those who made up their minds in the campaign's final three days. Among those who had decided earlier, she held a 17-point advantage.

Clinton ultimately lost the Democratic nomination contest to Obama in a historic battle that lasted until June 2008. Obama's campaign employed a strategy focused on mobilizing new voters, winning large delegate victories in low-turnout caucus states, and financially planning for a long race (Kenski et al. 2010; McDonald and Schaller 2011). Nevertheless, Clinton's efforts during the early months of the primaries serve as an example of how early voting has encouraged campaigns (particularly those of early front-runners) to seek protection from negative momentum. Candidates, sensing an early advantage over less well-known challengers, can actively mobilize voters in later states where they are popular, thus securing votes before an opponents' momentum allows citizens to reconsider their preferences.

After her defeat in 2008, Clinton served as President Obama's Secretary of State. By the time she relinquished the position after Obama's reelection in 2012, she was one of the most popular politicians in the country. A January 2013 *Washington Post-ABC News* poll revealed that 67% of Americans had a favorable view of her. Even 37% of Republicans approved of the job she was doing as Secretary of State (Cohen and Blake 2013). As a result, for the second time in less than a decade, Clinton became the presumptive Democratic nominee for president entering the 2016 campaign. Her nomination seemed even more likely when few Democratic challengers entered the contest. By late 2015, her competition consisted only of former Senator Jim Webb of Virginia, former Governor and Senator Lincoln Chafee of Rhode Island, former Governor Martin O'Malley of Maryland, and the aforementioned Senator Bernie Sanders of Vermont. Webb, a former Navy Secretary under Ronald Reagan, was widely seen as both too moderate and too unknown to win a Democratic primary (Taylor 2015). Chafee and Sanders had not even been Democrats only a year before the contest began. Clinton's lead in the early polls was massive. A December 2015 Quinnipiac poll put her 31 points ahead of Sanders, the closest challenger. Other polls showed a smaller lead, but still exceeding 20 points in most cases.

Webb and Chafee dropped out of the race before the primaries and caucuses began. O'Malley was unable to gain any traction in polling and dropped out after winning less than 1% of the vote in the Iowa Caucuses. Sanders, however, emerged as a credible challenger to Clinton. He lost a very tight race to Clinton in Iowa and won the New Hampshire primary in convincing fashion. However, Clinton maintained a double-digit lead in most national polls after the first two contests. The perception was that the electorates of Iowa and New Hampshire were uniquely difficult for Clinton given the small percentage of non-White voters, who were often some of her strongest supporters. In the weeks and months that followed, a similar dynamic to the one previously seen with Clinton and Obama emerged. Sanders would frequently confront an early Clinton lead in the polls with several weeks remaining before a state's contest. Then, as he focused his attention on the state, the lead would shrink. As one commentator noted, "In every contest in every state, be it a primary or caucus, Bernie has started out far behind. And in every state that he has seriously contested . . . it has taken Sanders until the last week or so to significantly close that gap with Clinton, and in some cases actually surge ahead, in the final waning days and hours" (Rinaldo 2016).

Across the country, however, Clinton was again banking early votes. The campaign held early vote rallies in several states, urging voters to cast ballots both by mail and at in-person early voting sites. Before major contests in March, including in Ohio and Illinois, "her volunteers . . . phoned voters to get them to cast their ballots that day," rather than waiting for the primary day (Davis 2016). Even though Clinton won Ohio by 14 points, she won early voters by over 30 points. Perhaps these voters would have supported Clinton regardless, but given that Sanders cut Clinton's advantage in statewide polling by the final week, it is not entirely clear.

In the weeks leading up to the California primary, where Clinton had a commanding 11-point lead several weeks before the primary, her team worked hard to get early votes secured. Marlon Marshall, Clinton's director of state campaigns and political engagement, commented, "We mailed folks, we called them, we knocked on their doors, etc." to get early votes secured. Buffy Wicks, Clinton's California state director, added, "We told people to take that ballot off the kitchen cabinet, fill it out and put it in the mail" (qtd. in Osborne 2016). Doing so would limit any possible damage created by a surge in Sanders support. In addition, securing early votes allowed the campaign to narrow its focus in the final days of the campaign. Each voter that cast an early ballot was an additional voter that the campaign could bypass in its final get-out-the-vote efforts. By the time the primary date arrived, Clinton had a lead of about 400,000 votes. Sanders did surge as the campaign drew closer, narrowing the gap to four points in statewide polls. And among voters who voted on primary day, he tied Clinton. But Clinton's early margin was too great to overcome and her campaign won by seven percentage points.

One of the keys to Obama's victory in 2008 was his large victory margin in caucus states. With lower turnout that skews toward passionate supporters, caucuses tend to favor insurgent candidates with committed, youthful supporters. Sanders also benefited from caucus states, but Clinton was able to use early voting to minimize the damage. In 2016, Nebraska—for the first time—allowed voters to cast early ballots in the state's caucus. Sanders beat Clinton in the caucuses, earning 57% of the vote. However, Clinton secured a whopping 85% of early voters, narrowing the margin of defeat and reducing Sanders' delegate margin in the state from seven to five.

Jeff Weaver, who served as Sanders' campaign manager, conceded that Clinton's early voting operation was highly effective at blunting his candidate's momentum. He remarked, "Early voting requires a tremendous amount of infrastructure and a particular kind of organizing that they were just very good at. . . . Their early voting operation was extremely effective and I can't think of an exception" (qtd. in Bradner 2016).

MEASURING CLINTON'S EARLY VOTING ADVANTAGE

While Clinton clearly sought to exploit early voting in 2008 and 2016, measuring her effectiveness requires greater scrutiny. In conducting my analysis, I seek to build on the only academic piece to address the possibility of early voting and information asymmetries in presidential nomination contests. Meredith and Malhotra (2011) analyze the 2008 California presidential primaries, taking advantage of a natural experiment. In California, counties with precincts consisting of less than 250 people can choose to be universal vote-by-mail (VBM) counties. In these counties, all voters essentially become early voters. The authors assess whether voters in these counties were more likely to support candidates who ultimately dropped out of the 2008 presidential race before the state's primary date (February 5). Ultimately, they find that the all-VBM precincts gave a greater share of their vote to John Edwards, Rudy Giuliani, and Fred Thompson, three candidates who were actively seeking the nomination when the early voting period began (on January 7), but dropped out before February 5. Further, they find that candidates who polled better during the early voting period, including Hillary Clinton on the Democratic side, performed better before primary day than on it.

I seek to both confirm and extend Meredith and Malhotra's findings through individual-level data from the 2008 and 2016 Democratic primaries.

While the authors' findings are useful, they examine only a very small population in a single state that is essentially forced to vote early through the mail. More notable perhaps is the possibility that voters may *choose* to vote early, believing that their minds are set, when in reality they could be altered with new information. While such a phenomenon is difficult to prove, I construct models that attempt to do so with some confidence.

I seek to determine whether Clinton's early support in a handful of 2008 and 2016 states provided her with an advantage in the final vote tallies. In 2008, I focus on Florida (held on January 29), as well as three Super Tuesday (February 5) states—Arizona, California, and Tennessee. In 2016, I focus on three states—Florida, North Carolina, and Ohio—whose primaries were held on Tuesday, March 15. I choose these states for several reasons. First, my choices are severely limited in each year, as the National Election Pool—my data source for the analysis—only sampled early voters in a very limited number of states in 2008 and 2016.[4] In these states, exit-pollsters supplemented their traditional polling place surveys with telephone calls to early voters before the respective state's primary day (see Table 6.1). Second, each state held its contest early in the respective nomination process, making it more likely that the lesser-known candidate (Obama or Sanders) still lacked a national profile on par with Hillary Clinton.[5] Third, in each case, the lesser-known candidate recorded a significant victory after the early voting period in the selected states had begun. Obama won a large victory in South Carolina on January 26, 2008 after Florida, Arizona, California, and Tennessee had commenced early voting. Sanders won a surprise victory on March 8, 2016 in the critical state of Michigan after Florida, North Carolina, and Ohio had begun early voting. As a result, it is plausible to expect Clinton to have benefited from "banking" early votes in each case before her respective opponent improved his standing.

Simply noting that early voters preferred Clinton more than primary day voters is inadequate. Even if this is the case, it may be that more voters

Table 6.1   **Early Voters in National Election Pool Exit Polls (Democratic Party Primaries), 2008 and 2016**

State	Year	Early Voters in Sample	Total Voters in Sample
Florida	2008	294	1,525
Arizona	2008	308	1,226
California	2008	363	1,919
Tennessee	2008	344	1,351
Florida	2016	217	1,659
North Carolina	2016	172	1,764
Ohio	2016	342	1,867

Source: Created by Elliott Fullmer using data from Edison Research (accessed through the Roper Center for Public Opinion Research).

inclined toward Clinton chose to vote early for other reasons, such as work requirements, convenience, or age. It could also be that the Clinton campaign identified its supporters more effectively during the early voting period and better mobilized them. If so, Clinton did not necessarily gain an advantage through early voting. Rather, her voters simply cast ballots sooner than her opponents' voters did.

In order to gain more insight into the behavior of individual primary voters, I rely on the aforementioned National Election Pool's official 2008 and 2016 exit polls.[6] Exit-pollsters supplemented their polling place surveys with telephone calls to early voters in select states during the weeks before their respective primaries. Specifically, pollsters selected households using random-digit dialing, and a respondent was then randomly selected within each household. Callers then directly asked respondents whether they voted early. All early voters were asked the same questions asked at the polling place on the state's primary day. Before the telephone survey results were combined with the exit poll data from precincts, they were weighted to reflect the actual number of early voters in the state.[7]

In addition to identifying whether respondents voted early, pollsters asked a series of personal and demographic questions. I use this data to control for the independent effect of voting early on supporting Clinton. While the 2008 and 2016 primaries were tightly contested, in each case the candidates had clear demographic coalitions behind them. By controlling for these and other demographic traits in my model, I can estimate whether early voting itself, independent of other characteristics, helped bring voters into the Clinton column who otherwise may have chosen Obama or Sanders had early voting not been an option.

I develop two principal Probit models—one for both the 2008 and 2016 campaigns. In each model, the dependent variable is a binary measure signifying a Clinton vote in the relevant contest. Voters who supported Obama are coded as 0s in the 2008 model, while voters who supported Sanders are coded as 0s in the 2016 model.[8] The primary independent variable is a binary measure for voting early.

The 2008 model includes controls for numerous demographic and political characteristics, each of which is expected to have a positive relationship with Clinton support. These characteristics account for several vital Clinton constituencies in her race against Obama. Gender is an important consideration in the model, as women favored Clinton's bid to become the first woman president in both 2008 and 2016 (Sullivan 2008; Zitner et al. 2016). I also expect voters self-identifying as Democrats, rather than independents or Republicans, to be more likely to support Clinton, as she was more popular with party's base. Obama, conversely, was stronger with independents and disgruntled Republicans. In fact, self-identified Democrats gave Clinton over 800,000 more votes than Obama during the nomination fight (Beam 2008).

Race played a very important role in the 2008 Democratic primaries, as Black voters overwhelmingly supported Obama (typically with 80%–90% support), while non-Hispanic Whites and Hispanics backed Clinton by solid margins. In fact, on Super Tuesday, Clinton won the support of over 60% of Hispanic voters ("Behind the Obama-Clinton Draw," 2009). While income was not a particularly strong predictor of candidate support, education was a noted factor; Clinton tended to be stronger among those without a college education. Finally, Clinton earned more support from married voters, as well as those aged 65 and older (Harwood 2008).

The various controls are each expected to have positive effects on the dependent variable. If the effect of simply voting early survives the inclusion of these covariates, then I can be more confident in my hypothesis that Clinton benefited from her front-runner status during the early voting period. I include five specifications—one that includes respondents from all four states examined and one for each of the four states. This allows me to assess not only the overall effect of voting early on Clinton support, but how the relationship varied across states.

The 2016 model accounts for demographic indicators predictive of Clinton support in her race against Sanders. Most are the same as Clinton's contest against Obama, as she again performed well with women, older voters, registered Democrats, those without a college education, and Hispanics. Unlike 2008, however, Clinton also did consistently well among Black voters and not as well among non-Hispanic White voters. Support for Clinton and Sanders was again not predicted by income in any significant way (Zitner et al. 2016). While there is some evidence that a healthy majority of married voters again supported Clinton in 2016, the exit poll data has a considerable amount of missing data for this variable. As a result, I do not include it in my 2016 model.

2008 FINDINGS

Table 6.2 reports the findings of my five multivariate Probit specifications for 2008. Across all five tests, the expected predictors of Clinton support mostly behave as expected. Women, non-Hispanic Whites, Hispanics, self-identified Democrats, and those without a college education are consistently associated with higher levels of Clinton support. Married voters and those 65 and older are significant predictors of Clinton support in the primary model, though not in each individual state. Even with the inclusion of these highly significant and powerful covariates, the effect of a voter casting an early ballot has a positive and significant relationship with Clinton support in all five specifications. This offers strong evidence that Clinton indeed benefited from early voting programs in 2008.

Table 6.2 Predicting Support for Hillary Clinton in Democratic Party Primaries, 2008

	(1) Clinton Support (California)	(2) Clinton Support (Tennessee)	(3) Clinton Support (Arizona)	(4) Clinton Support (Florida)	(5) Clinton Support (All Four States)
Early voter	0.206***	0.150*	0.306***	0.195**	0.296***
	(0.047)	(0.084)	(0.102)	(0.094)	(0.105)
Woman	0.283***	0.272***	0.370***	0.223***	0.340***
	(0.038)	(0.064)	(0.087)	(0.083)	(0.081)
Married	0.0629*	−0.0266	0.128	0.135*	0.0239
	(0.037)	(0.064)	(0.086)	(0.081)	(0.081)
White	0.823***	0.211**	1.563***	0.592***	1.121***
	(0.049)	(0.087)	(0.100)	(0.130)	(0.100)
Hispanic	0.902***	0.574***	1.676***	0.722***	1.042***
	(0.062)	(0.099)	(0.277)	(0.155)	(0.133)
Democrat	0.382***	0.473***	0.584***	0.278***	0.251**
	(0.046)	(0.078)	(0.099)	(0.100)	(0.103)
No college degree	0.317***	0.191***	0.461***	0.263***	0.351***
	(0.037)	(0.066)	(0.086)	(0.080)	(0.079)
65 and older	0.280***	0.272***	0.175	0.416***	0.145
	(0.048)	(0.093)	(0.118)	(0.097)	(0.090)
Constant	−1.376***	−0.927***	−2.115***	−1.382***	−1.307***
	(0.070)	(0.115)	(0.159)	(0.170)	(0.152)
Observations	5,069	1,660	1,149	1,076	1,184

Source: Created by Elliott Fullmer using data from Edison Research (accessed through the Roper Center for Public Opinion Research).
Notes: *** $p < 0.001$; ** $p < 0.01$; * $p < 0.05$. Cell entries are Probit regression estimates with standard errors in parentheses.

Marginal effects help determine the size of any significant relationships in the Probit tests. Figure 6.1 presents the marginal effects on Clinton support in the primary specification, which has a sample of over 5,000 respondents and includes all four states. Each covariate in this model is statistically significant at conventional levels. The marginal effects of being non-Hispanic White (0.32) or Hispanic (0.33) are easily the best predictors of Clinton support. Each, holding the effects of the other factors constant, raises the likelihood that a voter will support Clinton over Obama by a whopping 32 and 33 percentage points, respectively. The next highest predictors are self-identified Democrats (0.15), voters without a college degree (0.13), women (0.11), and those 65 and older (0.10). One's identification as an early voter is the next predictive characteristic, as it makes a voter eight percentage points (0.08) more likely to support Clinton over Obama, independent of all other covariates in the model. Finally, married voters are just three percentage points more likely to support Clinton over Obama.

With each state isolated, the marginal effects of early voting on Clinton support are consistent. The weakest effect is in California, where early voters are found to be six percentage points more likely to back Clinton; the strongest effect is in Arizona, where Clinton support is predicted to be 12 points higher when accounting for all controls. In between are Tennessee and Florida, where the effects sizes are 8 and 11 points, respectively.

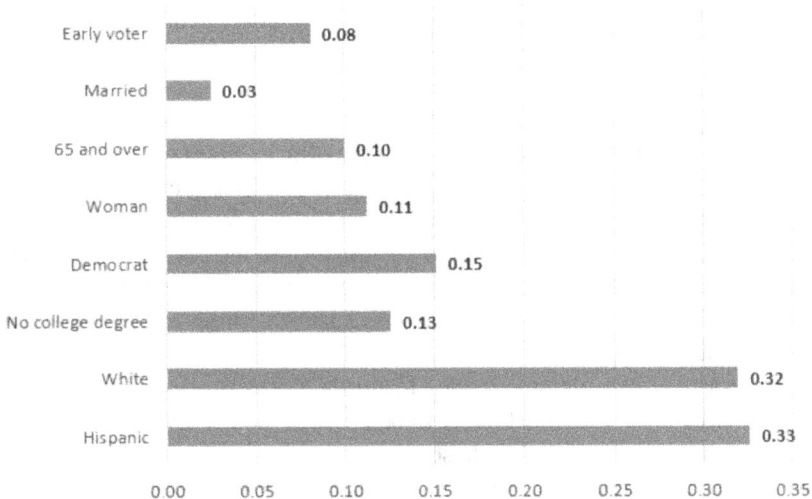

Figure 6.1   Marginal Effects on Support for Hillary Clinton across Four States, 2008.
Source: Created by Elliott Fullmer using data from Edison Research (accessed through the Roper Center for Public Opinion Research).

These findings suggest with strong credibility that Clinton meaningfully benefited from early voting during the 2008 presidential primaries; this edge was likely a result of her early front-runner status and early voting mobilization program. Had voters waited until their respective primary dates to vote, some may have become Obama supporters, increasing both his overall vote share and delegate haul.

More generally, these findings reveal an important potential unintended consequence of early voting. During nomination campaigns, programs may serve to further assist certain types of candidates, namely early front-runners and those with high levels of name recognition.

2016 FINDINGS

Table 6.3 reports my 2016 Probit findings. Again, I include a primary model that includes all respondents across the three states examined—Florida, North Carolina, and Ohio—along with separate models for each individual state. In the primary model, I find that early voters are significantly more likely to support Clinton, even when accounting for a range of highly significant covariates. When the three states are isolated, the effect is significant in both the North Carolina and Ohio models, though it is not significant in Florida.

Most of the other covariates behave as expected. With all three states included, women, Hispanics, self-identified Democrats, and those over 65 are significantly more likely to support Clinton. Unlike 2008, but as I expected in 2016, Blacks are also more likely to back Clinton. I do not report any significant relationship between college education and candidate preference in 2016.

Figure 6.2 presents the marginal effects on Clinton support in the primary 2016 specification, which again has a sample of over 5,000 respondents from the states examined. Because it was not a significant predictor of Clinton support in the primary model, no marginal effect is presented for lacking a college degree. All other variables were significant and therefore have marginal effects. Generally, the effects are quite similar to those reported in 2008. Most notably, being an early voter is again associated with an eight percentage-point increase in supporting Clinton (0.08). The fact that this effect remained the same across two election cycles featuring different opponents is somewhat remarkable. Those most likely to be 2016 Clinton supporters are Blacks (0.27), Democrats (0.24), and those who were at least 65 years old (0.23). The finding regarding self-identified Democrats is particularly unsurprising, as Sanders was a self-identified democratic socialist who only formally registered as a Democrat in 2015. Hispanics (0.14) and women (0.10) are also found to be strong Clinton supporters once again.

Table 6.3 Predicting Support for Hillary Clinton in Democratic Party Primaries, 2016

	(1) Clinton Support (Florida)	(2) Clinton Support (Ohio)	(3) Clinton Support (North Carolina)	(4) Clinton Support (All Three States)
Early voter	−0.0284	0.264***	0.483***	0.211***
	(0.099)	(0.085)	(0.114)	(0.055)
Woman	0.233***	0.212***	0.330***	0.248***
	(0.066)	(0.065)	(0.065)	(0.037)
Black	0.748***	0.882***	0.528***	0.730***
	(0.085)	(0.069)	(0.081)	(0.044)
Hispanic	0.240***	0.301	0.135	0.370***
	(0.086)	(0.196)	(0.244)	(0.070)
Democrat	0.544***	0.609***	0.617***	0.612***
	(0.077)	(0.068)	(0.071)	(0.041)
65 and older	0.453***	0.633***	0.755***	0.619***
	(0.081)	(0.082)	(0.081)	(0.047)
No college degree	0.0437	0.000312	−0.0812	0.00388
	(0.066)	(0.064)	(0.064)	(0.037)
Constant	−0.549***	−0.949***	−0.877***	−0.820***
	(0.091)	(0.078)	(0.080)	(0.047)
Observations	1,659	1,867	1,764	5,290

Source: Created by Elliott Fullmer using data from Edison Research (accessed through the Roper Center for Public Opinion Research).
Notes: *** $p < 0.001$; ** $p < 0.01$; * $p < 0.05$. Cell entries are Probit regression estimates with standard errors in parentheses.

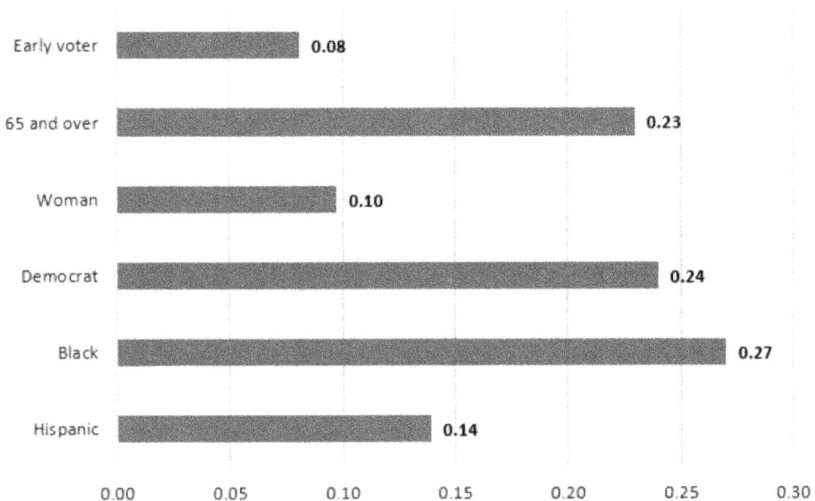

Figure 6.2 Marginal Effects on Support for Hillary Clinton across Three States, 2016.
Source: Created by Elliott Fullmer using data from Edison Research (accessed through the Roper Center for Public Opinion Research).

When the three states are separated, casting an early vote is strongly predictive of Clinton support in both North Carolina and Ohio. In North Carolina, with all controls included, early voting is associated with a 10 percentage-point spike in one's likelihood of backing Clinton. In Ohio, the effect soars to 19 points. In Florida, however, I do not report a significant effect between early voting and Clinton support.

CONCLUSIONS

Research has long focused on how institutions affect the types of candidates that ultimately ascend to the presidency. More specifically, changes in rule structures have been known to affect presidential nomination campaigns. Using 2008 and 2016 exit poll data from the National Election Pool, I report strong evidence that early voting makes it more likely that some voters will support front-running candidates. Aware of this possibility, Hillary Clinton effectively exploited her early name recognition and polling lead in both 2008 and 2016, actively mobilizing Democrats to vote early in states where the option existed. By securing votes before Barack Obama gained momentum by winning the Iowa Caucuses and (especially) the South Carolina primary in 2008, she may have won the support of some who would have backed Obama had they been forced to wait until their state's respective primary date. Eight years later, Clinton's far superior early vote operation banked votes across numerous states before the insurgent Bernie Sanders was able to effectively communicate his message to primary voters. My findings suggest that early voters were eight percentage points more likely to support Clinton in each election, even when a series of highly predictive demographic variables are considered. Ultimately, Clinton lost her party's presidential nomination in 2008 and won it in 2016. Whether early voting was a decisive factor in her 2016 victory is unclear. It *is* clear, however, that she built (and seemingly benefited from) a strategy that considered the new realities of early voting. As programs continue to expand in the coming years, other front-running presidential campaigns will likely seek to follow her example.

If my central findings are confirmed across even more elections, then officials may wish to consider the normative implications of early voting during nomination contests. Many believe that early front-runners and those with deep campaign coffers need no additional advantage in their quest to secure presidential nominations. Rather, some argue that the process is healthier when voting occurs in fewer locales at once, allowing lesser-known candidates to compete and generate momentum for later contests. Indeed, it has been said that the sequencing of state contests "embraces the little guy" (Delahayeal 2009). On the other hand, some suggest that front-runners with ample cash gain their advantage through meaningful experience and strong managerial skills, attributes we tend to seek in presidents. Whether a new advantage for front-runners is a problem is surely a matter of debate.

The findings in this chapter raise broader normative considerations. If early voting leads to premature votes that would shift in light of more information (by a campaign's end), then it is reasonable to ask whether elections truly represent the will of a determinate majority (or plurality). Thompson (2004) argues that when voters participate at different times, electoral outcomes cannot credibly claim to represent a majority (or plurality) of voters at any snapshot in time. Instead, final tallies are an amalgamation of votes cast by citizens operating in distinct information realities. With voters not operating on "equal terms," he argues that the legitimacy of election results is less assured. While Thompson raises valid concerns, the sequential nature of presidential nomination contests means that voters are already—with or without early voting—operating in different information environments. Those who vote in the Iowa Caucuses have no access to media reports, debates, and candidate statements made immediately before primaries held in April. Voters who support a candidate in the New Hampshire primary (in January or February) cannot know whether that candidate will still be around in May; citizens voting in June primary states, however, can. Early voting appears to make it more difficult for lesser-known candidates to build momentum by performing well in sequential contests, but it has not *introduced* information asymmetries into the nomination process; those existed long before early voting.

Thompson's critique of early voting, however, is worth considering with regards to general elections—which are not designed to be sequential. As I noted earlier in this chapter, late developments are relatively common in U.S. elections. And while partisan polarization suggests that most voters are unlikely to change their minds in contests between the two major parties, there are still millions of undecided voters in the final weeks of national campaigns (CNN 2020). Furthermore, research suggests that some citizens who *believe* that their minds are set could be swayed by new information. In the interest of minimizing the effects of information asymmetries, institutions surrounding campaigns need to better adjust to the realities of early voting. There is no reason why the major party candidates for president (and other offices) should begin debating in October. Citizens should have at least one opportunity to watch candidates compete on stage before polls open. Media outlets should aim to release major stories regarding the candidates before millions are casting ballots at early voting sites; high-profile interviews and town hall events with candidates should also air before this time. Donors should understand that early contributions are essential, as they allow candidates—especially down-ballot candidates—to begin communicating with voters before early voting begins.

Finally, there is some question as to whether early voting may begin *too early* in some states. I would proceed very carefully before cutting early voting options, but as my findings in chapters 2 and 3 indicate, the length of a state's early voting window has a minimal effect on turnout. If a state were to reduce its period from 45 days to 30 days *and* use the savings to invest in additional early voting locations, then it may (1) increase its turnout and (2) decrease the likelihood that citizens cast votes that they will regret. Both developments, if realized, would be positives for democracy.

NOTES

1. The three presidential debates would include two debates between the presidential candidates (Donald Trump and Joe Biden) and one debate between the vice presidential candidates (incumbent Mike Pence and Senator Kamala Harris of California). Trump and Biden were originally scheduled to meet three times, but the second debate was canceled due to Trump's COVID-19 diagnosis (and his unwillingness to debate virtually).

2. In 1992, the Democratic field for president included Tom Harkin, a popular U.S. senator from Iowa. As a result, most Democrats—including Clinton—largely conceded the state to him and did not aggressively campaign in that year's caucuses.

3. While Clinton eventually anticipated a loss to Obama in South Carolina, the 28 percentage-point margin was larger than her campaign or pre-election polls predicted.

4. In 2008, early voters were sampled in Florida, Arizona, California, Tennessee, and Texas. In 2016, early voters were sampled in Arkansas, Florida, Georgia, North Carolina, Ohio, Tennessee, and Texas.

5. In 2008, the first nomination contest (Iowa) was held very early (January 3). In 2016, the Iowa Caucuses were held much later (February 1). As a result, my 2008 and 2016 cases mark relatively comparable stages in the respective nomination contests.

6. National Election Pool data is accessed through the Roper Center for Public Opinion Research at Cornell University.

7. Edison Research, who conducts the polls for the National Election Pool (a consortium of ABC, CBS, NBC, CNN, Fox and the Associated Press), did not provide specific dates regarding their calls to early voters.

8. By the time the four 2008 contests occurred, only Clinton and Obama remained as active, campaigning candidates for the Democratic nomination. John Edwards, who dropped out during the early voting period, did receive a notable number of early votes in many states, as Meredith and Malhotra (2011) report. My analysis, however, is interested in how voters evaluated the candidacies of Clinton and Obama. The inclusion of Edwards's voters would skew the findings by suggesting that both Obama and Clinton performed much better among primary date voters than early voters. This is the case only because each faced only one major opponent on primary day rather than two during the early voting period. In order to best assess the performance of Clinton and Obama across the electorates, I include only voters in my analysis that chose one of them, regardless of when they voted.

Conclusion

In 1867, Christopher Latham Sholes filed a patent for a writing machine he developed with the help of two friends. The machine, called a "Type Writer," would soon become an office necessity in a rapidly industrializing United States. The machine, however, was not without flaws. The characters were mounted on metal arms that had a tendency to jam when consecutive keys were typed. As a result, Sholes (with the assistance of others) arranged the keys in a manner that would minimize the need to click consecutive keys. Commonly used letter pairs, such as 'th' or 'st,' were therefore separated. The resulting arrangement became known as the "QWERTY" keyboard after the first six letters on the top row. The design was a practical solution to a major problem and certainly helped the typewriter become a commercial success in the late 1800s (Weller 1918). What is less obvious, however, is why this book (completed in the early 2020s) was written on a keyboard with the same "QWERTY" arrangement.

The answer lies in the concept of path dependence, or the idea that decisions made in the present are affected (and highly constrained) by choices made in the past. While it no longer seems sensible to use the "QWERTY" keyboard, altering the design is easier said than done. Parents and teachers, having learned on the design themselves, are inclined to teach their children using the same arrangement. Businesses have little incentive to alter a widely practiced design that generates few complaints (even if it is not optimal). In other words, we continue to use "QWERTY" today because we used it yesterday. We used it yesterday because we used it the day before. We inherit a world created by millions of decisions made before our time. In crafting our society, we do not begin with a clean slate; we begin with a baseline molded by past decisions.

Path dependence affects all aspects of politics and government, including the U.S. electoral system. When Congress first set a universal Election Day for presidential elections in 1845, it chose to hold such contests on the first Tuesday following the first Monday in November. The most accepted rationale is that November 1 was unappealing because it was the day that merchants typically did their books from the preceding month.[1] By setting the date as the first Tuesday that followed a Monday in November, possible dates would only include November 2 through November 8. As for the day of the week, Sunday was not an option because it is the Sabbath for Christians. Monday was difficult because it often took a full day for farmers to travel to town (where they would vote). Wednesday was market day (in town), where farmers would sell their crops. So Tuesday made sense. Travelers could leave on Monday, vote on Tuesday,[2] and be in town for market day on Wednesday. Again, this arrangement was logical in 1845. But while it has less practical application in 2020, Election Day has not changed.

Like the QWERTY keyboard, old habits die hard.

Americans often lament that political institutions, laws, and programs are unnecessarily complicated. They blame self-interested politicians, corrupt lobbyists, and disconnected technocrats. Setting aside the culpability of these actors, some blame should also be reserved for path dependence. Much of the reason why government and politics are complicated and sometimes inefficient is because generations must build on the systems they inherit. The resulting aggregation of policy is often a clunky patchwork designed to both preserve imbedded traditions and address new problems. Examples are abundant. I doubt anyone would have designed the Patient Protection and Affordable Care Act of 2010 (Obamacare) if they were not constrained by existing arrangements. The comprehensive healthcare bill signed into law by President Barack Obama in 2010 was drafted with the intention of addressing contemporary problems, including millions of uninsured Americans and the high cost of coverage for those with insurance. But Congress and the president could not draft a program from scratch. Existing government plans for the elderly (Medicare), the poor (Medicaid), children (CHIP), and veterans (the VHA) had created a complicated web of benefits for citizens that could not easily be discarded or replaced. Millions of American citizens and businesses already had private insurance plans that they liked. Powerful organized interest groups on behalf of hospitals, doctors, drug companies, and insurance companies were ready to organize and lobby against measures that compromised their interests. Any healthcare plan needed to acknowledge these existing structures and minimize disruptions in order to achieve sufficient political support. The resulting bill was therefore complicated and confusing, opening it up to both fair criticisms and unfair distortions. But the

Affordable Care Act was not atypical; clear and efficient policies are rarely achievable in systems burdened with path dependence.

The development and effects of early voting laws in the United States have also been affected by path dependence. Early voting developed as a response to the electoral system that preceded it. Tuesday is not the most convenient day for most citizens to vote. It is a work day for most adults and a school day for nearly all children aged five and older. Efforts to make Election Day a national holiday have repeatedly failed. And even if it were a holiday, no one single day would be convenient for all to vote. One way to improve voter convenience was to expand the number of days available for citizens to vote. For those hoping to ease the burden of voting, early voting made sense.

Meanwhile, the decentralized nature of elections in the United States means that counties (or towns) are largely responsible for election administration. Burdened by a growing electorate, election officials found the need to spread voting across a longer period of time. While doing so increased administrative burdens in the weeks preceding Election Day, it also reduced the likelihood of being overwhelmed on Election Day.

Today, early voting is practiced in some form in 42 states. By all accounts, it is exceptionally popular among voters. And while programs are now more polarized along party lines, those states that have already adopted early voting cannot realistically consider repealing their programs. Even marginal cuts lead to criticism and, in some cases, federal intervention. Republican-led states such as Arkansas, Louisiana, and West Virginia would probably not approve early voting (at least on a permanent basis) in 2021. But because they did in the 1990s and early 2000s (when it was not politically controversial), undoing their programs in 2021 is not politically feasible. Path dependence, yet again.

THE TURNOUT QUESTION

In addition to exploring the causes behind early voting's emergence, one of the major goals of this book has been to assess the effects (if any) of early voting on turnout. Doing so is challenging, as early voting has not developed (and does not exist) in a vacuum. As states have expanded early voting, many have also eased registration requirements. Meanwhile, other states (and in some cases the same states) have cut polling places and adopted restrictive voter identification laws. Any effort to isolate the effects of early voting must carefully consider the effects of other predictors of voting.

While many others have addressed the turnout question, new approaches help build on these contributions. In modeling early voting and turnout, past studies have often omitted any consideration of past (or lagged) turnout in

respective states and counties, missing potentially important local turnout
norms not captured by conventional covariates. Many have not distinguished
between different types of early voting, omitting any distinction between
early in-person voting and liberalized absentee laws. Finally, most studies
lack consideration of local (mostly county) early voting implementation,
instead using states as their units of analysis.

In fact, early voting options do vary considerably both across and within
states. Five states, as well as some counties in other states, now mail ballots
to all registered voters. Thirty additional states allow any citizen to receive an
absentee ballot. Thirty-seven states offer in-person early voting, though the
number of sites provided by counties varies considerably. While most Ohio
counties typically have only one site, Illinois and Nevada counties often have
dozens. Even within early voting states, site availability often ranges from
very low to very high. In California, San Diego County offered its voters
just one early voting site in 2016. Santa Clara County, with barely half of
the population, offered six. These important implementation decisions are
often path dependent. My conversations with local election administrators
highlighted the importance of budget constraints, local parking and traffic
concerns, language diversity, and other factors in constraining municipal
decisions regarding site density. County clerks often wish to ease the voting
process, but lack the resources for idiosyncratic reasons out of their control.

In chapter 2, I construct a county-level model designed to account for variation in site offerings. My early voting sites per capita variable measures the
number of early voting sites in a county for every 1,000 voting-age residents.
With county turnout as the dependent variable, I assess the effect of sites
per capita, a no-excuse absentee program, a universal vote-by-mail (VBM)
program, and the number of days early voting is offered. I control for other
voter convenience options, as well as county demographics, political considerations, and lagged county turnout. Ultimately, I report that early voting is
indeed a catalyst of higher turnout when local governments offer more sites
per capita. An additional site per 1,000 voting-age residents is consistently
associated with an additional two points of turnout or more, even with highly
significant covariates included in the model. In urban counties, the effect size
is much larger, suggesting that even an additional site per 10,000 residents
can bring meaningful turnout gains. These findings are significant across two
presidential (2012 and 2016) and two national midterm election (2014 and
2018) cycles. Liberalized absentee rules—including universal VBM and no-
excuse absentee laws—are generally associated with higher county turnout as
well. In chapter 2, I find that the interaction between no-excuse absentee policies and site density is positive and significant in 3 of 4 elections analyzed;
adding an additional site per 1,000 voting-age residents yields greater turnout
increases in counties that also allow anyone to receive a ballot through the

mail. My findings regarding the length of time a state offers early voting (measured in days) are less consistent across the various specifications.

In chapter 3, I expose my findings to new scrutiny through an individual-level analysis. Using Current Population Survey (CPS) data from over 30,000 respondents, I find that those who reside in counties with higher site density were more likely to vote in both the 2014 and 2016 elections. The substantive effects are strong, as citizens were up to 14 and 6 percentage points more likely to vote if their counties offered greater levels of site density in 2014 and 2016, respectively. By confirming my county-level findings with individual-level data, I gain greater confidence that early in-person programs have a meaningful effect on participation when aggressively implemented. I also confirm my significant findings regarding universal VBM programs in the CPS analysis, though no-excuse absentee laws are only found to be positive turnout predictors in 2016 (not 2014).

UNINTENDED CONSEQUENCES

While early voting appears capable of producing higher levels of participation, it is not without externalities. These unintended consequences present new problems, challenges, and dynamics for various political stakeholders. In chapters 4 through 6, I examine the role of early voting in worsening down-ballot roll-off, creating (or expanding) racial disparities in polling offerings, and aiding front-runners in presidential nominating contests.

In the United States, elections for federal, state, and local elections are often held on the same day. As a result, those voting early are asked to cast votes for offices at all levels of government. My findings in chapter 4 suggest that early voting may be increasing down-ballot roll-off in some cases. As more complete ballots weeks before Election Day—before down-ballot candidates become visible to the electorate—some are choosing to leave lower-tier races blank. Examining the state of Ohio, where over a quarter of voters consistently vote early, I report that early voting reduces down-ballot turnout by several percentage points in state supreme court races. Turnout in some partisan statewide elections also appears to suffer (more modestly) in counties with higher levels of early voting.

The relationship between early voting and roll-off was smaller in 2018 than 2010, suggesting that a learning effect may be taking place. Recognizing that many citizens are casting early ballots, down-ballot campaigns may be knocking on doors, making phone calls, distributing direct mail, and holding local events sooner. If this adjustment *is* occurring in Ohio, however, my 2018 findings suggest that it has not (yet) eliminated all roll-off increases due to early voting. As my analysis is one of the first to explore the relationship between early voting and roll-off, I strongly encourage additional work in this area. I am hopeful that future analyses will examine states with higher early voting rates (e.g., Arizona, Nevada, and North Carolina), as well as possible differences between states depending on the length of their early voting periods.

Given the importance of early voting sites, it is important to investigate their distribution across the country. In chapter 5, I respond to a challenge by Gronke and McDonald (2008) by exploring whether early voting sites are less available in heavily non-Hispanic White counties. Ultimately, I find a county's percent Black to be negatively correlated with site density in every national election between 2012 and 2018. The effects are significant in both urban and less-populated counties and survive the inclusion of numerous covariates—including a county's mean household income and percent college-educated. In each election, the substantive effects are large. In a county of about 20,000 persons, a 20 percentage-point increase in the share of residents identifying as Black is associated with close to two fewer early voting sites. This finding is alarming, as it suggests that early voting is not yet achieving its potential in heavily Black counties. Furthermore, the Voting Rights Act forbids states and localities from adopting voting laws that disadvantage racial or ethnic minority groups.

Meanwhile, sites tend to be more available than usual in heavily Hispanic counties—at least those with 200,000 residents or less. This is not terribly surprising, as many of the states with the highest shares of Hispanic voters are also those who spearheaded early voting in the late 1980s and early 1990s (e.g., Arizona, California, Colorado, New Mexico, and Texas). With long traditions of early voting, counties in these states typically offer ample sites. Lending evidence to this explanation, a county's percent Hispanic no longer predicts more sites per capita in any year when state-fixed effects are included in the model.

In chapter 6, I explore whether early voting affects the competitive environment in presidential nominating contests. In these contests, each state and territory holds a primary or caucus. Because the contests are sequential, candidates seek to gain momentum in later contests by performing well in earlier primaries and caucuses. Early voting may allow candidates to secure votes before an insurgent opponent can gain momentum and woo them to their side. Examining both the 2008 and 2016 Democratic nominating contests, I find that early voting appeared to help Hillary Clinton in both cases. As an early front-runner with high name recognition, Clinton was able to "bank" early votes while her support was high, potentially preventing some voters from shifting their support to her chief competitors—Barack Obama and Bernie Sanders—after each gained more momentum. In both 2008 and 2016, I report that early voters were eight percentage points more likely to support Clinton, even when numerous other predictors of Clinton support are considered. While additional elections with early front-runners and insurgent candidates should certainly be studied, this finding suggests that early voting may provide a systematic advantage to front-runners in presidential nominating campaigns. Furthermore, it raises normative questions about whether early voting—by raising the likelihood of voter regret—produces election outcomes that imperfectly reflect the popular will.

The externalities created by early voting are consequential and must be taken seriously. Nevertheless, I do not believe that these unintended consequences suggest that early voting (and robust implementation of it) is a net negative for American democracy. Early voting brings millions of additional voters to the polls on a regular basis; in 2020, it allowed voting to be conducted safely in many communities, undoubtedly saving lives. Rather, the aforementioned issues simply remind us that all institutional reforms produce externalities that must be identified and addressed. Congress and the U.S. Justice Department may need to intervene to guarantee that racial disparities do not exist with regard to early voting sites. Modest federal investments could ensure that all communities have funds to invest in ample site density. My limited Ohio analyses suggest that candidates, parties, outside groups, and voters are already adjusting to the new realities of early voting in down-ballot races. To the extent that stakeholders can encourage donors to contribute earlier in campaign cycles, down-ballot candidates will be better prepared to communicate with voters before polls open. Local institutions, including media networks and civic groups, can also help prepare voters in advance by scheduling town halls, debates, and other events earlier in the process.

Parties may wish to consider the implications of early voting for their presidential nominating contests. Some may actually celebrate changes that aid early front-runners, though if sequentialism and its role in aiding insurgent (or lesser-known) candidates is something valued, then the ramifications of early voting could be problematic. Furthermore, while I did not examine the effect of information asymmetries in general elections, my findings suggest that institutions should better adapt to a campaign environment where nearly half of all votes are cast in advance. Again, those responsible should schedule debates, town hall events, interviews, and media exposés sooner. In 2020, *60 Minutes* aired interviews with both major party presidential tickets on October 25, after tens of millions of Americans had already voted. These sorts of events could easily take place in mid-September instead. In addition, states choosing where to allocate early voting resources would be wise to opt for extra sites rather than exceedingly long (45-day) windows. Not only do my findings consistently indicate that site density brings greater turnout returns, but longer windows increase the possibility of citizens voting without access to important information about candidates.

The bottom line is that early voting's negative externalities are fixable. And given that more early voting sites and liberalized absentee rules generate clear and meaningful increases in voter participation, it is important that they are addressed.

A MODEST PROPOSAL

Throughout this book, I have emphasized the importance of decentralization in understanding the U.S. electoral system. The Constitution, existing legal precedents, and norms all reinforce the authority granted to states and localities to manage elections within their borders. The positives are clear. States are able to experiment with innovative programs like early voting. Counties are able to place early voting locations outside grocery stores and college campuses to make voting most convenient for citizens. Administrators at all levels can assess and accommodate the specific needs of their constituents and adjust polling locations and voter outreach as needed.

The negatives of decentralization in election administration are also glaringly apparent. The complex web of jurisdictions and their policies breeds confusion and inconvenience. Voters often do not know the nuances of registering and voting in a new jurisdiction. Voter files throughout the country are full of errors, in some part due to the complexities involved in record sharing across states and localities. Inequality across the country is extreme. In Colorado, a voter is not required to present a photo ID, will have a ballot sent to their home (without needing to request it), can vote early at physical locations in their county, and can register as late as Election Day. In Mississippi, a photo ID is required, all voters must provide an excuse to either obtain an absentee ballot in the mail or vote early in-person, and registration must be completed at least 30 days before Election Day.

Given the confusion, inefficiency, and inequality that pervades our electoral system, the argument for better national standards is a strong one. In 2016, then-candidate Hillary Clinton proposed a national program of automatic voter registration (AVR), an updated Voting Rights Act that would reinstate preclearance requirements, and a minimum of 20 days of early voting in all 50 states (Berman 2015). In an election dominated by scandal, populist appeals, and histrionics, Clinton's proposal received little attention. But voter convenience has since gained momentum in Congress. In 2019, the Democratic-led House of Representatives approved the For the People Act (H.R. 1), a sweeping measure that would—among other things—end partisan gerrymandering, require AVR, undo strict ID laws, require at least 15 days of early in-person voting (for at least 10 hours a day), and mandate no-excuse absentee voting options.

Regarding early voting site density, H.R. 1 was somewhat vague, declaring, "The State shall ensure that polling places which allow voting during an early voting period . . . will be located in rural areas of the State, and shall ensure that such polling places are located in communities which will provide the greatest opportunity for residents of rural areas to vote during the early voting period." Furthermore, the bill required that sites be located within "walking distance of a stop on a public transportation route." When the House again passed the For the People Act in 2021 (the Senate had failed to consider it in 2019–2020), the language regarding early voting mostly remained the same. It did, however, include an important new requirement that states ensure that early voting sites be established on college campuses.

Given my findings, I believe mandating no-excuse absentee voting would be a sound policy. Regarding in-person sites, I would certainly amend the bill to include more specific requirements requiring site density in all communities. Simple mandates, however, are insufficient. As I have documented, discrepancies in site availability are generally not due to a lack of will on behalf of county clerks. The problem often lies in resources. Any congressional measure to advance early voting must provide federal dollars to states and localities for the purpose of offering a minimum number of locations per capita. Counties could still have considerable leeway with regards to their total number of sites and their locations, but in exchange for federal funds a minimum standard could be set. Given my conversations with dozens of local administrators across the country, I suspect that such assistance would be mostly welcomed. A national standard for early voting (and site density) could build on the turnout gains reported in chapters 2 and 3, as well as address the racial inequity issues raised in chapter 5.

When the House considered H.R. 1 in 2019 and 2021, the votes were entirely partisan. Not a single House Republican supported the measure on either occasion. This is not surprising, given the polarized nature of voting rights today. As I discussed in chapter 1, many Republicans have operated under the assumption that voter convenience measures will hurt them politically. Truthfully, many Democrats, academics, commentators, and operatives agree. But I question whether this assumption is entirely accurate. Both the 2018 and 2020 elections proved that many low-propensity voters will cast Republican ballots when they choose to participate. Even in a losing effort, the Republican ticket received more presidential votes in 2020 than ever before. As David Weigel wrote in *The Washington Post* a few days after the election, "Democrats won the White House and lost a myth about turnout (in 2020)." With the caveat that the 2020 election may have limited external validity, the last few campaigns do at least raise the possibility that many potential Republican voters are among those who often stay home. If this is true, then the party would be wise to reconsider its resistance to voter convenience efforts. Given Republican efforts to further restrict voting rights in Florida, Georgia, Texas, and other states in 2021, however, party officials do not appear to share my perspective.

Beyond partisan considerations, some look to the 2018 and 2020 elections and conclude that the United States no longer has a turnout problem. With the highest turnout in midterm and presidential elections in over 100 years, Americans have indeed been heading to the polls (or the mailbox) at greater rates. For those who believe increased electoral participation is good for democracy, this is a good thing! But there are many reasons why turnout still demands our attention. First, even the unusually high participation levels seen in 2018 and 2020 are mediocre when compared to the industrialized world. Many democracies routinely record turnout rates above 80%. Second, the presidency of Donald Trump was a uniquely polarizing period in the United States. Strong support and opposition to Trump undoubtedly mobilized voters in unusual ways. We cannot assume that engagement will remain high when more conventional politicians lead tickets. Third, the 2020 election was also held amid the backdrop of a global pandemic that affected nearly all aspects of American life. Not only were the stakes of the election seen as atypically high, but citizens were living unusual lifestyles and voting options were often expanded in (so far) temporary ways. There is plenty of reason for doubt, or at least uncertainty, regarding the broader applicability of any voting observations in 2020.

Fourth, and most importantly, many Americans still find it very burdensome to vote. Young people are often unprepared to navigate the processes required to get registered and cast ballots (Holbein and Hillygus 2020). While my findings regarding voter ID laws are mixed, there is anecdotal evidence that they prevent at least some citizens from casting ballots. Consider the example of Eddie Lee Holloway Jr., a 58-year-old Black man who moved from Illinois to Wisconsin around the time the state implemented a strict ID law in 2016. When he sought to get an ID in Wisconsin, his application was rejected because his birth certificate read "Eddie Junior Holloway," the result of a clerical error when it was issued. Holloway would make seven trips to different public agencies in Illinois and Wisconsin and spend over $200 in an attempt to rectify the issue. In the end, he could not obtain an ID in time to vote in 2016 (Berman 2017). Confusing or restrictive absentee rules can lead to ballots being discarded, in some cases without voters having an opportunity to correct minor errors. At least 4,000 ballots were discarded in Philadelphia alone in 2020 because Pennsylvania would not count absentee ballots that were placed in one envelope, rather than two (Winberg 2020). Lines are still too long in many jurisdictions, a result of insufficient polling sites in many places. In Georgia, some voters waited for 11 hours in 2020 to cast ballots—during a deadly pandemic (Tarbous 2020). Hardly anyone who studies election administration in the United States believes the system maximizes citizen convenience.

Of course, not all nonvoters will be moved to the polls by convenience voting reforms. Many Americans feel disconnected from their government, believe their votes do not matter, are dejected by polarization and legislative inertia, or simply do not care. Addressing these problems is a herculean task and involves rethinking civic education, the media's role in disseminating information, electoral institutions that do not breed competition, and much, much more.

But while electoral reforms such as early voting cannot alone make U.S. electoral participation the envy of the democratic world, they can help. Even one or two additional points of turnout equates to millions of new citizens choosing to participate in their democracy. Their engagement may generate other forms of political activism, including participating in local meetings, talking about government with their children, and taking more care to follow national political developments. Systems which discourage otherwise (even mildly) interested citizens from participating only further the distance between the American ideal of democracy and American reality. Those who wish to vote but cannot get to the polls on a Tuesday, or who find it burdensome to drive across their county to the one early voting site provided, only become more disenchanted with politics and their role in it. Electoral reform is not only about turnout; it is about making a clear statement to the American electorate that this government is theirs to be shaped. American history is a story of progress in this regard. The original U.S. electorate began as a limited group of (mostly) land-owning White males. It gradually grew to include White males without land, women, Native Americans, Blacks, those with a native language other than English, those who could not pay a poll tax, and those 18 and older. Electoral reforms such as same-day registration (SDR) and early voting have faced setbacks, but have generally expanded over time. Progress is often slow and fragile, but it does happen.

Momentum for electoral reform is insufficient to ease participation. When momentum grows, it is essential that it be matched with effective action. Momentum that breeds unproductive reforms only leads to disillusionment. For this reason, continued research into these areas is key. In this book, I have subjected various policies to close scrutiny in an effort to identify the possibilities and potential pitfalls of early voting reforms. But as developments in this area remain in flux, I expect that new reforms and approaches will present additional opportunities and externalities that cannot yet be anticipated. As new ideas emerge in the years to come, we can only verify their effectiveness through objective, empirical studies that assume no conclusions. As always, this work requires careful data collection, modeling, and interpretation. The study of voting, which Riker (1982) once said represents "the heart of both the method and the ideal of democracy," is worth it.

NOTES

1. It has also been suggested that November 1 was unappealing to Catholics because it is All Saints Day, a holy day of obligation. Given the minimal political power of Catholics in 1840s America, however, it seems unlikely that this was heavily weighed by Congress.

2. In those days, Election Day often featured lavish celebrations that spanned an entire day.

Bibliography

Abramowitz, Alan I. 1989. "Viability, Electability, and Candidate Choice in a Presidential Primary Election: A Test of Competing Models." *Journal of Politics* 51 (4): 977–992.

Ahmed, Hauwa. 2020. "States Must Maintain and Expand In-Person Voting Locations During COVID-19." Center for American Progress. September 24, 2020. https://www.americanprogress.org/issues/democracy/news/2020/09/24/4907 44/states-must-maintain-expand-person-voting-locations-covid-19/

Aldrich, John H. 1980. *Before the Convention: Strategies and Choices in Presidential Nominating Campaigns.* Chicago: University of Chicago Press.

Aldrich, John H. 1993. "Rational Choice and Turnout." *American Journal of Political Science* 37 (1): 246–278.

Alvarez, R. Michael, Delia Bailey, and Jonathan N. Katz. 2008. "The Effect of Voter Identification Laws on Turnout." Social Science Working Paper 1267R, California Institute of Technology.

Alvarez, R. Michael, Dustin Beckett, and Charles Stewart III. 2011. "Voting Technology, Vote-by-Mail, and Residual Votes in California, 1990–2010." *Political Research Quarterly* 66 (3): 658–670.

American Bar Association. 2020. "Law Day Survey: Americans like Online Voting, Early Voting, and the ERA." May 2020. https://www.americanbar.org/news/ab anews/publications/youraba/2020/youraba-may-2020/aba-civic-survey/

Anderson, Bill. 1994. "Arapahoe Dems Run Uphill." *The Denver Post*, October 26, 1994.

Ansolabehere, Stephen, and Gary King. 1990. "Measuring the Consequences of Delegate Selection Rules in Presidential Nominations." *Journal of Politics* 52 (2): 609–621.

Ashenfelter, Orley, and Stanley Kelley Jr. 1975. "Determinants of Participation in Presidential Elections." *The Journal of Law and Economics* 18 (3): 695–733.

Bailey, Michael A., and Mark C. Rom. 2004. "A Wider Race? Interstate Competition across Health and Welfare Programs." *Journal of Politics* 66 (2): 326–347.

145

Baker, Michael, Jonathan Gruber, and Kevin Milligan. 2008. "Universal Child Care, Maternal Labor Supply, and Family Well-Being." *Journal of Political Economy* 116 (4): 709–745.

Baker, Mike. 2008. "N.C. GOP Lashes Out at Voting Sites Near Obama Rally." *WRAL.com*, October 19, 2008. https://www.wral.com/news/state/story/376 9394/

Balz, Dan, Anne E. Kornblut, and Shailagh Murray. 2008. "Obama Is Big Winner in S.C. Primary." *The Washington Post*, January 28, 2008. http://www.washingto npost.com/wp-dyn/content/article/2008/01/26/AR2008012601018.html

Barber, Brad, and Terrence Odean. 2001. "Boys Will Be Boys: Gender, Overconfidence, and Common Stock Investment." *Quarterly Journal of Economics* 116 (February): 261–292.

Bardes, Barbara A., Mack C. Shelley II, and Steffen W. Schmidt. 2009. *American Government and Politics Today: Essentials*, 15th edition. Boston: Cengage.

Baretto, Matt A., Matthew J. Streb, Mara Marks, and Fernando Guerra. 2006. "Do Absentee Voters Differ from Polling Place Voters? New Evidence from California." *Public Opinion Quarterly* 70 (2): 224–234.

Bartels, Larry M. 1985. "Expectations and Preferences in Presidential Nominating Campaigns." *American Political Science Review* 79 (3): 804–815.

Bartels, Larry M. 1988. *Presidential Primaries and the Dynamics of Public Choice.* Princeton: Princeton University Press.

Beam, Christopher. 2008. "A Number You Probably Haven't Seen." *Slate*, February 28, 2008. http://www.slate.com/content/slate/blogs/trailhead/2008/02/28/a_n umber_you_probably_havent_seen.html

"Behind the Obama-Clinton Draw." 2009. *CBS News*, June 18, 2009. http://www .cbsnews.com/2100-250_162-3795497.html

Benac, Nancy. 2008. "Early Voting in 2008 Presidential Race Playing an Important Role." *Memphis Daily News*, January 23, 2008. https://www.memphisdailynews .com/news/2008/jan/23/early-voting-in-2008-presidential-race-playing-an-impor tant-role//print

Berinsky, Adam, Nancy Burns, and Michael Traugott. 2001. "Who Votes by Mail? A Dynamic Model of the Individual-Level Consequences of Voting-By-Mail Systems." *Public Opinion Quarterly* 65 (2): 178–197.

Berman, Ari. 2015. "Hillary Clinton's Bold Plan for Voting Rights." *The Nation*, June 4, 2015. https://www.thenation.com/article/archive/hillary-clintons-bold-plan -voting-rights/

Berman, Ari. 2017. "Wisconsin's Voter-ID Law Suppressed 200,000 Votes in 2016 (Trump Won by 22,748)." *The Nation*, May 9, 2017. https://www.thenation.com /article/archive/wisconsins-voter-id-law-suppressed-200000-votes-trump-won-by -23000/

Bernstein, Alan, and Jo Ann Zuniga. 1992. "Early Voting is Big Winner in Popularity." *The Houston Chronicle*, October 27, 1992.

Bitler, Marianne P., Jonah Gelbach, and Hilary Hoynes. 2005. "Welfare Reform and Health." *Journal of Human Resources* 40 (2): 309–334.

Bomboy, Scott. 2016. "Early Voting Looms as Key Election Factor." *Constitution Daily*, October 11, 2016. https://constitutioncenter.org/blog/early-voting-looms-as-key-election-factor

Bond, Michaelle. 2011. "Maryland Looks for Improvement When Early Voting Starts on Friday." *Capital News Service*, October 21, 2011. http://www.journalism.umd.edu/cns/wire/2010-editions/10-October-editions/101021-Thursday/EarlyVoting_CNS-UMCP.html

Bowler, Shaun, and Todd Donovan. 1994. "Information and Opinion Change on Ballot Measures." *Political Behavior* 16 (4): 411–435.

Bradner, Eric. "Why Wait for November? Campaigns Look to Lock in Support before Election Day." *The Oklahoman*, September 12, 2016. https://oklahoman.com/article/feed/1073553/why-wait-for-november-campaigns-look-to-lock-in-support-before-election-day

Brams, Steven J. 1978. *The Presidential Election Game*. New Haven: Yale University Press.

Brennan Center for Justice. 2012. "Election 2012: Voting Laws Roundup." http://www.brennancenter.org/analysis/election-2012-voting-laws-roundup

Brewer, Mike. 2007. "Welfare Reform in the UK: 1997–2007." IFS Working Papers W07/20, Institute for Fiscal Studies.

Brians, Craig Leonard, and Bernard Grofman. 1999. "When Registration Barriers Fall, Who Votes?" *Public Choice* 99: 161–176.

Bright, Chelsie L. M., and Michael S. Lynch. 2017. "Kansas Voter ID Laws: Advertising and Its Effects on Turnout." *Political Research Quarterly* 70 (2): 340–347.

Brockington, David. 2003. "A Low Information Theory of Ballot Position Effect." *Political Behavior* 25 (1): 1–27.

Broder, John M. 2007. "In Clinton Aide's Advice, an Early Voting Dilemma." *The New York Times*, May 25, 2007. http://www.nytimes.com/2007/05/27/us/politics/27ballot.html?pagewanted=print&_r=0

Burden, Barry, David Canon, Kenneth Mayer, and Donald Moynihan. 2014. "Election Laws, Mobilization, and Turnout: The Unanticipated Consequences of Election Reform." *American Journal of Political Science* 58 (1): 95–109.

Bush, George W. 2010. *Decision Points*. New York: Random House Inc.

California Secretary of State. 2012. "Historical Vote-By-Mail (Absentee) Ballot Use in California." http://www.sos.ca.gov/elections/hist_absentee.htm

Calvan, Bobby Caina. 2020. "Settlement Reached in Florida Dispute Over College Voting." *AP News*, April 3, 2020. https://apnews.com/article/2331b5398ca1908c64ec3fe03c95e4d5

Camerer, Colin, and Dan Lovallo. 1999. "Overconfidence and Excess Entry: An Experimental Approach." *American Economic Review* 89 (1): 306–318.

Campbell, Angus. 1966. "Surge and Decline: A Study of Electoral Change." In *Elections and the Political Order*, edited by Angus Campbell, Philip E. Converse, Warren E. Miller and Donald E. Stokes. New York: Wiley.

Campbell, James E. 1997. *The Presidential Pulse of Congressional Elections*. Lexington: University of Kentucky Press.

Cavala, William. 1974. "Changing the Rules Changes the Game: Party Reform and the 1972 California Delegation to the Democratic National Convention." *American Political Science Review* 68 (1): 27–42.

Clayton, Mark. 2012. "Voting-Machine Glitches: How Bad was it on Election Day around the Country?" *The Christian Science Monitor*, November 7, 2012. https://www.csmonitor.com/USA/Elections/2012/1107/Voting-machine-glitches-How-bad-was-it-on-Election-Day-around-the-country

CNN. 2020. "Exit Polls." https://www.cnn.com/election/2020/exit-polls/president/national-results

Cohen, Jon, and Aaron Blake. 2013. "Hillary Clinton Reaches New Heights of Political Popularity." *The Washington Post*, January 23, 2013. https://www.washingtonpost.com/news/the-fix/wp/2013/01/23/record-high-for-hillary-clinton-as-she-faces-little-regarded-congress/?utm_term=.81fcb7989fee

Corasaniti, Nick, and Reid J. Epstein. 2021. "What Georgia's Voting Law Really Does." *The New York Times*, May 13, 2021. https://www.nytimes.com/2021/04/02/us/politics/georgia-voting-law-annotated.html

Cotterell, Bill. 2013. "Florida Restores Early Voting Days, Moves Back Primary." *Reuters*, May 3, 2013. https://www.reuters.com/article/us-usa-florida-voting/florida-restores-early-voting-days-moves-back-primary-idUSBRE94300K20130504

Crews, Ed. 2007. "Voting in Early America." *Colonial Williamsburg*, Spring 2007. https://www.history.org/foundation/journal/spring07/elections.cfm

Darcy, R., and Anne L. Schneider. 1989. "Confusing Ballots, Roll-off, and the Black Vote." *Western Political Quarterly* 42 (3): 347–364.

Davis, Bob. 2016. "Early Voting Seen as a Boost for Front-Runners in Super Tuesday Polls." *The Wall Street Journal*, March 1, 2016. https://www.wsj.com/articles/early-voting-seen-as-a-boost-for-presidential-front-runners-1456782068

Delahayeal, Shannon. 2009. "The Democratic Party Primary Process." *Harvard Negotiation Law Review*, Winter 2009.

DeSilver, Drew. 2021. "Turnout Soared in 2020 as Nearly Two-Thirds of Eligible U.S. Voters Cast Ballots for President." *Pew Research Center*, January 28, 2021. https://www.pewresearch.org/fact-tank/2021/01/28/turnout-soared-in-2020-as-nearly-two-thirds-of-eligible-u-s-voters-cast-ballots-for-president/

Domurat, Stephanie. 2008. "Early Voting." *KULR 8*, September 8, 2008. http://www.kulr8.com/news/local/27977079.html

Downs, Anthony. 1957. *An Economic Theory of Democracy*. New York: Harper and Brothers.

Drinkard, Jim. 2004. "Long Lines on Election Day Enhance Appeal of Early Voting." *USA Today*, November 18, 2004.

Drutman, Lee, and Charlotte Hill. 2020. "America Needs a Federal Elections Agency." *New America*, November 4, 2020. https://www.newamerica.org/political-reform/reports/america-needs-federal-elections-agency/

Dubin, Jeffrey A., and Gretchen A. Kalsow. 1996. "Comparing Absentee and Precinct Voters: A View over Time." *Political Behavior* 18 (4): 369–392.

Dyck, Joshua J., and James Gimpel. 2005. "Distance, Turnout, and the Convenience of Voting." *Social Science Quarterly* 86 (3): 531–548.

"Early Bird Gets the Vote." 2009. *WDTN.com*, September 16, 2009. http://www.wdtn .com/dpp/news/early-bird-gets-the-vote

"Early Bird Gets the Vote? Pols Hunt Early Ballots." 2010. *KMOV*, September 20, 2010. http://www.kmov.com/news/politics/103263839.html

"Early Voters Key to Victory in Florida." 2008. *CBS News*, January 21, 2008. http:// www.cbsnews.com/stories/2008/01/21/politics/main3734796.shtml

"Early Voting adds yet Another Note of Uncertainty to Super Tuesday." 2008. *PBS*, February 5, 2008. http://www.pbs.org/newshour/updates/politics-jan-june08-earl y_voting_02-05/

"Early Voting Grows in Popularity." 2008. *NPR*, November 7, 2008. http://www.npr. org/templates/story/story.php?storyId=96756705

Eggert, David. 2004. "Secretary of State Hopes to Expand Early Voting in Michigan." *The Associated Press*, November 7, 2004.

"Elections Officials Hope New Early Voting Law Increases Turnout." 2002. *The Associated Press State and Local Wire*, April 25, 2002.

Erikson, Robert S., and Lorraine C. Minnite. 2009. "Modeling Problems in the Voter Identification—Voter Turnout Debate." *Election Law Journal* 8 (2): 85–101.

Ewald, Alec C. 2009. *The Way We Vote: The Local Dimension of American Suffrage*. Nashville: Vanderbilt University Press.

FairVote. 2012. "Presidential Tracker 2012." https://www.fairvote.org/presidential_tr acker_2012#2012_campaign_spending

FairVote. 2016. "Tracking the Candidates Through the Final Campaign Push: Lots of Stops but Few States." November 2, 2016. https://www.fairvote.org/tracking_t he_candidates_through_the_final_campaign_push_lots_of_stops_but_few_states

Farr, Alix. 2010. "Light Turnout Marks Early Voting Debut." *Capital News Service*, September 3, 2010.

Fenster, Mark J. 1994. "The Impact of Allowing Day of Registration Voting on Turnout in US Elections from 1960 to 1992." *American Politics Quarterly* 22 (1): 74–87.

Ferejohn, John, and Morris Fiorina. 1974. "The Paradox of Not Voting: A Decision Theoretic Analysis." *American Political Science Review* 68 (2): 525–536.

Figlio, David N., Van W. Kolpin, and William E. Reid. 1999. "Do States Play Welfare Games?" *Journal of Urban Economics* 46 (3): 437–454.

Fitzgerald, Mary. 2005. "Greater Convenience but Not Greater Turnout: The Impact of Alternative Voting Methods on Electoral Participation in the United States." *American Politics Research* 33 (6): 842–867.

"Florida Republicans Push to Cut Early Voting." 2011. *Miami Herald*, April 15, 2011. http://election2010.illumen.org/latest-news/florida-republicans-push-to-cut -early-voting-to-single-week-2

Fortier, John C. 2006. *Absentee and Early Voting: Trends, Promises, and Perils*. Washington: The AEI Press.

Francesconi, Marco, and Wilbert van der Klaauw. 2007. "The Socioeconomic Consequences of 'InWork' Benefit Reform for British Lone Mothers." *Journal of Human Resources* 42 (1): 1–31.

Fullmer, Elliott. 2015a. "Early Voting and Presidential Nominations: A New Advantage for Front-Runners?" *Presidential Studies Quarterly* 45 (3): 425–444.

Fullmer, Elliott. 2015b. "Early Voting: Do More Sites Lead to Higher Turnout?" *Election Law Journal* 14 (2): 81–96.

Fullmer, Elliott. 2015c. "The Site Gap: Racial Inequalities in Early Voting Access." *American Politics Research* 43 (2): 283–303.

Fulwood, Sam, III. 2016. "A Voting Rights Story." *Center for American Progress*, July 22, 2016. https://www.americanprogress.org/issues/race/reports/2016/07/22/1 41713/a-voting-rights-story/

"Gallup Editors: New Hampshire in Context." 2004. *Gallup*, January 28, 2004. http://www.gallup.com/poll/10435/gallup-editors-new-hampshire-context.aspx

Garcia, Arturo. 2013. "NC GOP Official Fired After Bragging Voter ID Law Would 'Kick the Democrats' Butt.'" *Raw Story*, October 24, 2013. https://www.rawstory.com/2013/10/nc-gop-official-fired-after-bragging-voter-id-law-would-kick-the-democrats-butt/

Geer, John G. 1986. "Rules Governing Presidential Primaries." *Journal of Politics* 48 (4): 1006–1025.

Geer, John G. 1989. *Nominating Presidents*. New York: Greenwood.

Giammo, Joseph D., and Brian J. Brox. 2010. "Reducing the Costs of Participation: Are States Getting a Return on Early Voting?" *Political Research Quarterly* 63 (2): 295–303.

Gimpel, James G., J. Celeste Lay, and Jason E. Schuknecht. 2003. *Cultivating Democracy: Civic Environments and Political Socialization in America*. Washington: Brookings Institute Press.

Graham, Bob. 2012. "Voting Rights are Hindered in Florida." *Sun Sentinel*, January 29, 2012.

Graham, David. 2016. "Ohio's 'Golden Week' of Early Voting is Dead, Again." *The Atlantic*, August 23, 2016. https://www.theatlantic.com/politics/archive/2016/08/ohio-voting-decision/497066/

Granowsky, Alvin. 2008. "No Child Left Behind: A Tale of Unintended Consequences." Paper presented at the LDA Texas Annual State Conference, Austin, TX.

Greene, Andrea D., and Alan Bernstein. 1992. "Added Polling Sites Fail to Boost Voters' Turnout." *The Houston Chronicle*, February 28, 1992.

Griffiths, Brent. 2016. "When does Early Voting Start in Every State?" *Politico*, September 21, 2016. https://www.politico.com/story/2016/09/early-voting-states-228435

Grogger, Jeffrey, and Lynn A. Karoly. 2005. *Welfare Reform: Effects of Decade of Change*. Cambridge: Harvard University Press.

Gronke, Paul. 2005. "Ballot Integrity and Voting by Mail: The Oregon Experience." Commission on Federal Election Reform, June 15, 2005. https://blogs.reed.edu/earlyvoting/files/2013/04/Ballot-Integrity-and-Voting-by-Mail-The-Oregon-Experience.pdf

Gronke, Paul, Eva Galanes-Rosenbaum, and Peter Miller. 2007. "Early Voting and Turnout." *PS: Political Science and Politics* 40 (4): 639–645.

Gronke, Paul, Eva Galanes-Rosenbaum, and Peter Miller. 2008. "Convenience Voting." *Annual Review of Political Science* 11: 437–455.

Gronke, Paul, and Michael McDonald. 2008. "Tracking the Early Electorate?" http://www.princeton.edu/csdp/events/Election050108/McDonaldElection.pdf

Gronke, Paul, and Peter Miller. 2012. "Voting by Mail and Turnout in Oregon: Revisiting Southwell and Burchett." *American Politics Research* 40 (6): 976–997.

Guillen, Joe. 2011. "Ohio Lawmakers Set to Approve Election Overhaul Legislation." *Cleveland Plain-Dealer*, May 24, 2011. http://www.cleveland.com/open/index.ssf/2011/05/ohio_lawmakers_set_to_approve.html

Hall, Melinda Gann. 1999. "Ballot Roll-off in Judicial Elections: Contextual and Institutional Influences on Voter Participation in the American States." Paper presented at the annual meeting of the American Political Science Association, Atlanta, GA, 1999.

Hall, Thad, and Dan Tokaji. 2007. "Money for Data: Funding the Oldest Unfunded Mandate." *Equal Vote Blog*, June 5, 2007. http://moritzlaw.osu.edu/blogs/tokaji/2007_06_01_equalvote_archive.html

Hammond, Thomas H. 1980. "Another Look at the Role of 'The Rules' in the 1972 Democratic Presidential Primaries." *Western Political Quarterly* 33 (1): 50–72.

Hanmer, Michael. 2009. *Discount Voting*. Cambridge: Cambridge University Press.

Harrison, Bobby. 2020. "'Practices Aimed to Suppress the Vote': Mississippi is the Only State Without Early Voting for All During Pandemic." *Mississippi Today*, October 13, 2020. https://mississippitoday.org/2020/10/13/practices-aimed-to-suppress-the-vote-mississippi-is-the-only-state-without-early-voting-for-all-during-pandemic/

Harwood, John. 2008. "The White Working Class: Forgotten Voters No More." *The New York Times*, May 26, 2008. http://www.nytimes.com/2008/05/26/us/politics/p26caucus.html

Haspel, Moshe, and H. Gibbs Knotts. 2005. "Location, Location, Location: Precinct Placement and the Costs of Voting." *Journal of Politics* 67 (2): 560–573.

Hassan, Adeel. 2021. "What's in Florida's New Voting Law?" *The New York Times*, May 10, 2021. https://www.nytimes.com/article/florida-voting-law.html

Heimlich, Russell. 2012. "Early Voting Increased in 2008." Pew Research Center, October 26, 2012. https://www.pewresearch.org/fact-tank/2012/10/26/early-voting-increased-in-2008/

Henninger, Daniel. 2008. "The Financial Crisis Is McCain's Katrina." *RealClearPolitics*, October 16, 2008. http://www.realclearpolitics.com/articles/2008/10/the_financial_crisis_is_mccain.html

Herron, Michael C., and Daniel A. Smith. 2014. "Race, Party, and the Consequences of Restricting Early Voting in Florida in the 2012 General Election." *Political Research Quarterly* 67 (3): 646–665.

Higgins, Tucker, and Nate Rattner. 2020. "When does vote by mail and early voting start? A state by state guide." *CNBC*, September 4, 2020. https://www.cnbc.com/2020/09/04/election-early-absentee-mail-voting-every-state.html

"High Court Rules Early Vote in 16 States Gets Nod." 2000. *Tulsa World*, June 13, 2000.

Highton, Benjamin. 2005. "Self-Reported versus Proxy-Reported Voter Turnout in the Current Population Survey." *Public Opinion Quarterly* 69 (1): 113–123.

Hochschild, Jennifer. 2003. "Introduction and Comments." *Perspectives on Politics* 1 (2): 247–248.

Holbein, John B., and D. Sunshine Hillygus. 2020. *Making Young Voters: Converting Civic Attitudes into Civic Action.* Cambridge: Cambridge University Press.

Holmes, Sue Major. 2002. "About 30 Percent of New Mexicans Generally Vote Early." *The Associated Press State and Local Wire*, October 24, 2002.

Hylton-Austin, Hilary. 2008. "Clinton-Obama Rodeo Lassos Texas." *Time*, February 21, 2008. http://content.time.com/time/politics/article/0,8599,1715329,00.html

"Interlude: Toner on Election Administration." 2006. *The Hotline: National Journal's Daily Briefing on Politics*, November 2006. hotlineblog.nationaljournal.com/arc hives/2006/11/interlude_toner.html

Issenberg, Sasha. 2012. "Early Bird Gets the Delegates." *Slate*, March 12, 2012. http://www.slate.com/articles/news_and_politics/victory_lab/2012/03/mitt_romney_s _early_voting_mastery_his_rivals_never_stood_a_chance_.html

Jewitt, Caitlin E. 2019. *The Primary Rules: Parties, Voters, and Presidential Nominations.* Ann Arbor: University of Michigan Press.

Joslyn, Richard A. 1976. "The Impact of Decision Rules in Multi-Candidate Campaigns: The Case of the 1972 Democratic Presidential Nomination." *Public Choice* 25 (Spring): 1–17.

Kam, Dara. 2012. "Former Florida GOP Leaders Say Voter Suppression was Reason They Pushed New Election Law." *The Palm Beach Post*, November 27, 2012. https://www.palmbeachpost.com/article/20121125/NEWS/812021098

Kamarck, Elaine C. 1987. "Delegate Allocation Rules in Presidential Nomination Systems: A Comparison between the Democrats and Republicans." *Journal of Law and Politics* 4 (2): 275–310.

Kamarck, Elaine C. 2018. *Primary Politics: Everything You Need to Know About How America Nominates Its Presidential Candidates*, 3rd edition. Washington: Brookings Institution Press.

Kenney, Patrick J., and Tom W. Rice. 1989. "An Empirical Examination of the Minimax Hypothesis." *American Politics Research* 17 (2): 153–162.

Kenski, Kate, Bruce W. Hardy, and Kathleen Hall Jamieson. 2010. *The Obama Victory: How Media, Money, and Message Shaped the 2008 Election.* Oxford: Oxford University Press.

Keyssar, Alexander. 2001. *The Right to Vote: The Contested History of Democracy in the United States.* New York: Basic Books.

Kimball, David C., Chris T. Owens, and Katherine McAndrew. 2001. "Who's Afraid of an Undervote?" Paper presented at the annual meeting of the Southern Political Science Association, Atlanta, GA, 2001.

King, Erika G. 1990. "Thematic Coverage of the 1988 Presidential Primaries: A Comparison of USA Today and The New York Times." *Journalism Quarterly* 67 (1): 83–87.

Knack, Stephen. 2001. "Election-Day Registration." *American Politics Research* 29 (1): 65–78.

Kousser, J. Morgan. 1999. *Colorblind Injustice*. Chapel Hill: UNC Press.

Kuk, John, Zoltan Hajnal, and Nazita Lajevardi. 2020. "A disproportionate burden: strict voter identification laws and minority turnout." *Politics, Groups, and Identities*. DOI: 10.1080/21565503.2020.1773280

LaPolt, A. 2002. "GOP gets Florida Absentee Vote Down to a Science." *Gannett News Service*, November 9, 2002.

Larocca, Roger, and John S. Klemanski. 2011. "Election Reform and Turnout in Presidential Elections." *State Politics & Policy Quarterly* 11 (1): 76–101.

Leighley, Jan E., and Jonathan Nagler. 2013. *Who Votes Now? Demographics, Issues, Inequality, and Turnout in the United States*. Princeton: Princeton University Press.

Lengle, James I., and Byron Shafer. 1976. "Primary Rules, Political Power, and Social Change." *American Political Science Review* 70 (1): 25–40.

Levine, Sam. 2018. "Wisconsin Voting Rights Groups Promise Lawsuit Over Early Voting Cuts." *HuffPost*, December 14, 2018. https://www.huffpost.com/entry/wisconsin-early-voting_n_5c141be8e4b049efa7524568

Levine, Sam. 2019. "Federal Judge Blocks Wisconsin GOP's Cuts to Early Voting." *HuffPost*, January 17, 2019. https://www.huffpost.com/entry/wisconsin-early-voting-cuts-blocked_n_5c40ddd5e4b041e98ffc00d8

Lichter, S. Robert, Daniel Amundson, and Richard Noyes. 1988. *The Video Campaign: Network Coverage of the 1988 Primaries*. Washington: American Enterprise Institute.

Lieb, David A. 2011. "Nixon Vetoes Photo ID, Early Voting Bill." *The Southeast Missourian*, June 19, 2011.

Lyons, William, and John M. Scheb II. 1999. "Early Voting and the Timing of the Vote: Unanticipated Consequences of Electoral Reform." *State and Local Government Review* 31 (2): 147–152.

Macedo, Stephen, and Christopher Karpowitz. 2006. "The Local Roots of American Inequality." *PS: Political Science & Politics* 39 (1): 59–64.

Magers, Phil. 2004. "Analysis: Early Voting Gaining Popularity." *United Press International*, November 19, 2004.

Magleby, David. 1985. "Participation in the Initiative and Referendum Elections in Switzerland and the United States." Presented at the 13th World Congress of the International Political Science Association, Paris, France.

Maine Secretary of State. 2007. "Report and Pilot Program for Early Voting - Survey of Maine Municipal Clerks Regarding Early and Absentee Voting."

Maisel, Louis, and Gerald J. Lieberman. 1977. "The Impact of Electoral Rules on Primary Elections: The Democratic Presidential Primaries in 1976." In *The Impact of the Electoral Process*, edited by Louis Maisel and Joseph Cooper. Beverly Hills: Sage.

Man, Anthony. 2010. "Residents Love Early Voting but Palm Beach and Broward Counties Cut Locations." *Sun Sentinel*, August 3, 2010. http://www.palmbeach

post.com/news/news/state-regional/residents-love-early-voting-but-palm-beach
-and-bro/nL8xp/

Mannies, Jo. 2004. "Holden Says State Would Have to Pay for Early Voting." *St. Louis Post-Dispatch*, July 11, 2004.

Marble, William. 2020. "The Neutral Partisan Effects of Vote-by-Mail: Evidence from County-Level Rollouts." Stanford University Institute for Economic Policy Research. https://siepr.stanford.edu/sites/default/files/publications/20-015.pdf

Marley, Patrick. 2020. "Appeals Court Limits Wisconsin Early Voting to 2 Weeks Before Election, Stops Voters from Receiving Ballots via Email, Fax." *Milwaukee Journal Sentinel*, June 29, 2020. https://www.jsonline.com/story/news/politics/2020/06/29/wisconsin-early-voting-limited-appeals-court-tightens-election-law/3283006001/

Marshall, Thomas. 1979. "Caucuses and Primaries: Measuring Reform in the Presidential Nomination Process." *American Politics Quarterly* 7 (2): 155–174.

"Maryland Early Voting Shot Down; Ruling Upheld by Highest Court in the State." 2006. *Southern Maryland Online,* August 25, 2006.

Massachusetts. 2019. "Massachusetts Communities to be Reimbursed Over $1.1 million for 2018 Mandated Early Voting Expenses." *Mass.gov*, January 1, 2019. https://www.mass.gov/news/massachusetts-communities-to-be-reimbursed-over-11-million-for-2018-mandated-early-voting

Mathews, Donald R. 1978. "Winnowing: The News Media and the 1976 Presidential Nomination." In *Race for the Presidency*, edited by James David Barber. New Jersey: Prentice-Hall.

Mayer, William G., and Andrew E. Busch. 2004. *The Front-Loading Problem in Presidential Nominations*. Washington: Brookings Institution Press.

Mayes, Brittany Renee, and Kate Rabinowitz. 2020. "Since 2016, 11 States and D.C. have Expanded Voting Rights for the Currently and Formerly Incarcerated." *The Washington Post*, August 12, 2020. https://www.washingtonpost.com/politics/2020/08/12/since-2016-11-states-dc-have-expanded-voting-rights-currently-formerly-incarcerated/

McAvoy, Audrey. 2019. "Hawaii Lawmakers Pass All-Mail Elections, Automatic Recounts." *AP News*. May 1, 2019. https://apnews.com/article/2de69fb1f88c4112b3a6da3625d886aa

McDonald, Michael P. 2012. "2012 November General Election Early Voting." United States Elections Project. http://www.electproject.org/2012_early_vote

McDonald, Michael P. 2016. "2016 November General Election Early Voting." United States Elections Project. "http://www.electproject.org/early_2016

McDonald, Michael P. 2018. "2018 November General Election Early Voting." United States Elections Project. http://www.electproject.org/early_2018

McDonald, Michael P. 2020. "2020 General Election Early Vote Statistics." United States Elections Project. https://electproject.github.io/Early-Vote-2020G/index.html

McDonald, Michael P., and Thomas Schaller. 2011. In *The Change Election: Money, Mobilization, and Persuasion in the 2008 Federal Elections*, edited by David Magleby. Philadelphia: Temple University Press.

Menger, Andrew, Robert M. Stein, and Greg Vonnahme. 2018. "Reducing the Undervote with Vote by Mail." *American Politics Research* 46 (6): 1039–1064.

Meredith, Marc, and Neil Malhotra. 2011. "Convenience Voting Can Affect Election Outcomes," *Election Law Journal: Rules, Politics, and Policy* 10 (3): 227–253.

Merton, R.K. 1936. "The Unanticipated Consequences of Purposive Social Action." *American Sociological Review* 1 (6): 894–904.

Mica, Jason D., Michael W. Wagner, and David C. Wilson. 2007. "The Effect of Voter Identification Laws on Aggregate and Individual Level Turnout." Paper presented at the annual meeting of the American Political Science Association, Chicago, IL, 2007.

Morgan, Edmund S. 1988. *Inventing the People: The Rise of Popular Sovereignty in England and America.* New York: Norton & Company.

Morrill, Jim. 2011. "GOP Proposal Would Cut a Week from Early Voting." *The Charlotte Observer*, April 27, 2011.

National Association of Secretaries of State. 2012. "Early Voting Dates and Absentee Ballot Deadlines for the 2012 General Election." http://www.nass.org/elections-voting/early-voting-dates-and-absentee-ballot-deadlines-2012-general-election/

National Conference of State Legislatures. 2020a. "State Laws Governing Early Voting." October 22, 2020. https://www.ncsl.org/research/elections-and-campaigns/early-voting-in-state-elections.aspx

National Conference of State Legislatures. 2020b. "Straight Ticket Voting States." March 25, 2020. https://www.ncsl.org/research/elections-and-campaigns/straight-ticket-voting.aspx.

National Conference of State Legislatures. 2021a. "Automatic Voter Registration." February 8, 2021. https://www.ncsl.org/research/elections-and-campaigns/automatic-voter-registration.aspx

National Conference of State Legislatures. 2021b. "Same Day Voter Registration." May 7, 2021. https://www.ncsl.org/research/elections-and-campaigns/same-day-registration.aspx

National Conference of State Legislatures. 2021c. "Voter Identification Requirements." May 21, 2021. https://www.ncsl.org/research/elections-and-campaigns/voter-id.aspx

National Election Pool (ABC News, Associated Press, CBS, CNN, Fox News, NBC). "2008 Arizona Democratic Primary Exit Poll." Edison Research. Accessed through the Roper Center for Public Opinion Research, Cornell University, Ithaca, NY. Dataset #31093451.

National Election Pool (ABC News, Associated Press, CBS, CNN, Fox News, NBC). "2008 California Democratic Primary Exit Poll." Edison Research. Accessed through the Roper Center for Public Opinion Research, Cornell University, Ithaca, NY. Dataset #31093453.

National Election Pool (ABC News, Associated Press, CBS, CNN, Fox News, NBC). "2008 Florida Democratic Primary Exit Poll." Edison Research. Accessed through the Roper Center for Public Opinion Research, Cornell University, Ithaca, NY. Dataset #31093459.

National Election Pool (ABC News, Associated Press, CBS, CNN, Fox News, NBC). "2008 Tennessee Democratic Primary Exit Poll." Edison Research. Accessed through the Roper Center for Public Opinion Research, Cornell University, Ithaca, NY. Dataset #31093501.

National Election Pool (ABC News, Associated Press, CBS, CNN, Fox News, NBC). "2016 Florida Democratic Primary Exit Poll." Edison Research. Accessed through the Roper Center for Public Opinion Research, Cornell University, Ithaca, NY. Dataset #31115172.

National Election Pool (ABC News, Associated Press, CBS, CNN, Fox News, NBC). "2016 North Carolina Democratic Primary Exit Poll." Edison Research. Accessed through the Roper Center for Public Opinion Research, Cornell University, Ithaca, NY. Dataset #31115231.

National Election Pool (ABC News, Associated Press, CBS, CNN, Fox News, NBC). "2016 Ohio Democratic Primary Exit Poll." Edison Research. Accessed through the Roper Center for Public Opinion Research, Cornell University, Ithaca, NY. Dataset #31115245.

Neale, Thomas H. 1983. "The Eighteen-Year-Old Vote: The Twenty-Sixth Amendment and Subsequent Voting Rates of Newly Enfranchised Age Groups." *Congressional Research Service.* http://digital.library.unt.edu/ark:/67531/metacrs8805/.

Neeley, Grant W., and Lilliard E. Richardson, Jr. 1996. "The Impact of Early Voting on Turnout: The 1994 Elections in Tennessee." *State and Local Government Review* 28 (3): 173–179.

Newton-Small, Jay. 2008. "The Battle for the Latino Vote." *Time*, February 1, 2008. http://www.time.com/time/politics/article/0,8599,1709033,00.html.

"N.H. Voters Boost Insurgents – But Does It Translate Nationally?" 1999. *ABC News*, December 16, 1999. http://abcnews.go.com/images/pdf/806a2NHNational.pdf

Nichols, Stephen M. 1998. "State Referendum Voting, Ballot Roll-off, and the Effect of New Electoral Technology." *State and Local Government Review* 30 (2): 106–117.

Nicholson, Stephen P. 2003. "The Political Environment and Ballot Proposition Awareness." *American Journal of Political Science* 47 (3): 403–410.

Nicholson, Stephen P. 2005. *Voting the Agenda: Candidates, Elections and Ballot Measures*. Princeton: Princeton University Press.

Norrander, Barbara. 1996. "Presidential Nomination Politics in the Post-Reform Era." *Political Research Quarterly* 49 (4): 875–915.

Oliver, J. Eric. 1996. "The Effects of Eligibility Restrictions and Party Activity on Absentee Voting and Overall Turnout." *American Journal of Political Science* 40 (2): 498–513.

Osborne, Matt. "Here Are Six Ways the Clinton Machine Can Destroy Trump." *Breitbart Unmasked*, June 15, 2016. https://www.breitbartunmasked.com/2016/06/15/here-are-six-ways-the-clinton-machine-can-destroy-trump/

Osinski, Bill. 1993. "Early-Ballot System May Replace Ga. Absentee Voting." *The Atlanta Journal-Constitution*, October 17, 1993.

Paterson, Blake. "Bipartisan Furor as North Carolina Election Law Shrinks Early Voting Locations by Almost 20 Percent." *ProPublica*, September 24, 2018. https ://www.propublica.org/article/bipartisan-furor-as-north-carolina-election-law-sh rinks-early-voting-locations-by-almost-20-percent

Patterson, Samuel C., and Gregory A. Caldeira. 1985. "Mailing in the Vote: Correlates and Consequences of Absentee Voting." *American Journal of Political Science* 29 (4): 766–789.

Perman, Michael. 2001. *Struggle for Mastery: Disfranchisement in the South, 1888–1908*. Chapel Hill: University of North Carolina Press.

Pew Research Center. 2020. "The Voting Experience in 2020." November 20, 2020. https://www.pewresearch.org/politics/2020/11/20/the-voting-experience-in-2020/

Piven, Frances Fox, and Richard A. Cloward. 1989. *Why Americans Don't Vote*. New York: Pantheon.

"Poll: Bradley Still an Unknown." 1999. *CBS News*, November 4, 1999. http://www .cbsnews.com/news/poll-bradley-still-an-unknown/

Polsby, Nelson, and Aaron Wildavsky. 2008. *Presidential Elections*. Lanham: Rowman and Littlefield.

Primo, David M., Matthew I. Jacobsmeier, and Jeffrey Milyo. 2007. "Estimating the Impact of State Policies and Institutions with Mixed-Level Data." *State Politics and Policy Quarterly* 7 (4): 446–459.

Rakich, Nathaniel. 2020. "More States Are Using Ballot Drop Boxes. Why Are They So Controversial?" *FiveThirtyEight*, October 5, 2020. https://fivethirtyeight.com /features/more-states-are-using-ballot-drop-boxes-why-are-they-so-controversial/

Ratcliffe, Donald. 2013. "The Right to Vote and the Rise of Democracy, 1787—1828." *Journal of the Early Republic* 33 (2): 219–254.

Redlawsk, David, Caroline Tolbert, and Todd Donovan. 2010. *Why Iowa? How Caucuses and Sequential Elections Improve the Presidential Nominating Process*. Chicago: University of Chicago Press.

Reilly, Shauna, and Sean Richey. 2011. "Ballot Question Readability and Roll-off: The Impact of Language Complexity." *Political Research Quarterly* 64 (1): 59–67.

Rein, Lisa. 2008. "Decision Time for Early Voting in Md." *The Washington Post*, October 26, 2008.

Riccardi, Nicholas, and Bobby Caina Calvan. "Here's how Trump's opposition to mail voting hurts the GOP." *The Washington Post,* July 28, 2020. https://www .washingtonpost.com/politics/heres-how-trumps-opposition-to-mail-voting-hurts-t he-gop/2020/07/28/efc45c04-d088-11ea-826b-cc394d824e35_story.html

Riker, William H., and Peter C. Ordeshook. 1968. "A Theory of the Calculus of Voting." *American Political Science Review* 62 (1): 25–42.

Riker, William H. 1982. *Liberalism Against Populism*. San Francisco: W. H. Freeman.

Rinaldo, Tom. "Hillary's Surge Protector: Early Voting and the Sanders Campaign." *Daily Kos*, March 30, 2016. https://www.dailykos.com/stories/2016/3/30/1508030 /-Hillary-s-Surge-Protector-Early-Voting-and-the-Sanders-Campaign

Roberts, John. 2007. "Hillary Clinton Launches White House Bid: I'm In." *CNN.com*, January 22, 2007. http://www.cnn.com/2007/POLITICS/01/20/clinton.announce ment/index.html

Rom, Mark Carl, Paul E. Peterson, and Kenneth F. Scheve. 1998. "Interstate Competition and Welfare Policy." *Publius* 28 (3): 17–38.

Rosenstone, Steven J., and John Mark Hansen. 1993. *Mobilization, Participation, and Democracy in America*. New York: Macmillan.

Ross, Brian, and Rehab El-Buri. 2008. "Obama's Pastor: God Damn America, U.S. to Blame for 9/11." *ABC News*, March 13, 2008. http://abcnews.go.com/Blotter/DemocraticDebate/story?id=4443788

Sabato, Larry J. 1998. "Bill Clinton and Gennifer Flowers." *The Washington Post*. http://www.washingtonpost.com/wp-srv/politics/special/clinton/frenzy/clinton.htm

Scanlan, Quinn. 2020. "Here's how states have changed the rules around voting amid the coronavirus pandemic." *ABC News*, September 22, 2020. https://abcnews.go.com/Politics/states-changed-rules-voting-amid-coronavirus-pandemic/story?id=72309089

Schaffner, Brian, Matthew Streb, and Gerald Wright. 2001. "Teams without Uniforms: The Nonpartisan Ballot in State and Local Elections." *Political Research Quarterly* 54 (1): 7–30.

Scheele, Raymond H., Joseph Losco, Gary Crawley, and Sally Jo Vasicko. 2008. "Assessing the Impact of Vote Centers on Electoral Behavior: An Examination of Indiana Vote Centers in the 2007 Municipal Elections." Paper presented at the annual meeting of the Midwest Political Science Association, Chicago, IL, 2008.

Schroeder, Alan. 2001. *Presidential Debates*. New York: Columbia University Press.

Schoenberg, Shira. 2014. *Mass Live*, May 22, 2014. "Massachusetts Gov. Deval Patrick signs early voting into law." https://www.masslive.com/politics/2014/05/massachusetts_gov_deval_patric_32.html

Siegel, J. 2011. "Elections overhaul sent to Kasich without photo-ID provision." *The Columbus Dispatch*, June 30, 2011. http://www.dispatch.com/content/stories/local/2011/06/30/elections-overhaul-sent-tokasich-without-photo-id-provision.html

Southwell, Priscilla, and Justin Burchett. 2000. "The Effect of All-Mail Elections on Voter Turnout." *American Politics Quarterly* 28 (1): 72–79.

Southwell, Priscilla L. 2009a. "Analysis of the Turnout Effects of Vote by Mail Elections, 1980–2007." *The Social Science Journal* 46 (1): 211–217.

Southwell, Priscilla L. 2009b. "A Solution for Voter Fatigue? Vote by Mail in the State of Oregon." *The Journal of Political and Military Sociology* 37 (2): 195–203.

Stein, Robert M., and Patricia A. Garcia-Monet. 1997. "Voting Early, but Not Often." *Social Science Quarterly* 78 (3): 657–671.

Stein, Robert M. 1998. "Early Voting." *Public Opinion Quarterly* 62 (1): 57–69.

Stein, Robert M., Jan E. Leighley, and Chris Owens. 2004. "Voting, Early Voting, and Party Mobilization: Is Timing Everything?" Paper presented at the annual meeting of the Midwest Political Science Association, Chicago, IL, 2004.

Stein, Robert M., and Greg Vonnahme. 2008. "Engaging the Unengaged Voter: Voter Centers and Voter Turnout." *Journal of Politics* 70 (2): 487–497.

Stein, Robert M., and Greg Vonnahme. 2012. "When, Where and How We Vote: Does it Matter?" *Social Science Quarterly* 93 (3): 692–712.

Sullivan, Amy. 2008. "Why Didn't More Women Vote for Hillary?" *Time*, June 5, 2008. http://www.time.com/time/magazine/article/0,9171,1812050,00.html

Sullivan, Andy. 2019. "Southern U.S. states have closed 1,200 polling places in recent years: rights group." *Reuters*, September 10, 2019. https://www.reuters.com /article/us-usa-election-locations/southern-u-s-states-have-closed-1200-polling-pl aces-in-recent-years-rights-group-idUSKCN1VV09J

Svenson, Ola. 1981. "Are We All Less Risky and More Skillful Than Our Fellow Drivers?" *Acta Psychologia* 47 (2): 143–148.

Swanstrom, Todd. 2008. "Regional Resilience: A Critical Examination of the Ecological Framework." Paper presented at the annual meeting of the Urban Affairs Association, Baltimore, MD, 2008.

Taebel, Delbert A. 1975. "The Effect of Ballot Position on Electoral Success." *American Journal of Political Science* 19 (3): 519–526.

Tarbous, Ken. 2020. "Voters Wait Up to 10 Hours in Line to Vote in Critical Georgia County." *Newsweek*, October 21, 2020. https://www.newsweek.com/voters-wait -10-hours-line-vote-critical-georgia-county-1541132

Taylor, Matt. 2012. "Romney's Early Vote Strategy Mirrors Obama's." *National Memo*, March 8, 2012. http://www.nationalmemo.com/romneys-early-vote-str ategy-mirrors-obamas/

Taylor, Jessica. 2015. "Jim Webb Exits Democratic Primary, Leaves Door Open for Independent Bid." *NPR*, October 20, 2015. https://www.npr.org/sections/itsallpolit ics/2015/10/20/450239642/jim-webb-ends-his-presidential-campaign

Teixeira, Ruy. 1992. *The Disappearing American Voter*. Washington: Brookings Institution.

"Texans Begin Voting Early." 1992. *The Associated Press*, October 14, 1992.

Texas House of Representatives. 1988. Committee on Elections, Interim Report to the 71st Texas Legislature. http://www.lrl.state.tx.us/scanned/interim/70/e125 .pdf

"They Want to Make Voting Harder?" 2011. *The New York Times*, June 5, 2011. http: //www.nytimes.com/2011/06/06/opinion/06mon1.html

Thompson, Dennis F. 2004. "Election Time: Normative Implications of Temporal Properties of the Electoral Process in the United States." *American Political Science Review* 98 (1): 51–63.

Tobin, Thomas C. 2002. "Expect More Early Voting." *St. Petersburg Times*, November 25, 2002.

Tocqueville, Alexis de. *Democracy in America*. New York: G. Dearborn & Co., 1838.

Tucker, Cynthia. 2011. "Hardball with Chris Matthews." *MSNBC.com*, November 3, 2011. http://www.msnbc.msn.com/id/45163637/ns/msnbc_tv-hardball_with_ch ris_matthews/t/hardball-chris-matthews-thursday-november-rd/#.T-E0lBfLzE0

Tucker, Spencer. 2011. *The Encyclopedia of the Vietnam War [4 volumes]: A Political, Social, and Military History*. Santa Barbara: ABC-CLIO.

Tumulty, Karen. 2008. "Women and Absentee Ballots Were the Key." *Time*, January 9, 2008. http://www.time.com/time/politics/article/0,8599,1701752,00 .html#ixzz1B3O3OL8m

United States Census Bureau. 1992. Current Population Survey: November Voting and Registration Supplement.

United States Census Bureau. 2012. American Community Survey, 5-year Estimates, 2008–2012.

United States Census Bureau. 2014. Current Population Survey: November Voting and Registration Supplement.

United States Census Bureau. 2016. Current Population Survey: November Voting and Registration Supplement.

United States Election Assistance Commission. 2012. Election Administration & Voting Survey.

United States Election Assistance Commission. 2014. Election Administration & Voting Survey.

United States Election Assistance Commission. 2016. Election Administration & Voting Survey.

United States Election Assistance Commission. 2018. Election Administration & Voting Survey.

Valdemoro, Tanya. 2005. "McCain-Feingold Hasn't Changed a Thing." *Western Knight Center for Specialized Journalism.* http://www.wkconline.org/index.php/ seminar_showcase/cc_story/mccainfeingold_hasnt_changed_a_thing/

Vanderleeuw, James M., and Richard L. Engstrom. 1987. "Race, Referenda and Roll-off." *Journal of Politics* 49 (4): 1081–1092.

Vercellotti, Timothy, and David Anderson. 2006. "Protecting the Franchise, or Restricting It?" Paper presented at the annual meeting of the American Political Science Association, Philadelphia, PA, 2006.

Volden, Craig. 2002. "The Politics of Competitive Federalism: A Race to the Bottom in Welfare Benefits?" *American Journal of Political Science* 46 (2): 352–363.

Wagner, John. 2010. "Ehrlich Votes Early, Downplays Primary Challenge." *The Washington Post*, September 9, 2010.

Waldman, Michael. 2016. *The Fight to Vote.* New York: Simon & Schuster.

Walker, Jack L. 1966. "Ballot Forms and Voter Fatigue: An Analysis of the Office Block and Party Column Ballots." *Midwest Journal of Political Science* 10 (4): 448–463.

Wattenberg, Martin P. 1991. *The Rise of Candidate-Centered Politics.* Cambridge: Harvard University Press.

Weeks, Luther. 2009. "Is Early Voting a Good Idea for Connecticut?" CTVotersCount .org, July 14, 2009. http://www.ctvoterscount.org/connecticut-vs-minnesota-part-2/

Weigel, David. 2020. "The Trailer: Democrats won the White House and lost a myth about turnout." *The Washington Post*, November 8, 2020. https://www.washingt onpost.com/politics/2020/11/08/trailer-democrats-won-white-house-lost-myth-about-turnout/

Weiser, Wendy R., and Lawrence Norden. 2012. "Voting Law Changes in 2012." Brennan Center for Justice. https://www.brennancenter.org/sites/default/files/ 2019-08/Report_Voting_Law_Changes_2012.pdf

Weller, Chas. E. 1918. *The Early History of the Typewriter.* La Porte: Chase & Shepherd Printers.

Whittenburg, Catherine. 2011. "Scott Signs Bill that Cuts Early Voting Days and Adds Restrictions." *Tampa Bay Online*, May 19, 2011. http://www2.tbo.com/news/politics/2011/may/19/2/scott-signs-bill-that-cuts-early-voting-days-and-a-ar-208573/

"Why People Don't Vote Down-Ballot." 2009. *Democratic Blog News*, February 1, 2009. http://collindemsnews.blogspot.com/2009/02/why-people-dont-vote-down-ballot.html.

Wilkinson, Howard. 2010. "Parties: Don't Forget the Supreme Court." *Cincinnati.com*, October 17, 2010. http://news.cincinnati.com/article/20101017/NEWS0108/10180303/Parties-Don-t-forget-Supreme-Court

Winberg, Michaela. 2020. "Good job, Philly: Only 1% of City Mail Ballots Were 'Naked.'" *Billy Penn*, November 11, 2020. https://billypenn.com/2020/11/11/philly-naked-ballots-pennsylvania-mail-votes-november-election/

Wines, Michael. 2016. "Texas Agrees to Soften Voter ID Law After Court Order." *The New York Times*, August 3, 2016. https://www.nytimes.com/2016/08/04/us/texas-agrees-to-soften-voter-id-law-after-court-order.html

Wolfinger, Raymond E., and Steven J. Rosenstone. 1980. *Who Votes?* New Haven: Yale University Press.

Yang, John E. 1992. "Jackson Delivers the Vote in Denver Drive." *Chicago Sun-Times*, October 18, 1992.

Zitner, Aaron, Dante Chinni, and Brian McGill. 2016. "How Hillary Clinton Overcame the Challenge from Sen. Bernie Sanders." *The Wall Street Journal*, June 8, 2016. http://graphics.wsj.com/elections/2016/how-clinton-won/

Index

Note: *Italic* page numbers refer to figures and tables; page numbers followed by "n" denote endnotes.

AFL-CIO, 90
Aldrich, John H., 37
Alvarez, Michael, R., 48
Anderson, David, 48
Ashenfelter, Orley, 37
automatic voter registration (AVR), 31, 48, 51, 64, 70–71, 77, 79, 81, 140

Barrett, Amy Coney, 1, 114
BCRA. *See* Bipartisan Campaign Reform Act (BCRA)
Biden, Joe, 1, 26, 114
Bipartisan Campaign Reform Act (BCRA), 6, 88
Blackwell, Ken, 19, 92
BLS. *See* Bureau of Labor Statistics (BLS)
Blunt, Matt, 19
Bradley, Bill, 117
Bright, Chelsie L. M., 48
Brox, Brian J., 38, 47
Burden, Barry, 38, 44, 46, 47, 50
Bureau of Labor Statistics (BLS), 76
Bush, George W., 16–18, 114, 117
Bush, Jeb, 17, 18

Caddell, William, 19
Campbell, Angus, 59
Campbell, James E., 59
Chafee, Lincoln, 120
Chesney, Kelly, 18
CHIP, 134
citizen's decision to vote, 36–39; costs and benefits of voting, 36–37; effect of early voting, past research on, 7–8, 37–39; effect of same-day registration, past research on, 37; rational choice approach, 36–37
Civil Rights Movement, 28
Clinton, Bill, 115
Clinton, Hillary, 10, 71, 113–16, 122, 123, 129, 138, 140; effect of early voting on support for, 2008, *127*; effect of early voting on support for, 2016, *130*; predicting support for, 2008, *126*; predicting support for, 2016, *129*. *See also* Clinton's early vote strategies
Clinton's early vote strategies, 118–22; in California, 119–20; in New

Hampshire, 118–19; in 2008, 118–20; in 2016, 120–22

Cordray, Richard, 92, 95

county turnout and early voting: importance of site density, 43–45; midterm election findings, 60–69, *61–63, 66–67, 69*; midterm election model, 58–60; presidential election findings, 49–58, *50–55, 57*; presidential election model, 45–49

COVID-19 outbreak, 1, 3–5, 23, 26, 32, 33, 35, 43–45, 74n17, 114, 132n1, 142

Current Population Survey (CPS) data, 3–4, 6, 8–9, 39, 76–77, 81, 86n1, 86n2, 101, 137

Davidson, Donetta, 15

Davis, Jim, 25

decentralization, 11, 88, 140. *See also* decentralized nature of elections

decentralized nature of elections, 135; national reforms, 12; problems with, 12–13; in US history, 11–12

DeGenaro, Mary, 97

Dendahl, John, 16

DeWine, Mike, 92, 93, 95

down-ballot roll-off and early voting: AFL-CIO efforts to combat roll-off, 2010, 90; causes of ballot roll-off, 88–90; Democratic Party efforts to combat roll-off, 2010, 90; measuring effect of early voting on roll-off in Ohio, 2010, 90–93; need for future research on, 99–100; Ohio findings, 2010, 93–96, *94, 95*; Ohio findings, 2018, 96–99, *98*

Downs, Anthony, 37, 71

Drutman, Lee, 12

Dubin, Jeffrey A., 37

EAC. *See* Election Assistance Commission (EAC) data

early in-person voting, 3, *4*, 7–9, 10n1, 13–16, 21, 32, 36, 38–40, 43–44, 46, 70, 72, 91, 136, 140

early voting: effect of Voting Rights Act on, 29–31; increased use of, 3–4; in US, 2021, *4*; outrage at 2021 Georgia law, 33; Republican efforts to limit early voting, 23–27. *See also* county turnout and early voting; down-ballot roll-off and early voting; emergence of early voting; expansion of early voting; implementation of early voting in counties; individual turnout and early voting; racial inequity and early voting; Supreme Court approval of, 16; variations of, 3

ecological inference, 8, 85

Edwards, John, 115, 118, 122

Ehrlich, Bob, 20

Election Assistance Commission (EAC) data, 6, 36, *50, 51, 61*, 76, *80, 84*, 102

Election Day Vote Centers (EDVCs), 44

electoral reform, 5, 72, 75, 111, 143

emergence of early voting: in Arizona, 16; in Colorado, 15–16; concerns about turnout, 14, 15; concerns about voter fraud, 13–15; in Georgia, discussion of, 15; in Nevada, 15; in New Mexico, 16; no-excuse absentee voting laws, 13; "no-excuse voting by personal appearance," 13–14; Texas as pioneer in, 13–15

endogeneity, 47

expansion of early voting, 2000s: in Florida, 17–18; in Maine, 21; in Maryland, 20; in Massachusetts, 21–22; in Michigan, 18–19; in Missouri, 19; in New England states, resistance to, 20–22; in Ohio, 19; in West Virginia, 18

Fasano, Mike, 24

Ferejohn, John, 37

Fiorina, Morris, 37

Fitzgerald, Mary, 38

For the People Act in 2021, 140–41

Garcia-Monet, Patricia A., 38
get-out-the-vote (GOTV) efforts, 38, 121
Giammo, Joseph D., 38, 47
Giuliani, Rudy, 115, 122
GOTV. *See* get-out-the-vote (GOTV)
  efforts
Granholm, Jennifer, 18
Gronke, Paul, 9, 37, 38, 45, 101, 102,
  116, 138

Hajnal, Zoltan, 48
Hall, Thad, 12
Hammerstrom, Beverly, 19
Hanmer, Michael, 4
Hart, Gary, 117
Herron, Michael C., 46
Hickenlooper, John, 22
Hill, Charlotte, 12
Hochschild, Jennifer, 12
Holmes, Bob, 15

implementation of early voting in counties:
  advertisement of programs, 42; clerks,
  40–43; decisions about site placement,
  41–42; factors, determining site
  locations, 40–41; lack of site density,
  negative effects, 42; limitations, 40;
  role of the state and county, 39–40;
  stress for election officials, 43; student
  convenience as a factor, 41
individual turnout and early voting:
  early voting and likelihood of voting,
  in 2014 midterm election, 77–81,
  78–80; early voting and likelihood
  of voting, in 2016 presidential
  election, 81–85, *82–84*; measuring
  relationship between, 76–77
information asymmetries, 2, 9; effect
  on presidential primary outcomes,
  116; late developments in 2016 and
  2020, 114; "October Surprise," 114;
  in presidential elections, general,
  114; in presidential nominating
  campaigns, 115–16
"I Voted" stickers, 1

Jackson, Reverend Jesse, 15
Johnson, Lyndon B., 28, 29, 114

Kalsow, Gretchen A., 37
Kasich, John, 25
Kelley, Stanley Jr., 37
Kenney, Patrick J., 37
Klemanski, John S., 39, 44
Kuk, John, 48

Lamb, Denise, 16
Larocca, Roger, 39, 44
liberalized absentee rules, 13, 45, 136,
  140
Lynch, Michael S., 48
Lyons, William, 37

Malhotra, Neil, 115, 122
McCain, John, 114, 117
McCrory, Pat, 25
McDonald, Michael P., 9, 101, 102,
  138
McGovern-Fraser Commission, 1971, 6
Medicaid, 134
Medicare, 134
Meredith, Marc, 115, 122
Merton, R.K., 87
midterm elections: electoral context
  across states, difference, 60; lack of
  "wow factor," 59. *See also* county
  turnout and early voting; individual
  turnout and early voting; racial
  inequity and early voting
Miller, Thomas Vincent Jr., 20
Mondale, Walter, 117
Montgomery, Betty, 92

National Conference of State
  Legislatures (NCSL), 3–4, 18, 31,
  53, 55, 57, 63, 67, 69, 80, 84, 105,
  108, 110
NCLB. *See* No Child Left Behind
  (NCLB) Act of 2001
Neeley, Grant W., 38
Nixon, Jay, 19

Nixon, Richard, 114
No Child Left Behind (NCLB) Act of
    2001, 6
no-excuse absentee program, 4, 49, 68,
    70, 106, 136, 141

Obama, Barack, 23–25, 29, 49, 71, 90,
    114, 115, 117–25, 127, 128, 130,
    134, 138
O'Connor, Maureen, 93
Oliver, Eric J., 37
OLS regression models, 45, 49, 59, 60,
    73n2, 73n3, 73n4, 88, 91, 93–94,
    97, 104
O'Malley, Martin, 120, 121
Ordeshook, Peter C., 37
Organization for Economic Cooperation
    and Development, 2

partisan polarization, 1, 7, 131
path dependence, 133–35
Patient Protection and Affordable Care
    Act of 2010 (Obamacare), 134
Patrick, Deval, 22
Peterson, James, 31
Petro, Jim, 92
political polarization and tribalism, 33
pre-Election Day voting, 1, 3, 45, 47
presidential debates, 16, 132n1
presidential nominations: information
    asymmetries in, 115–16; normative
    implications of early voting in,
    130–31. *See also* Clinton, Hillary;
    Clinton's early vote strategies
Probit regression models, 76, 77, *78*, 81,
    82, 85, 124, 125, *126*, 127, 128, *129*

"QWERTY" arrangement, 133

racial inequity and early voting:
    demographics and early voting
    site density, 2012 and 2016, *105*;
    demographics and early voting
    site density, 2014 and 2018, *108*;
    differences between Black and

Hispanic populations, 104, 111;
    fixed effects models, 109–10, *110*;
    inequality in election administration,
    examples, 111; measuring
    relationship between, 102–3;
    midterm election findings, 107–9;
    presidential election findings, 103–6;
    racial and ethnic site disparities,
    speculated by others, 101–2; role of
    the Voting Rights Act, 101–2; site
    inequities, potential causes, 111
rational choice theory, 37, 43, 71
Rice, Tom W., 37
Richards, Ann, 14
Richardson, Lilliard E. Jr., 38
Riker, William H., 4, 37, 144

same-day registration (SDR) laws, 26,
    31, 37, 38, 48, 50, 64, 70, 71, 74n11,
    77, 79, 81, 143
Sanders, Bernie, 117, 120, 130, 138
Scheb II, John M., 37
SCLC. *See* Southern Christian
    Leadership Conference (SCLC)
Scott, Rick, 24, 30
SDR. *See* same-day registration (SDR)
    laws
Shank, Christopher, 20
Sholes, Christopher Latham, 133
Smith, Daniel A., 46
SNCC. *See* Student Nonviolent
    Coordinating Committee (SNCC)
"Souls to the Polls," 24
Southern Christian Leadership
    Conference (SCLC), 28
Stein, Robert M., 38, 44, 47, 116
Stewart, Melody, 97
Stratton, Evelyn, 93
Student Nonviolent Coordinating
    Committee (SNCC), 28

Taft, Bob, 20
Taylor, Matt, 23
Thompson, Dennis F., 131
Thompson, Fred, 115, 122

Tokaji, Dan, 12
Toner, Michael, 12
Traugott, Michael, 19
Trump, Donald, 1, 26, 59, 71, 114, 142

unintended consequences, 5, 6, 9, 87, 88, 137–40: addressing externalities created by early voting, 139; of early voting, on ballot roll-off, 137–38; of early voting, on presidential nominating campaigns, 138–39; of early voting, on racial inequity, 138
universal vote-by-mail (VBM), 2, 3, 8–9, 38, 46, 50–51, 58–59, 64–65, 70, 72n1, 75–77, 81, 85, 89, 103, 122, 136–37; adoption of, 22–23
U.S. Election Assistance Commission (EAC), 36, 50, 51, 61, 80, 84

variations in early voting, 3, 136
Vercellotti, Timothy, 48
VHA, 134
Vonnahme, Greg, 44, 47
vote-by-mail (VBM) programs. *See* universal vote-by-mail (VBM)
Voter turnout, 2, 7–8, 15, 18, 43, 70, 71, 73, 73n2, 77
Voting Integrity Project, 16
Voting Rights Act, 140; adoption in 1965, 28; effect on Black participation, 29; events preceding, 27–28; pre-clearance requirement, 29–30; role in adjudicating early voting cuts in the 2010s, 29–31

Webb, Jim, 120
Weigel, David, 141

Yost, Dave, 92, 97

About the Author

Elliott Fullmer is an associate professor of political science at Randolph-Macon College in Ashland, Virginia. His research on voting behavior has been published in various scholarly journals, including *American Politics Research*, *Election Law Journal*, *Presidential Studies Quarterly*, *State Politics & Policy Quarterly*, and *The Forum*. He has authored opinion pieces on election reform for *USA Today*, *Richmond Times-Dispatch*, and *Virginia Capitol Connections*, and is a frequent guest on local public radio (VPM News). In 2019, Fullmer coauthored an introductory textbook, *Basics of American Politics* (16th ed.), with Gary Wasserman. He is currently completing a book project on democracy reform in the United States.

In the classroom, Fullmer teaches a wide variety of undergraduate courses, including identity politics, interest group politics, political parties, presidential elections, research methods, the American presidency, and the federal budget. Every four years, he also leads a travel course to New Hampshire, where students volunteer for candidates competing in the state's first-in-the-nation presidential primary. In 2017, he received Randolph-Macon College's Thomas Branch Award for Excellence in Teaching.

Fullmer enjoys traveling, good coffee and beer, rooting for his Philly sports teams, and looking at the ocean. He lives in Richmond, Virginia with his wife and young daughter.

www.ingramcontent.com/pod-product-compliance
Lightning Source LLC
Chambersburg PA
CBHW050607280326
41932CB00016B/2945